*Architectural Variability in the Southeast*

A Dan Josselyn Memorial Publication

# Architectural Variability in the Southeast

Edited by
Cameron H. Lacquement

THE UNIVERSITY OF ALABAMA PRESS
*Tuscaloosa*

The University of Alabama Press
Tuscaloosa, Alabama 35487-0380

Manufactured in the United States of America

Typeface: ACaslon

∞
The paper on which this book is printed meets the minimum requirements of American National Standard for Information Sciences-Permanence of Paper for Printed Library Materials, ANSI Z39.48-1984.

Library of Congress Cataloging-in-Publication Data

Architectural variability in the Southeast / edited by Cameron H. Lacquement.
p. cm.
Papers originally presented at a symposium titled "Variability in Native American Architecture of the Late Prehistoric and Early Historic Southeast," presented at the 62nd Southeastern Archaeological Conference in Columbia, South Carolina, in 2005.
Includes bibliographical references and index.
ISBN-13: 978-0-8173-1591-7 (cloth : alk. paper)
ISBN-10: 0-8173-1591-8
ISBN-13: 978-0-8173-5459-6 (pbk. : alk. paper)
ISBN-10: 0-8173-5459-X
1. Mississippian culture—Southern States—Congresses. 2. Indians of North America—Dwellings—Southern States—Congresses. 3. Indians of North America—Southern States—Antiquities—Congresses. 4. Southern States—Antiquities—Congresses. I. Lacquement, Cameron H., 1978–
E99.M6815A74 2007
720.975′0902—dc22

2007008277

# Contents

# Illustrations

## Figures

## Tables

# Acknowledgments

The origins of this project on Native American architecture began in the fall of 2005 as a symposium titled "Variability in Native American Architecture of the Late Prehistoric and Early Historic Southeast," presented at the 62nd Southeastern Archaeological Conference in Columbia, South Carolina. Several of the presenters from the symposium were not able to contribute to the publication, while other archaeologists not involved with the symposium were gracious enough to supply their research for this volume. I would like to thank everyone who participated. I would also like to extend my appreciation to David Hally for being the discussant at the 2005 symposium and providing critical comments on the research that was presented. His initial impressions had an important impact on the direction of the manuscript.

Many individuals assisted me in various aspects of the publication process. Bob Scott provided assistance in digitizing several images. I would like to thank Bonnie Styles, Marcelyn Love, Lynne Sullivan, Rachael Popma, Larry Conrad, Saundra Taylor, Stephanie Ogeneski, Scot Danforth, and Lewis Larson for granting permission to use various illustrations. I would especially like to extend my thanks to Charles Swan of the Chucalissa Museum for assistance with the Nash photograph and for figuring out the history behind the reconstruction of the structure depicted.

My appreciation also extends to Paul Welch and an anonymous reviewer for commenting on the chapters and providing vital observations for improvement. I would also like to thank the staff at the University of Alabama Press. In addition, I would like to thank each of the authors for their willingness to participate and for their excellent research.

Appreciation for the broader aspects of the completion of this volume also needs to be recognized. I would like to extend my appreciation to my many anthropology and archaeology professors over the years, including Jane Brown, Anne Rogers, Philip Coyle, Nyaga Mwaniki, Ian Brown, John Blitz, Kathryn Oths, James Bindon, William Dressler, Charles Nuckolls, Keith Jacobi, Jeffrey Schwartz, Richard Krause, Marysia Galbraith, Richard Diehl, Michael Murphy, and especially Vernon J. Knight. Without his guidance and patience, this project would not have been possible.

I am also especially grateful to those individuals who assisted me in an experimental reconstruction of a flexed pole house. Monique Billeaud, Bill Bomar, and Betsy Gilbert of the Moundville Archaeological Park graciously allowed the use of the site and its resources. Kristi Wheeler-Griffin advertised the structure's demise (see cover), and Brock Rester and the Moundville Fire Department made sure I did not burn down the park in the process. I am also indebted to those volunteers who assisted me with the construction of the house. Steve Barry, Bob Scott, Brian Padgett, Tom Lewis, and Matt Grunewald especially deserve recognition as they endured several battle wounds, including red ant bites, bee stings, blisters, splinters, poison ivy, and sprained ankles, during the material preparation and construction process. Also, other volunteers who supported me in the preparation and construction—Sarah Szurek, Katie Gillespie, Christine Newkirk, Erica Gibson, Becky and Andy Kelso, Kyle Lubsen, Charles Redwine, Ben Staneland, and Pam Johnson—should also be recognized for their assistance in various ways.

Most importantly, I would like to thank James and Sarah Caldwell for their financial support in awarding me the David and Elizabeth DeJarnette Scholarship to complete the experimental reconstruction.

Finally I would like to thank my family and my fiancée, Sarah.

# *Architectural Variability in the Southeast*

# 1
# Introduction to Architectural Variability in the Southeast

*Cameron H. Lacquement*

Native (or indigenous) architecture throughout the world differs substantially in building styles, materials, and construction techniques. Varieties in architectural form are not only found among the different cultural, geographical, and temporal regions of the globe but within these regions as well. For instance, a survey of contemporary South African houses alone would show several forms of architecture including round, oval, square, and rectangular houses, with flexed, hipped, gabled, or conical roofs, or combinations of these roof styles (Biermann 1971; Denyer 1978; Frescura 1981; Guidoni 1975). Despite the differences in location, climate, and time, the intraregional variability found in contemporary South African houses is very similar to that of prehistoric houses of the southeastern United States. A variety of house shapes, including round, oval, square, rectangular, and cross-shaped, which are believed to represent a variety of construction techniques, have also been uncovered in the Southeast United States. The variability of architectural forms in the southeastern United States is the focus of this manuscript. The authors provide their research on the variation of construction techniques in the Southeast United States concerning both above-ground and below-ground architectural analyses in order to investigate the various structural forms in this region.

Through the study of architectural remains, the archaeologist can infer the cultural patterns and behaviors associated with the creation of a particular type of structure. As several archaeologists and other social scientists have stated (Alexander 1979; Alexander et al. 1977; Lewis et al. 1998; Mitchell 1990; Rapoport 1969; to name a few), some of the most visible expressions of human culture are illustrated architecturally. Unfortunately for the archaeologist, the architecture being studied is not always visible, making this underlying manifestation of culture difficult to analyze. With the exception of the occasional preservation of burned structural remains, this lack of visible prehistoric architecture is certainly the case for the southeastern United States.

In this volume, several archaeologists address almost a millennium of Native American architecture in the form of both public and domestic structures in the southeastern United States. The research presented here is used to create a more complete picture of the variation of Native architecture in the Southeast and the changes that occurred both before and after the arrival of Europeans. The areas of interest include but are not limited to the American Bottom, central and southern Illinois, northeastern Arkansas, west-central Alabama, northern and central Georgia, and eastern and western Tennessee during the Mississippian (ca. A.D. 1000–1550) and Historic (A.D. 1550–1820) stages (Figure 1.1).

The majority of architectural studies in archaeology tend to focus on large monumental structures such as the Maya temples or the Mississippian platform mounds. The overall concept of this book is unique in the sense that it addresses architecture mainly at a household level with additional emphasis on community-level structures. This relatively narrow focus of architecture allows for the identification of construction trends in public and domestic houses. The research presented in this book is not concerned with architecture in the sense of large-scale planning and construction such as earthen mounds, plazas, town designs, palisades, or defensive structures (as in Dalan et al. 2003; Lewis and Stout 1998; Rogers and Smith 1995; to name a few). Therefore, from this point forward when the term architecture, structure, building, or any other synonym is used, it refers only to Native houses, both public and domestic, consisting of covered walls and a roof, unless stated otherwise.

The authors use an array of approaches in examining architecture in the Southeast, including ethnohistory, ethnography, multivariate data analysis, architectural grammar, experimental archaeology, wood science, and structural engineering. Each chapter focuses on at least one of two objectives in examining Native architecture. The first objective addresses the above-ground appearance of prehistoric houses. This is typically accomplished through the use of ethnography and experimental archaeology. The second objective is to inspect architectural floor plans and structural remains in order to classify the variety of foundation types. Based on the analysis of these forms, a second part of the latter objective involves categorizing these floor plans based on their similarities from samples recovered in the specific region of study. In order to create these typologies, different methodologies at the house level, both public and domestic, are fashioned based on variables documented in the archaeo-

1.1. Location of some of the related Mississippian and Historic sites.

logical record. These variables include but are not limited to wall post size, floor area, wall trench width and depth, burned wall and roof material, and other structural characteristics.

A recurring aspect in many of these chapters is the study of experimental archaeology. A number of archaeologists have conducted full-sized experimental recreations ranging from a single dwelling (Blanton this volume; Callahan 1992; Cheatham 1992; Gorman and DuChemin 2004; Harn 1972; Iseminger and Williams 1998; Lacquement 2004, 2005; Litchford 2002; Nash 1968; Norrish 1989; Reed this volume; Sullivan this volume) to an entire Mississippian

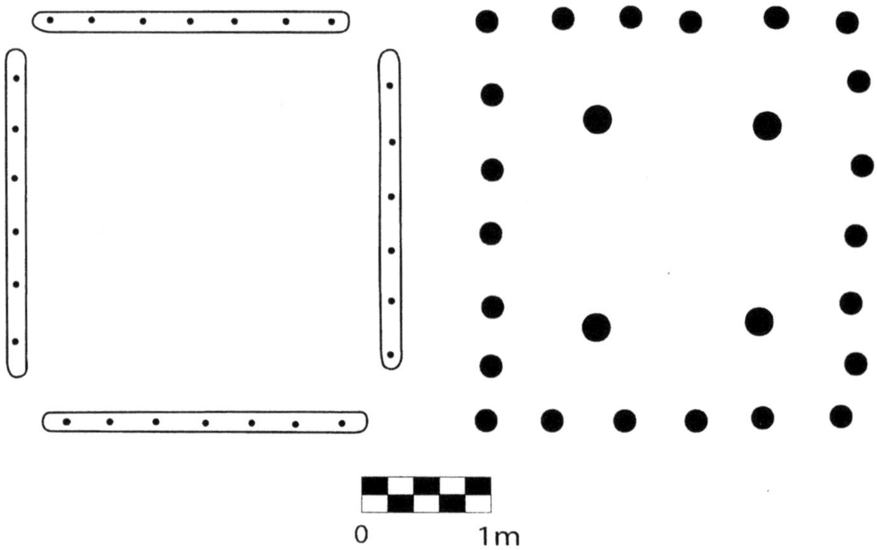


1.2. Floor plans from the two main forms of domestic architecture, (left) the small closely set pole design and (right) the large widely spaced post design.

village (Kennedy and Sawyer 2005; Reed n.d.). However, as Knight (this volume) points out, the majority of experimental research remains unpublished. These experiments are like Native folklore, in that, after the structures have been destroyed the only evidence that remains are their stories. This makes it difficult for one to comparatively study what archaeologists have learned from their architectural triumphs and setbacks. Regardless, the authors in this publication bring together many of these sources, some their own research, along with other references concerning the general thoughts and interpretations of Native architecture.

## Early Mississippian Wall Trench House Debate

The subsequent chapters of this book are dedicated to exposing a long-running and unsolved debate concerning the above-ground appearance of early Mississippian wall trench architecture. Varieties of floor plans have been discovered in the southeastern United States, among which two most common floor plans emerge—a wall trench design and a large individually set post design (Figure 1.2). Early southeastern archaeologists in the 1930s speculated that the wall trench design of the Native Americans during the Mississippian stage represented a curved roof structure covered in bark, cane matting, or grass thatching

1.3. Flexed pole architecture as illustrated by Charles Nash's experimental reconstruction in 1955 (from Nash 1968:Plate 2A, courtesy of the Chucalissa Museum, the University of Memphis).

(Jones and DeJarnette 1936; Lewis 1937; Lewis and Kneberg 1941, 1946; Sullivan this volume; Webb 1938) (Figure 1.3). The same archaeologists believed that the chronologically later form, the large individually set post design, was a different architectural form that possessed a hipped or gabled roof as opposed to a curved or flexed roof (Figure 1.4). Note that throughout this book, this earlier type of proposed architecture is referred to as curved roof, flexed roof, flexed pole, arbor roof, or wigwam interchangeably, whereas architecture proposing a hipped or gabled roof is referred to as rigid roof structures unless the two variants of this roof style can be distinguished.

The perception of early Mississippian architecture changed very rapidly in the 1940s. Although DeJarnette, Lewis, Kneberg, and Webb maintained the idea of a flexed pole appearance for the early Mississippian wall trench foun-

1.4. Rigid roof architecture as portrayed in an illustration by Glenn Black in 1944 (from Black 1944:485, Figure 2, courtesy of the Indiana Historical Society Press).

dations, other archaeologists began advocating a more European or Mesoamerican style of architecture for the wall trench design (Black 1944, 1967; Harn 1972; Hoebel 1949; Martin et al. 1947; Price 1969; Walthall 1977), one slightly similar to the notion of late Mississippian rigid post buildings. This view that there was no architectural difference in roof style between structures of the early Mississippian and late Mississippian floor plans dominated the subsequent decades. Yet, within the last twenty years, a growing number of archaeologists have again begun to support a curved or flexed roof style for the early Mississippian wall trench foundation (Blanton and Gresham this volume; Lacquement 2005, this volume; Polhemus 1985, 1987; Reed n.d., this volume; Scarry 1995, 1998; Wilson 2005). However, it appears based on current museum displays, paintings, dioramas, book covers and illustrations, and full-scale reproductions that the rigid roof concept is still more widely accepted.

Chapters in support of each side of the debate are presented in order to address distinguishing characteristics of both views. Archaeologists supporting either of the two positions have had success and failure in the experimental reproduction of Mississippian wall trench houses, as well as supporting and contradicting evidence from ethnohistory, structural engineering, and wood science technology. The point of contention in the debate seems to be post size and the presence or absence of corner posts and internal support posts.

Archaeologists supporting the idea of a flexed roof typically argue that a hipped or gabled roof cannot be supported without posts in the corners of structures and posts placed inside of the structure in strategic locations in order to support the independent roof component. From this point of view, flexed pole architecture is ideal, as open corners are considered necessary to weave the wall poles together into a roof framework. In addition, only small diameter poles would have been able to be manipulated in this fashion, whereas larger, widely set posts would be more appropriate for a hipped or gabled roof. This interwoven framework of the flexed roof form is believed to resist inward pressures and therefore requires no internal roof supports.

In contrast, archaeologists in favor of rigid construction argue that a hipped or gabled roof is both possible and plausible for an open corner wall trench foundation that lacks interior roof supports. From this point of view, internal roof supports, though frequently present, are not always necessary when proper internal roof bracing and suitable lashing are used in supporting the independent roof unit. On the one hand this standpoint typically embraces the idea that one or more roof supports will and did support an independent roof unit. Archaeologists who advocate a flexed roof style, on the other hand, argue that one or two supports may have been necessary in building larger flexed pole houses, or perhaps these internal postholes represent interior roof bracing or a scaffolding system that was used in the construction process and removed after completion.

Chapters that address this above-ground architectural debate are presented in this book in order to fully understand each point of view. Perhaps by acknowledging the debate and presenting the perspectives of the two opposing sides, a consensus will be reached and the criteria necessary to solve the dispute will be established in future research. Presenting both architectural views also allows readers to make up their own minds concerning the interpretation of the architectural data in the archaeological record. It may also be possible that both sides are correct and that this single foundation design possessed two above-ground architectural forms. However, the general consensus from both sides does not support this double interpretation of above-ground layout at present.

## Survey of Architectural Foundations in the Southeast

Many of the chapters present various characteristics of archaeological floor plans in the southeastern United States. These studies include architectural forms such as domestic houses, larger public/ceremonial houses, and sweat lodges. The main objective of these chapters is to distinguish which architectural floor plans can be grouped together based on similar characteristics to establish a particular structural form. In other words, the authors of these chapters are not as concerned with describing the above-ground features of houses as with focusing on the architectural characteristics that are consistent among certain building types. Regardless of which side of the flexed pole/rigid post debate one sympathizes, these chapters are important in the chronology of foundation styles in particular regions of the Southeast. In addition, by investigating regions independently, the results can be slowly merged together to assemble the beginnings of a regional chronology for prehistoric architecture in the southeastern United States.

The examination of foundation variability is accomplished in several ways. One method utilized is to construct an architectural grammar, as Lewis and Stout (1998) did in their assessment of Mississippian town designs. Here, classifications are created using linguistic methodology to pinpoint and categorize common trends in architecture. In addition to architectural grammars, another method in examining floor plan variability is to create typologies based on shared characteristics and/or multivariate analysis as Brown (1985) and Polhemus (1985) have done with Plaquemine culture architecture in the Lower Mississippi Valley, and Hiwassee, Dallas, and Mouse Creek phases in eastern Tennessee, respectively.

Additionally, a chapter addressing the variability in architecture focuses on one particular type of structure, the sweat lodge. Although the main objective of this author is to examine the architectural details of structures used both historically and prehistorically for the purpose of sweating, this chapter also indirectly addresses the above-ground debate mentioned previously. Many archaeologists group function and architecture together in stating that the majority of circular sweat lodges were created in a flexed roof form, even though this architectural form is not the norm for a particular area (McConaughy 1985, this volume; Milner 1984; Pauketat and Woods 1986; Simon 2002). This statement possesses implications that the only forms of flexed pole architecture in these areas were circular buildings utilized as sweat lodges, and therefore any suspected curved-roof buildings are automatically considered to be sweat lodges. It then appears that flexed pole architecture would most likely not be a construction method used in the simply domestic (nonsweating) structures. The chapter that addresses the architectural characteristics of sweat lodges provides a means for addressing the idea that a particular type of architecture accommodated a specific function.

## Organization of Chapters

Five of the chapters in this book were originally papers presented in a symposium at the 62nd annual Southeastern Archaeological Conference in Columbia, South Carolina, in November of 2005. Robert Lafferty's paper was also presented at the same meeting in a different symposium. Four additional chapters were added after the symposium, including those by Ramie Gougeon, Vernon Knight, Lynne Sullivan, and Mark McConaughy. The first three authors created chapters specifically for this publication. McConaughy's chapter is a revised version of a paper originally given at the 31st annual Midwest Archaeological Conference in East Lansing, Michigan, in 1985 and has been cited in numerous books and Cultural Resource Management reports in archaeology throughout the Southeast.

Nelson Reed, in Chapter 2, explores the archaeological, experimental, and ethnohistorical evidence of Mississippian wall trench houses in the southeastern United States. Based on his evidence, Reed suggests that the curved roof design is the most suitable above-ground architecture given the design of the wall trench foundation. This argument, like many that advocate curved roof architecture, is based on archaeological signatures such as small, closely spaced wall poles set in a wall trench, with no corner poles or strategically placed roof supports. According to Reed, his experimental reconstruction of several curved roof houses fits the given floor plan as well as providing a more suitable framework than a small pole wall trench structure with a hipped or gabled roof.

In Chapter 3, Dennis Blanton and Thomas Gresham create and test hypotheses concerning construction techniques for early Mississippian flexed pole architecture. In order to test these hypotheses, the authors conducted a rather unique experimental construction at the Etowah site in northwestern Georgia. Based on the floor plan of a house located beneath Mound C, Blanton created and then burned a flexed pole, wattle-and-daub house. After being covered with earth for nearly a decade, Gresham excavated the burned structure without any prior knowledge of the experimental replica. What follows is an interesting interpretation of the successes and failures of the experiment from the point of view of both the architect and the excavator.

In Chapter 4, I attempt a typology and chronology of the domestic houses in west-central Alabama. Data in the sample consist of houses from Moundville, Lubbub Creek, Bessemer, and a few farmsteads along the Black Warrior River Valley. Two objectives are accomplished in this chapter. First, the idea of two distinct domestic floor plans for Mississippian houses is formally tested, an idea that has been around for nearly 70 years. These tests reveal whether the floor plans represent two distinct forms or a continuum of the same form. The second objective is to build a typology and chronology of house types from these six sites in west-central Alabama and determine if the transition in architecture is related to environmental or sociocultural change.

Rebuttals to the flexed pole interpretation of early Mississippian houses are put forth by Brennan in Chapter 5 and McConaughy in Chapter 6. Both authors argue that the typical Mississippian wall trench houses possessed hipped or gabled roofs. However, neither author argues that the flexed pole form never existed, only that it was not the norm for Mississippian architecture.

Tamira Brennan, in Chapter 5, explores the roof debate based on her evaluation of the architecture at the Kincaid site in the Black Bottom of southern Illinois. The bulk of her chapter concentrates on advancing a multidisciplinary method of determining both construction and roof styles of Mississippian structures archaeologically. The remainder of the chapter applies these methods to the Kincaid Mounds site. She addresses the argument supported by flexed roof advocates that rigid roof architecture cannot be created with small wall poles and no corner or roof supports. In her chapter, she argues that a hipped or gabled roof is possible without these features with the addition of internal roof bracing and specifically designed rafter notching.

Mark McConaughy, in Chapter 6, conducts a survey of 39 burned house structures from 16 sites throughout Illinois, including sites in the Central Illinois Valley, the Lower Illinois Valley, the American Bottom, and southern Illinois. McConaughy examines the floor plans and surviving structural data to determine which roof type was most prevalent, a flexed roof or a hipped or gabled roof. Even though McConaughy concludes that most of the structures in his area of study possessed a hipped or gabled roof, he also infers that the flexed roof or wigwam form was used, only less frequently. As the paper was revisited 20 years after its initial presentation, the author has added an addendum to the original paper concerning his thoughts and reinterpretations of the architectural evidence in the interim.

Lynne Sullivan in Chapter 7 describes the details of an experimental reconstruction conducted by George A. Lidberg and the WPA in 1939 at the Thompson Village site of the Kentucky Lake Reservoir in western Tennessee. The foundation for this reconstruction was created in an excavated Mississippian wall trench house. Even though the house was constructed in a flexed pole form, it differs from other flexed pole reconstructions in that the poles came to a point in the middle of the structure similar to other early architectural reconstructions in the Southeast (Jones and DeJarnette 1936). The wall posts of this reconstruction were not intertwined to form a rounded roof as in Lewis and Kneberg's (1946) recreations or Nash's (1968) experimental reconstruction at the Chucalissa Museum in eastern Tennessee in 1955, but instead resembled the construction methods of the Caddo and Witchita of the south-central United States (Bushnell 1922:Plate 55; Swanton 1942).

In Chapter 8, Ramie Gougeon examines late Mississippian domestic winter houses in northwest Georgia. Gougeon examines the typical layout and common construction materials utilized in the area during the last 200 years of the Mississippian stage. Examples from Georgia and nearby regions comprising an area approximately 400 km centering on Carters Lake create the sample for this study. Examples are used to elaborate on the idea that while there may be broad, pan-Mississippian architectural patterns, the smaller patterns will likely reflect localized cultural expressions.

Robert Lafferty, in Chapter 9, examines one particular Mississippian structure in northeastern Arkansas in order to address its architecture and function. This building, uncovered at the East site, possessed artifactual and architectural characteristics similar to that of historic sweat lodges. Based on this evidence and a survey of ethnohistorical literature, Lafferty suggests that this particular prehistoric structure's function was that of a sweat lodge.

In Chapter 10, Robert Scott addressed historic Creek architecture at the turn of the nineteenth century. In examining changes in domestic architecture, the data are utilized to understand Creek responses to the direct contact experience of colonization and American frontier expansion. Based on the ethnohistorical evidence, people within core communities maintained traditional forms of domestic architecture, while those Creek who began settling away from the larger towns began to adopt the construction techniques of the Europeans.

Vernon Knight, in Chapter 11, brings all the research together in order to expose the larger archaeological and anthropological implications of these chapters as well as the implications of this research for future endeavors.

# 2
# Evidence of Curved Roof Construction in Mississippian Structures

*Nelson A. Reed*

Most recent descriptions, interpretations, and museum visual recreations of prehistoric rectangular structures assume the use of a hipped or gabled roof as the typical house form during the Mississippian stage (A.D. 900–1550) in the eastern United States. This perception of Mississippian houses has not always been dominant. DeJarnette, Lewis, Kneberg, and Webb were among the first archaeologists to publish architectural interpretations of Mississippian houses in the Southeast. Overall, they interpreted these Mississippian designs as curved roof structures. However, this view of Mississippian architecture has been slowly pushed aside over the last 70 years. An illustration of a hipped roof house set in wall trenches, a depiction that may have been borrowed from Maya house construction by Black (1944:485) (see Figure 1.4) and used in several introductory textbooks in anthropology in the 1940s to represent the typical Mississippian house (Hoebel 1949:120; Martin et al. 1947:355), may have caused archaeologists to stray from a curved roof perspective (Lacquement 2004). In this chapter, evidence will be presented from experimental archaeology, ethnohistory, excavation, and structural engineering, with lessons from failures and interaction among these disciplines in order to suggest that the earlier curved roof perspective of DeJarnette, Lewis, Kneberg, and Webb was correct.

## The First Experimental Structure

A full-scale rectangular hipped roof house set in wall trenches and constructed in what was believed to be the typical Mississippian manner was erected in 1964 to serve as an interpretation of the archaeological evidence discovered at the Cahokia site (Figure 2.1). The experimental structure consisted of 55 wall posts, approximately 8 to 10 cm in diameter set 30 cm deep and roughly 25 cm

2.1. Experimental hipped roof wall trench structure in 1964.

apart. These wall posts supported a roof plate of four poles, and the roof plate in turn supported an A-frame for the hipped roof, thatched with cattails. To protect the wattle-and-daub walls, a 20-cm roof overhang was included when constructing the roof. In keeping with the archaeological evidence at the Cahokia site, there were no corner posts or internal roof supports. Under the load of thatch, the roof plate members bowed at the unsupported corners, cantilevering out, as the roof was insufficiently supported by the eight wall poles, the end poles of each wall. The other 47 wall poles served no structural purpose (Figure 2.2).

During its first year, the building developed a tilt on the long axis, the cattails came loose as they dried, and the following spring while it was being rethatched, the hut collapsed with five volunteers on the roof. The roof unit, an assembly of poles lashed in a grid pattern, maintained its integrity, landing on the ground in one piece together with the startled volunteers. It had previously been noted, before its collapse, that the roof became unstable during high winds, with the wall posts/spandrel beam and the separate roof element becoming the point of failure, as the supporting wall posts lacked stability in their anchorage and columnar movement.

Following the collapse, a survey of 11 different hipped or gabled Mesoameri-

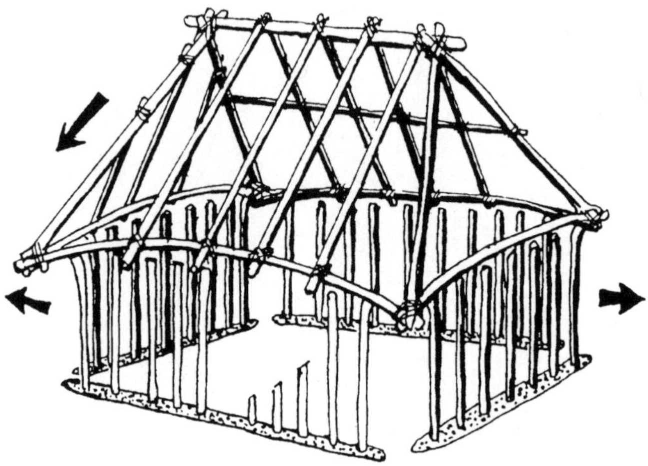

2.2. Structural problems of hipped roof wall trench architecture.

can house types was conducted by the author, who visited and lived in many of the examples (Table 2.1). The results indicated that most of these structures possessed heavy posts averaging 20 cm in diameter, which were widely spaced and set in individual postholes (Figure 2.3). Several of the wall posts of these Mesoamerican houses were not load bearing, only serving as a privacy screen. This arrangement is completely different from the Mississippian pattern and from the first experimental structure (Figure 2.1). This survey of Mesoamerican construction techniques and the results of the experimental wall trench hipped roof house led this author to question if the hipped or gabled roof technique could be built with a small wall post, open cornered, wall trench foundation.

## Ethnohistory

There are various terms used to describe the type of structures built by the Native people of the eastern United States. These terms describe either local variation such as Quonset, wigwam, and wickiup, or by analogy, barrel shaped, domed, vaulted, and arbor buildings. As these different names have come to have specific meaning but are all variations of a single, non-Western technology, the neutral term, "curved roof," is used here to cover the general category. It should also be noted that it is possible to have a curved roof added to rigid wall posts, which is also included under the category of curved roofs. Otherwise, structures utilizing a separate roof component are referred to as "rigid roof" structures, unless it is apparent which type of roof was used, hipped or gabled.

2.1. Location of Native Houses Observed by the Author and the Corresponding Number of Wall and Roof Supports in a Typical Construction.

| Location | Supporting Wall Posts | Interior roof supports |
|---|---|---|
| Maya, Yucatán | 4 | 0 |
| Maya, Quintana Roo | 4 | 0 |
| Gulf Coast, Olmec | 4 | 0 |
| Veracruz | 6 | 0 |
| Huastec | 6 | 3 |
| Totonec | 6 | 2 |
| Otomi | 8 | 0 |
| Colima, Nahuat | 6 | 0 |
| Colima | 4 | 2 (end walls) |
| Oaxaca | 4, 6, 8 | 0 |
| Coastal, Guerrero | 8 | 0 |

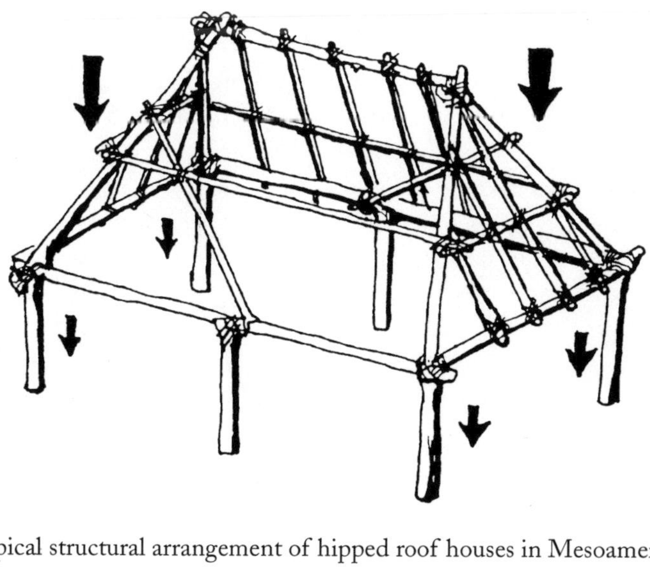

2.3. The typical structural arrangement of hipped roof houses in Mesoamerica.

Curved roof structures were the type of buildings found from Florida to Minnesota, from Massachusetts to Texas, reaching from the coast to the Great Plains, in historic times. The curved roof structures include several variations of curved roofs, such as the straight end wall longhouses of the Atlantic Coast and the beehive-shaped huts west of the Mississippi. Exceptions to this overall distribution of curved roof structures include the circular earth lodges of Macon Plateau, the Irene rotunda, the winter houses and town houses of the historic Creek and Cherokee, the round houses of the Chickasaw, and the open sided shelters of the Seminole. These houses typically employed concentric patterns of heavy posts (typically square or circular) in order to support rigid roof timbers that sloped into a central cribbed construction, which was covered with lathing and combinations of earth and thatch. On the one hand, these rigid roof houses of historic tribes are typically supported by a few large wall posts and internal roof supports. On the other hand, Mississippian wall trench houses are believed to be constructed with small, closely spaced poles, typically set in wall trenches, and bent in a strategic manner to form an interwoven basketlike framework (Figure 2.4). In this architectural form, there is no independent roof component and therefore no need for internal roof supports.

In describing the Siouan of eastern North Carolina at the beginning of the eighteenth century, Lawson (in Swanton 1946:410–411) stated, "These savages live in wigwams, or cabins, built of bark, which are made round, like an oven, to prevent any damage by hard gales of wind. . . . In building these fabrics, they get very long poles of pine, cedar, hickory, or any other wood that will bend." Ethnohistorical evidence of curved roof structures were also recorded as being utilized by the Virginia Algonquian, the Iroquois of New York, the Caddo of Oklahoma, the Yazoo, Natchez, and Tunica of the Lower Mississippi Valley, and the Yuchi of northern Georgia (Bushnell 1922; Speck 1909; Swanton 1942, several authors all listed in Swanton 1946:387–420; to name a few).

The most detailed account of this curved architectural form was provided by Le Page du Pratz in his description of the Natchez in the Lower Mississippi Valley in the 1720s (Swanton 1911:59–60, 1946:418–419). Although the description is too long to be included here (see Blanton and Gresham this volume:34–35), it does represent several important details. The most important aspect of his account was the description of the construction process with the roof and walls being created from the same architectural element and the bending and tying of corner posts together above to form a template upon which the wall poles were lashed and therefore controlling for the shape of the roof. Le Page du Pratz also gave information concerning construction tech-

2.4. Curved roof wall trench architectural arrangement.

niques such as the dimensions and material of wall members and horizontal supports, thatching, and the presence of internal scaffolding.

There is also evidence to suggest that flexed and rigid roof construction techniques were contemporaneous or transitional according to the ethnohistoric literature. The Chickasaw of northern Mississippi were described as using hipped or gabled roof architecture, but another curved roof form was also alluded to in the descriptions of their dwellings. In his account from the late eighteenth century, Adair (2005:417–418) stated that the Chickasaw "sink a large post in the center of each gable end, . . . in order to support the roof tree; to these they tie the rafters with broad splinters of white oak, or hickory, unless they make the choice of such long saplings, as will reach from side to side over the ridge pole." This account is important because it not only indicates the simultaneous use of or transition in roof forms, but it also indicates that both forms may be utilized in the construction of a single building. Such designs have been recreated for a large public structure found on Seven Mile Island in northern Alabama (Webb and DeJarnette 1942:46–48), and these designs are similar to the intermediate house forms described by Nash (1968), which may have utilized both flexed and rigid construction techniques.

The same transition was alluded to in a statement by Lawson in 1700 about the Tuscarora of eastern North Carolina. Lawson wrote, "They had made themselves Streets of Houses built with Pine-Bark, not with round roof Tops, as they commonly use, but Ridge-Fashion" (Lawson 1967:59). Frank Speck (1909) in his study of the Yuchi in eastern Oklahoma, originally from Tennessee and Georgia, mentioned a similar transition from a curved roof to a rigid roof structure: "The Yuchi remember still another type of family dwelling house which seems to show that the common house type of the Algonkian tribes bordering the Atlantic coast farther north was known to the Yuchi as well" (Speck 1909:40).

The housing of the Yazoo, Ofo, and Tunica was described by Gravier in 1700, in which he refers to these structures as "round and vaulted" (in Swanton 1911:315). Le Page du Pratz (in Swanton 1946:418–419) wrote that the housing of the Natchez was built with a curved roof in the early 1700s. Yet, as late as 1747, the Natchez, or rather their successors after the massacre, were shown building a mixture of curved and rigid roof houses (perhaps summer and winter houses), depicted in a drawing from that same year (Dumont de Montigny, Newbury Library Collection, Chicago). These rigid roof structures of the Natchez appear to be similar to the round houses of the Choctaw in 1775 (Romans, in Swanton 1946:Plate 89).

Father Anastasias, in 1685, is one of many who describe the Caddo houses as built like beehives. The Teran map of the Kadohadacho in 1691 illustrates these houses, together with a small round domed building and a ramada, grouped in a number of house lots (Swanton 1942:48). By 1868, as depicted in the Soulé photograph (Smithsonian Institution Archives, Bureau of American Ethnology Collection), the Caddo had replaced the "beehive" lodge with a post and clay wall hipped roof building while retaining the ramada and the round structure. The hipped roof houses are similar to the jacal, common in Texas and northern Mexico, and might have been brought from that area by the Indian servants of the Spanish priests who established missions there by 1690.

The Spanish built gabled churches, barracks, and governor's quarters at Saint Augustine, 1565–1595, covered with bark or thatch that was held down by the weight of exterior poles (Lorant 1946:21), an influencing form accompanied with elements of reverse borrowing from the local Native traditions. Other possible influences could be from the French at Mobile and New Orleans after 1700. The later renderings of the temple at Natchez are similar to the French Creole tradition of *poteau en terre,* posts set in earth. Finally, there was the Anglo-American influence beginning on the east coast a century earlier, which spread slowly into the interior. It is reasonable to assume that European influence played a role in the development of Native architecture in certain regions, particularly with the introduction of steel axes.

## Archaeological and Experimental Evidence of Roof Types

If we accept that the curved roof was a heavily utilized house form in the areas where the Mississippian culture had previously flourished, then we must con-

2.5. The experimental construction of a curved roof structure in 1974.

sider it a strong possibility that the Mississippians used this technique as well. In order to test the architectural designs described by early ethnohistorians, various types of houses were constructed, leading up to a village of 12 full-scale houses in 1974, including rectangular structures with rounded (Figure 2.5) and pointed arched roofs, rectangular structures with rounded and straight end walls, round houses, hot houses, ramadas, and granaries (Reed n.d.).

Prior to construction, the archaeological record was examined for evidence that would indicate curved roof construction. Archaeological data that are believed to support the idea of curved roof houses during the Mississippian stage include the use of wall trenches, many small wall posts, open corners, and the lack of internal supports. Burned structures throughout the Mississippian world also provide evidence of curved roof houses in the form of long slender poles, curved poles, burned interwoven roof framework, and the lack of any evidence of the survival of ridge pole.

### *Wall Trenches*

Perhaps the most direct evidence of the function of the wall trench was found by Webb (1938) at the Bowman Farm Mounds in northeastern Tennessee. Excavations revealed the use of horizontal log braces inside the trench, a lower one on the outside of the vertical posts, and an upper one on the inside, to resist the inward deflection of the wall poles (see Blanton and Gresham this volume:Figure 3.1). The two log braces inside the trench were reinforced with vertical stakes in Building 9 at Hiwassee Island (Lewis and Kneberg 1946:68; Webb 1938:23). "From the arrangement of braces and wedges it seems apparent that the builders were striving to overcome a force which was either pushing or pulling the top of the partition toward the center of the building" (Lewis and Kneberg 1946:68). This should have been the final word on the subject. Yet, it should be noted that not all wall trench houses utilized horizontal trench wedges. Trench braces may have been necessary when constructing curved roof houses on sandy or less compact soils, but were not common when the trench was dug into firm clay.

In general, Mississippian wall trenches typically range from 18 to 30 cm in width at the floor level, and 12 to 20 cm wide at the deepest point of the trench, which is typically 40 to 75 cm deep. In the construction of the replica village structures in 1974 (Reed n.d.), wall trenches were dug with primitive tools to get some idea of the problems and labor input involved: shell and flint hoes mounted in wood handles, pointed digging sticks, and wooden spades, all of which were modeled on tools marks found in the author's excavations at Cahokia. We could tap out a hole and haft the mussel shell hoe in fifteen minutes. We didn't knap flint hoes, which would take much more time, not to mention that the Mill Creek flint was traded in from Union County, Illinois, 120 km to the south. Our experiments with the flint "spade" were unsuccessful because of the weight and size. A digging stick 1.5 to 2 m served the equivalent of a pick and was used with a vertical and a prying movement, on trenches and in our agricultural experiments. A wooden spade with a 15-cm blade, which was designed based on tool marks found in deep pits on Monks Mound, served to excavate the relatively narrow and deep trenches, and the loosened dirt was removed with one of the hoes.

The nature of the wall trench indicates the above-ground architecture, but a wall trench is not always necessary in curved roof construction, particularly in the earlier Mississippian stage. Some Mississippian structures were built with wall trenches, while others were constructed with small individually set postholes. Based on the similar size, spacing, and material of these wall posts, it can be assumed that the two patterns were functionally equivalent (Blanton and Gresham this volume; Lacquement this volume). However, as the wall trench technique became more prevalent, there must have been some reason that it was favored. Lewis and Kneberg (1946:50) suggest that the wall poles and cross lathing might have been preassembled on the ground, and each section inserted into the trench as a unit (see Blanton and Gresham this volume).

Another labor-saving device made possible by the wall trench would be the preassembly of the curved pair units. Callahan (1981, 1985) used premanufactured and preassembled arched poles in his experimental replica of a Late Woodland Pamunkey longhouse excavated in 1981 at the Great Neck site (44VB7) in the Maryland Coastal Plains. To create preassembled units, poles were placed on the ground and bent around firmly anchored stakes. Once the individual poles were formed to the desired shape, the ends of the two poles were lashed together and held in position with the addition of a cross beam to each set. The process formed a symmetrical shape of uniform height and curvature before assembly, far more efficiently than wrestling with resistant poles in the air from a ladder or staging. The corner poles would then be individually added; in some cases the short or end wall trenches were not as deep.

Additional reasons for the favoring of the wall trench method over individually set posts is that it is easier to dig a trench with shell, flint hoe, or wooden spade, than to dig an individual hole. In digging individual postholes for the experimental reconstructions (Reed n.d.), we found that the most efficient method was to hammer a pointed stake into the ground at the desired place and then wiggle it back out, creating a ready-made posthole. In addition, it is easier to dig a straight trench of a controlled depth than to dig individual houses of the same depth and maintain a correct alignment.

### *Post Size and Spacing*

Architectural evidence discovered by Neitzel (1965) in his work at the Fatherland Site in western Mississippi suggests that post size and spacing was characteristic of curved roof houses. His excavation of Mounds B and C, which he identified as the Chief's House and Temple respectively, are very close to the description given by Le Page du Pratz, an eyewitness 250 years earlier. Neitzel's temple structures on Building Level 1, Mound C, were the ones seen by Le Page du Pratz in the 1720s. Le Page du Pratz's 4-in (10-cm) posts, placed 1 ft (30 cm) apart (in Swanton 1946:418–419) are almost identical to those reported by Neitzel (1965:34). Yet, Le Page du Pratz failed to mention the use of wall trenches in the construction process, while describing the use of larger end poles set in the corners, which were curved over to form a template for the other smaller wall posts, and which were not found in excavation. Except for this variation, Le Page du Pratz writes of the same village, the same people, and there should be no question that the same basic pattern in the earth reflects the same above-ground construction technique elsewhere.

*Upper Wall Braces*

In building the first experimental curved roof house (Reed n.d.), we found that the wall posts had a tendency to slope inward. To correct this, horizontal poles were added to the inside of the walls at head height. Le Page du Pratz described this method in Natchez construction (Swanton 1946:418). Le Page du Pratz wrote, "they plant the other poles in the earth in straight lines between those at the corners. When they are thus planted they are bound firmly to a cross pole on the inside of each face (or side) . . . at the height of 5 or 6 feet . . . This forms the walls."

This method of upper wall bracing would leave no evidence in the ground. For the same purpose, the Mijikenda people of Kenya, in building a house very similar to the proposed Mississippian house, erected a fencelike arrangement around the inside of their building, to stiffen the walls (Andersen 1977). This same pattern of internal postholes is shown in Feature 52 of the Mitchell site (Porter 1974) and Feature 173 at the Sponemann site (Jackson et al. 1992) (Figure 2.6), and occurs in houses H62 and H137 at Cahokia (Pauketat 1998). Charred evidence of horizontal braces has been found at the Emmons site (Emmons et al. 1960) and House 56 at Cahokia Tract 15B (McConaughy this volume). In addition, a variant of this pattern is found at Seven Mile Island, where a reconstruction of Feature 2 shows four vertical posts, one in each corner supporting horizontal braces (Webb and DeJarnette 1942).

A different solution to the same problem is the construction of a curved roof on independent vertical wall posts, as in the summer house of the contemporary Kickapoo (Figure 2.7). In this structure, three sets of heavy longitudinally running vertical posts support three horizontal roof forming (not supporting) braces. This was also true of larger buildings at Cahokia and Moundville discussed below.

*Open Corners*

Mississippian wall trenches normally have one or all open corners and in those that are closed, the corners are often not dug out to any depth and typically lack postholes (Figure 2.8). Occasionally, as in the "Charcoal House" at the Eveland site in the Central Illinois Valley (Caldwell 1967b), there is an individual posthole in each corner (Figure 2.8), which is like those large corner poles bent diagonally as a template to bend the other wall poles over as referred to by Le Page du Pratz above. (For alternative interpretation of this structure see McConaughy this volume.) This author has no doubt that "Charcoal House" possessed a curved roof, as at least four of the charred end poles

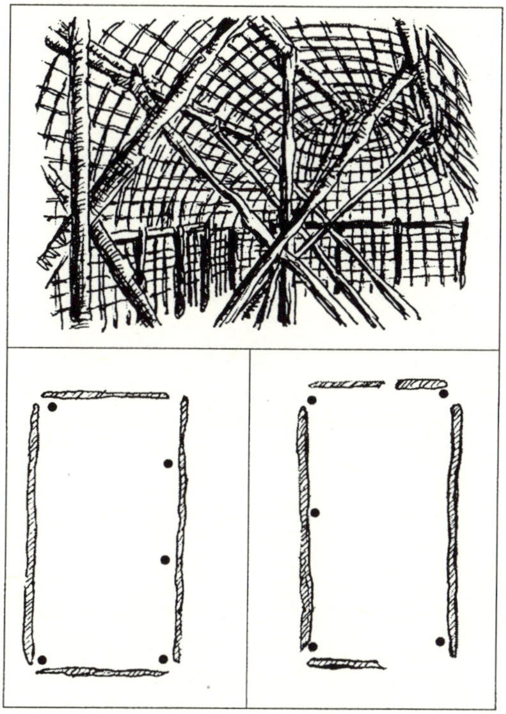

2.6. (Top) a Mijikenda house in Kenya and (bottom) two Mississippian floor plans demonstrating a similar posthole arrangement (top adapted from Andersen 1977:195).

are approximately 4 m long, too long to serve as separate wall or roof poles, and extend from near their posthole well into the roof crest area. The same point was made by Lewis and Kneberg (1946:51) in noting that 25-ft (7.6-m) charred poles found on the floor at the Hixon site, Chickamauga Basin, could only have functioned when bent to form a single wall and roof component.

The open corner layout is ideal for a curved roof construction as it allows room for independent "wall" poles to be bent inward and interwoven without conflict, forming a sturdy architectural framework. The open corners do not appear to serve as doors, as this would create a weakness in the structure, a weakness that was resolved by the horizontal braces. Doors were typically made along a long wall by cutting and removing lower sections of poles.

### *Roof Supports*

Wall trench structures have been classified as either curved or rigid roof depending upon whether the structure has internal postholes. Many archaeologists rarely consider the flexed pole form as a possibility, because wall trench structures with "central support posts" are assumed to have had a hipped or

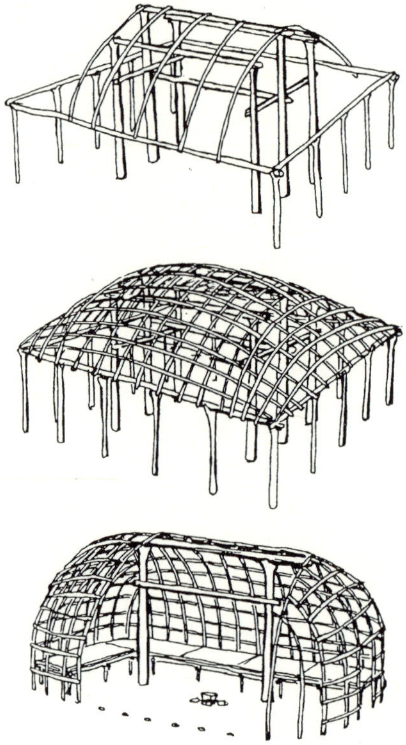

2.7. Illustration of two building stages of a Kickapoo summer house (top and middle) and cutaway drawing of a Kickapoo winter structure (bottom).

gabled roof, even if these supports were not strategically located within the structure. This type of oddly positioned internal roof supports typically occur off the center line of the building or spaced at irregular intervals. Some of these might be foundations for embedded mortars, partitions, or other facilities. Other examples of posts misidentified as internal roof supports include one central internal support. One central support posthole associated with open corner wall trench houses have been uncovered at Feature 1 at the Lawrence Primas site (Pauketat and Woods 1986; Simon 2002); Feature 7 at the Vaughn Branch site (Jackson 1996); Features 143 and 367 at ICT-II, Cahokia (Collins 1990); and Structure 5b on the Northwest Riverbank at Moundville (Scarry 1995, 1998), to name a few.

The winter house of the Kickapoo (Figure 2.7) has two interior roof support posts positioned longitudinally to the house axis and aligned to its midline. Just as in the Kickapoo summer house, these horizontal poles were props, not supports. The Mijikenda house in Kenya, Figure 2.6, has rooftree props, which together with two sets of mid-roof props help form the arched roof.

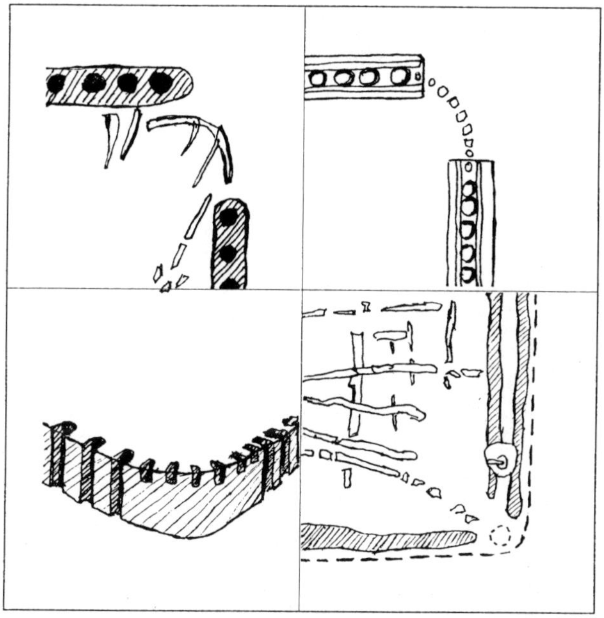

2.8. Diagram of various forms of corner arrangement in Mississippian wall trench foundations: (top left) an open corner wall trench, (top right) a closed wall trench, (bottom left) profile of closed wall trench corner, and (bottom right) an open corner wall trench with a single corner post.

These mid-roof props, placed diagonally, are removed once the arched poles have taken a set (Andersen 1977). It is also possible that the post molds that are being referred to as internal roof supports may be the remnants of a scaffolding system used during construction and removed after the building is completed.

In several cases at Toqua (40MR6) and Carden Farms (40AN44) in eastern Tennessee where structure floors were intact, individual centrally placed postholes were located beneath the hearth, indicating their removal prior to the completion of the building and possible use of a scaffolding system (Polhemus 1987). If a hearth was truncated by plowing or disturbances, the post pattern would appear to possess a single roof support. A series of large square houses at the Mitchell site, including F47, F55, and F56, had large central postholes, but also extraction trenches (Porter 1977:147–148). Espinosa gives a description of the construction of a Caddo lodge: "The laths [poles] are placed in a circle and in the middle they put up a very tall pole with knots on it for climbing. Two Indians are placed on top on a cross made of two pieces of wood. Each throws out a noose and seizes a lath [pole] by the top, working in unison. They continue to tie them until they have forced a figure like a half orange" (in Swanton 1942:150). To which Morfi adds, "They then cut the great log from the center, and the house is finished" (in Swanton 1942:151), indicating that "roof supports" were removed after the buildings were completed.

*Wood*

The identification of wood used in burned houses can be useful in recognizing curved roof construction techniques. Harvey (1977) found that hardwoods were preferred to softwoods for house construction in southeast Missouri, and that the prehistoric builders were careful in selecting wood based on the qualities important to them, in spite of the fact that they were not always available in the immediate vicinity. Le Page du Pratz reports hickory was used for curved roof construction among the Natchez. Harn (personal communication 1993) believed the Charcoal House at the Eveland site and many of the burned structures at the Orendorf village were constructed primarily using hickory, ash, and oak, while the structure at the Fingers site, Feature 1, was made up of 50 percent hickory, 19.2 percent red oak, and 36.8 percent willow (Kelly 1995:58). This preference for oak, hickory, and willow was found at Range (Kelly 1989), Julien (Johannessen in Milner 1984), and Radic sites (McElrath 1987), while at ICT-II, Cahokia, other woods were utilized, presumably out of necessity due to over-exploitation during times of peak building activity.

Simon (2002) studied the ethnobotanical remains of materials used in American Bottom house construction. She concluded that the most common wood used as wall posts in 27 structures with small postholes set relatively close together, and typically set in wall trenches, was predominantly white oak and hickory. She also found evidence of cane, red oak, and small percentages of several other wood types.

In examining above-ground architecture, it is important to determine which types of wood are most suitable for the task based on certain attributes. There are two attributes required of wood specimens for the construction of a curved roof house: rigidity and flexibility. The first characteristic, rigidity, is the ability to resist horizontal or axial deflection due to load-bearing functions. This attribute is needed in order to support the weight of thatch and the weight of the thatchers, as well as to maintain its shape in times of high winds and snow. In building a curved roof structure, species such as hickory (*Carya ovata*), white oak (*Quercus alba*), red oak (*Quercus rubra*), ash (*Fraxinus Americana*), and pine

(*Pinus unspecified*) would have provided the rigidity needed. The second attribute, flexibility, is important for curved roof construction, as the wood must be pliable enough to be bent into the desired shape. Species such as hickory, white oak, red oak, ash, hackberry (*Celtis occidentalis*), and black willow (*Salix nigra Marsh*) are all flexible, but some may be too weak to support a roof load of thatch and snow. Pine on the other hand meets the rigidity requirement but is one of the least flexible woods (U.S. Department of Agriculture) and therefore is not ideal for curved roof construction.

In 2004, Lacquement conducted an experimental study in which he bent various types of wood including pine, hickory, and white oak, around a fixed framework. The framework was meant to simulate the building pressures found in a curved roof house. In short, he concluded that both hickory and white oak were excellent species, being both flexible and rigid, but pine could not have been used in the creation of curved roof structures, as it was strong but not nearly flexible enough. Blanton and Gresham (this volume) made a similar statement in their creation and destruction of a curved roof house at Etowah. In the first attempt at building this curved roof house, pine was used as wall/roof members and almost every one of the pine poles split in the bending process.

What this information tells us is that houses that are predominately oak and hickory were probably constructed in a curved roof manner, whereas houses that are predominantly pine were most likely hipped or gabled houses, because the high crushing strength of pine makes it excellent as a rigid wall member supporting a roof plate or as an internal roof support, but it lacks the flexibility to make a curved roof house.

## Public Structures

If the basic Mississippian domestic house is built with a curved roof, we might expect that the larger public wall trench buildings used the same technique. The largest challenge to this progression from smaller to larger structures is that the larger wall trench structures occasionally possessed patterns of what appears to be internal roof supports. These rows of posts occur in structures in the American Bottom, such as Structural Feature 1 at the Galley Pond Mound (Binford et al. 1964) (see Figure 6.7); 7C and 52 at the Mitchell site (Porter 1974); F173 at the Sponemann site (Jackson et al. 1992); and Features 8, 12, 131, 143, 233, and 287 at ICT-II, Cahokia (Collins 1990). In addition, an unnamed structure in occupation level 7, Zone 2A, level 6 of Mx°7 at the Kincaid site (Cole et al. 1951) and Building 25 at Hiwassee Island (Lewis and Kneberg 1946) all share this pattern.

At first glance, these large structures would seem to be an example of hipped architecture based on their large floor area and the presence of longitudinally running "internal roof supports," which is how Binford et al. (1964) interprets the Galley Pond Mound structure. However, it should be noted that the central support posts of the Galley Pond Mound structure do not extend to the corners of the building, which would make it difficult to support roof rafters in the corners of the roof unit. In addition, the wall posts of this structure, averaging 16.4 cm, do not seem large enough to support the weight of a 17-m roof plate pole and several 9-m-long rigid rafters. The center support posts are all set at relatively shallow depths ranging from 14 to 61 cm, which is hardly deep enough to anchor the heavy framework of a separate roof component. This evidence indicates that Structural Feature 1 at the Galley Pond Mound site probably possessed a curved roof. The internal posts could, however, serve to support roof braces as in the Mijikenda house of Kenya (Figure 2.6).

In building their curved roof structures, the Mijikenda used a series of horizontal wall braces, which were supported by posts set just inside the line of wall posts in order to promote more vertical walls. A second set of braces applied much higher on the walls of the structure was forced outward with long props, and, finally, a ridge beam defined the crest of the building (Figure 2.8). Once the wooden poles and grid had cured, the props were removed (Andersen 1977:195). The same approach is used in South America where the Yawalapiti support their "shoulder high" braces with near vertical wall posts, while the Tupari use braced props to give form to their flexible structures as shown in models in the American Museum of Natural History, New York. Therefore, it seems that some kind of internal bracing would be necessary for curved roof construction larger than the simple dome. Lewis and Kneberg argue a similar point in discussing Building 25 at Hiwassee Island, which they believed possessed a curved roof; they also believed the four irregularly placed central supports represented internal roof supports that were used in areas that needed additional stability. Based on the typical arrangement for hipped or gabled structures, there should be a symmetrical arrangement of internal supports in order to support a separate roof component.

## Structural Engineering Questions

Questions of structural engineering, which might not seem vital in small huts, take on a new meaning when dealing with the reconstruction of large public buildings. Mississippians peoples had no theoretical knowledge of tensile and compressive forces, but they were the inheritors of over a thousand years of

2.2. Mississippian Public Structures and Their Structural Attributes.

| Location | Area ($m^2$) | Length/ Width (m) | Number of Roof Supports | Spacing between Roof Supports (m) | Distance from Roof Support to End Wall (m) |
|---|---|---|---|---|---|
| House 15 Powell Tract Cahokia | 172 | 18/9.75 | 3 | 3.4 | 4.6 |
| Structure 3 Moundville | 188 | 14.5/13 | 4 | 3.5 | 1.5–2.5 |
| Orendorf 8-4 | 308 | 19.5/15.9 | 4 | 2.2 | 6.25 |
| House 3 Tract 15A Cahokia | 321.4 | 22.8/13.7 | 4 | 3.7 | 4.8? |
| House 10 Dickson | 353 | 24.7/14.3 | ? | 3.6 | 5.48 |
| Major Structure—Monk Mound Cahokia | 427 | 29–40/13.8 | 5 | 3.7 | 7? |

construction experience, and they knew from practice what they could and could not do. In addressing the issue of curved roof technique on buildings with large floor plans, a group of Mississippian public buildings with a central row of "support" posts was examined (Table 2.2).

The Mississippian builders were limited to a roof-spanning technology of approximately 17 m, 8.5 m from either wall to the internally supported ridge pole. It would have taken a heavy timber to serve as a rigid rafter in covering this distance. In order to prevent vertical sagging of a horizontal member, the depth of the member or the distance between the compression and tension surface of a rafter would need to have been increased, thus increasing the weight of the rafter. This is a dead load upon the supporting posts and walls, to which must be added the weight of purlins and framework of the roof assembly, plus the load of thatch or matting.

A curved member, in contrast, would add no load, as its memory directs weight up and out. Much of the weight of living wood is attributed to water, held in the cells between wood fibers. This means that it is more flexible when freshly cut and that with curing it will stiffen and become stronger by up to two and one-half times depending on wood type, favoring an easier assembly (Scofield and O'Brian 1963; U.S. Department of Agriculture 1987). When first erected, a pair of poles would act as an arch, either round or pointed, with load dispersed from any point on the arch at a tangential angle, and with lateral stability temporarily assured by being lashed to the roof beam.

The Monks Mound and Moundville buildings probably had curving roofs mounted on a sturdy rigid wall, in the Kickapoo manner, while other large buildings apparently sprang directly from the wall trench. Once several arched pairs were installed, they would be joined to each other by lateral wall poles or purlins. The shape of the arch is important in giving strength and for symmetry, necessary for an efficient load path and to resist a lateral force such as would be created by wind. This is where upper braces would be required. They could have been of the temporary sort used by the Mijikenda (which seems easiest), or some kind of scaffolding attached to the roof tree support posts. There is no archaeological evidence, but there is a practical need.

At this point, the main section of the framework would act as a barrel shell, with an efficient dispersal of vertical and horizontal loads. Longitudinal movement was then dampened by the engagement of the end walls into the grid, supplying the great strength of the double curvature of a dome. The rigid wall frame, which kept the rafter poles suspended, now also served as a tension ring, as did the purlins to keep them in, while the latter also acted as anchors for the thatch or matting. This form of shell structure, a great deal stronger than the plate of a hipped or gabled roof, and its member could have been theoretically much reduced, limited only by the diameter of trees or saplings of sufficient length (Faherty and Williamson 1989). This weight factor is important considering the distance the wood must have been hauled by hand to the building site. The rounded shape and lack of right angles was also helpful under the wind load to be expected on mound top locations.

Quonset buildings (see Figure 6.6) lack the shell effect, as their end walls are vertical. It has been suggested that the principle advantage of this would be the opportunity to easily make additions at either end, without unfastening end poles, and this could be important in the case of longhouses, with the addition of more families. The only definite Mississippian "Quonset" structure, in this author's opinion, Structural Feature #1 at the Toothsome site (see McConaughy this volume:Figure 6.7), has this weakness in structure due to vertical end walls reinforced with three heavy posts in each end wall that supported a ridge pole and two braces.

## Conclusion

Familiarity with experimental hut construction demonstrates that the open corner Mississippian wall trench foundation is inappropriate for the use of a hipped or gabled roof, but serves excellently for a curved roof form, as it allows the corners to be rounded and merged with the rest of the building in a shell formation. First, curved roof houses in the Southeast involved the use of long, thin flexible saplings, which were planted closely together in the ground and then bent in a strategic manner to form a series of arches. These arches intersected, creating the internal framework. Architecturally, such structures possessed a domed roof with a basketlike integrity eliminating the need for internal roof supports. Second, hipped or gabled roof buildings leave a different footprint in the ground in precontact North America, namely corner posts and large, widely spaced wall posts and specifically arranged internal roof supports. Ethnohistorical accounts from the time of early European contact report that the majority of buildings of the eastern United States had curved roofs. A survey of burned structures demonstrated that this curved roof pattern was true of earlier Mississippian wall trench houses in the Tennessee-Cumberland Valley, the American Bottom, and the Illinois River Valley, including those with interior "support" postholes, which served with various systems of bracing necessary to achieve a symmetrical and effective curve for the shell formation. Therefore, it would appear that all open corner wall trench foundations are indicative of curved roof architecture.

There has been resistance to this "wigwam" approach, as though there is a cultural preference for a European style roof, or for that of Mesoamerican design, for a "high culture" building as opposed to one built by "primitives." It may be said that the curved roof technique— taking advantage of the structural integrity of the arch and the dome, allowing the use of thinner members to span greater distances, highly stable with relatively shallow foundations, and requiring considerably less material and labor—was the more elegant solution.

# 3
# An Experimental Perspective on Mississippian Small Pole Structures

*Dennis B. Blanton and Thomas H. Gresham*

This chapter presents the findings of a unique, long-term, experimental project designed to evaluate both the aspects of the so-called Mississippian small pole architectural style and the archaeological information produced from its creation. The first phase of the experiment, the construction of a full-scale replica, tested the plausibility of certain architectural features of small pole structures inferred from the archaeological record. The results inform most directly on structural design, level of effort, performance of building materials, and structural maintenance requirements. Archaeological method and reasoning were put to the test in the second phase, which involved a controlled excavation at the site of the experimental structure.

## Project Design

This project was carried out at the Etowah site near Cartersville, Georgia, on a small plot adjacent to the museum and visitor center. The first phase of work, involving the reconstruction of a small pole structure, took place between July and September of 1981, and the excavation phase was undertaken almost ten years later, between October and December of 1990. The project was conducted under the auspices of the Society for Georgia Archaeology based on a proposal prepared by the first author, who also directly supervised the experimental reconstruction (Blanton n.d). Gresham supervised the subsequent excavation phase organized as a blind test involving volunteers who were uninformed about the origin and nature of the experimental structure, and the fact that it had been intentionally burned a year after it was built. Even though both phases of the experiment were completed entirely on the effort of volunteers that stretched over a decade, procedures still followed a reasonably disciplined process guided by explicit goals and standards.

The leading goal of the first phase of the experiment was to test several inferences about the design of Mississippian stage (A.D. 1000–1550) small pole structures made by Lewis and Kneberg (1946). Their statements about design features for this style of architecture were derived from excavations of several remarkably well-preserved structures at Hiwassee Island and other sites in eastern Tennessee (Webb 1938). In effect, their explicit and well-reasoned interpretation of these buildings readily translated into a set of testable hypotheses.

Archaeological evidence from Tennessee, especially that from burned structures, made it abundantly clear to Lewis and Kneberg that a small pole, wall trench building design was typical of both public and domestic buildings during the early Mississippian stage (Lewis and Kneberg 1946:60, 74). This observation drew an important contrast with the large individually set post design that became a hallmark of the later Mississippian stage.

A very basic but important hypothesis made by Lewis and Kneberg (1946:51) was that small pole, wall trench buildings were framed by bending and weaving long, flexible, small-diameter poles. Such a mode of construction was abundantly clear in some of the burned Tennessee structures where 7.6-m-long (25-ft-long) flexed poles were preserved. This architectural form could also be surmised from the absence of large internal roof supports. Lewis and Kneberg proposed further that the flexible poles were interwoven at the top to create a sturdy latticelike frame to support roof covering. In addition, they suggested that the gaps at the corners of these buildings, created where wall trenches did not intersect, were merely a function of the woven, flexed pole design; a continuous rank of upright poles was simply unnecessary to create a sound framework.

Another hypothesis developed from their careful analysis of small pole structural evidence was that the walls of structures built in this design were prefabricated. Charred remains of horizontal braces bound to the flexible, vertical poles indicated that the braces held the principal vertical elements in a parallel position. In their words, "It is conceivable that this may have been done while all vertical poles composing a side of a building lay prone upon the ground, properly spaced parallel to one another" (Lewis and Kneberg 1946:50).

Excavation of small pole buildings also revealed that it was common to place horizontal poles inside the wall trenches, below ground level (Figure 3.1). Evidence of these poles was observed "near the bottom of the wall trench on

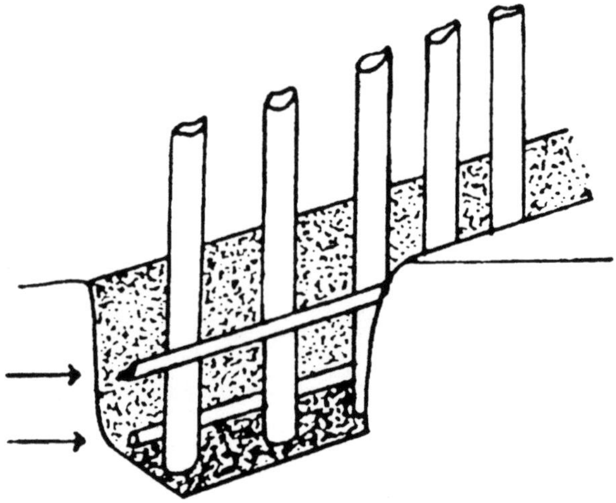

3.1. Diagram showing a wall trench with horizontal trench wedges (from Lewis and Kneberg 1946:51, Figure 4, courtesy of the Frank H. McClung Museum, the University of Tennessee).

the exterior side of the uprights, or near the top of the trench on the interior side; occasionally they have occurred in both positions within the same trench" (Lewis and Kneberg 1946:50). From this evidence Lewis and Kneberg (1946:50) hypothesized that the poles in the trenches acted as wedges, offering resistance "to the basal ends of the uprights when the tops were pulled inward and downward to form the roof. The wedges would prevent the basal ends from pushing outward under this stress. Similarly, a wedge placed along the interior, upper edge of the trench would prevent the inner side of the trench from giving way when the poles were pulled inward."

A multitude of ethnohistorical sources can be applied to reinforce the Lewis and Kneberg hypotheses concerning small pole design and, indeed, several were cited in their *Hiwassee Island* (1946) report. The most thorough and relevant description is by Le Page du Pratz (Swanton 1946:418–419) describing Lower Mississippi Valley Natchez architecture prior to the massacre:

> The natives go into the young woods in search of poles of young walnut [hickory] trees 4 inches [10.2 cm] in diameter by 18 to 20 feet [5.5 to 6.1 m] long . . . they plant the other poles in the earth in straight lines between those at the corners. When they are thus planted they are bound firmly to a cross pole on the inside of each face (or side). For this pur-

pose they use great cane splints to bind them, at the height of 5 or 6 feet [1.5 or 1.8 m] , according to the size of the cabin. This is what forms the walls. These erect poles are not more than about 15 inches [38.1 cm] apart. A young man then mounts to the top of a corner post with a cord between his teeth. He fastens the cord to the pole, and as he mounts inward the pole bends because those who are below draw the cord to make the pole curve as much as is needed. At the same time another young man does the same to the pole forming the angle opposite. Then the two poles, bent to a suitable height, are firmly and smoothly bound together. The same is done to the poles of the two remaining corners which are made to cross the first. Finally all the other poles are joined at the top, giving the whole the appearance of a bower in a greenhouse such as we have in France. After this work canes are fastened to the lower sides or walls crosswise about 8 inches [20.3 cm] apart, as high as the pole which I have spoken of as determining the height of the walls.

These canes being fastened in this manner, they make mud walls of adobe (mortier de terre) in which they put a certain amount of Spanish beard. These walls are not more than 4 inches [10.2 cm] thick. . . . Finally they cover the framework I have just described with cane mats.

For the North Carolina Siouan, another eighteenth-century account by Lawson (Swanton 1946:411) describes bent pole structures as follows:

In building these fabrics, they get very long poles . . . which they generally strip of the bark, and warm them well in the fire, which makes them tough and fit to bend. Afterwards, they stick the thickest ends of them in the ground, about two yards asunder, in a circular form, the distance they design the cabin to be (which is not always round, but sometimes oval) then they bend the tops and bring them together, and bind their ends with bark of trees . . . then they brace them with other poles to make them strong.

Then from seventeenth-century Virginia, we have this description of Algonquian dwellings: "They [Indian houses] are like garden arbours, at best like our sheppards' cottages, made yet handsomely enough, though without strength or gaynes(s), of such young plants as they can pluck up, bow, and make the greene toppes meete togither, in fashion of a round roofe" (Strachey, in Swanton 1946:414).

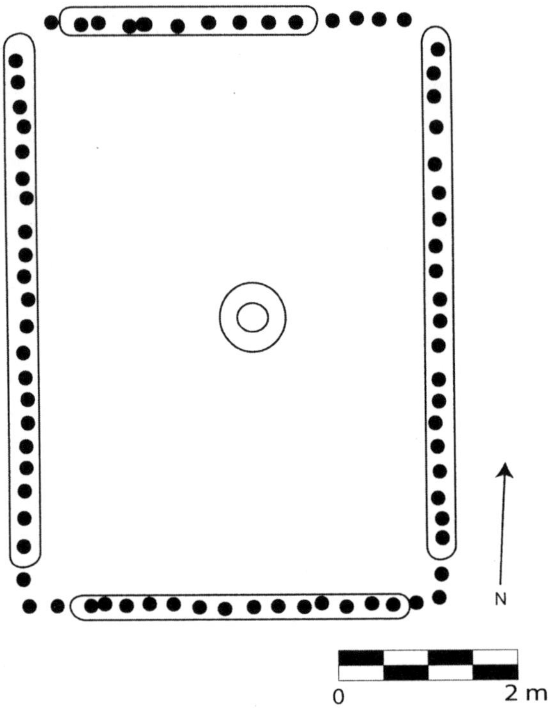


3.2. Floor plan of structure discovered by Larson under Mound C and the layout of the experiment structure (adapted from Lewis n.d. and Sheldon 1982:31, Figure 2, reproduced courtesy of Lewis H. Larson, Jr.).

As it happened, a classic small pole building had also been archaeologically documented at Etowah by Lewis Larson during his investigation of the site in the 1950s (Larson n.d.; Sheldon 1982:31). This structure was identified beneath the fill of Mound C and served as the model used for this reconstruction (Figure 3.2). Structure 4, as this building was named by Larson, was clearly constructed by setting 89 small-diameter uprights into wall trenches. The postholes averaged about 10 cm in diameter and were spaced an average of 27.5 cm apart. The wall trenches averaged about 25 cm in width. The floor of the structure was within a shallow basin excavated to approximately 40 cm below the general ground surface. A round, puddled clay hearth was documented at the center of the floor. The overall dimension of the house, measured from the center lines of the wall trenches, was 6.8 x 4.9 m (22 x 16 ft). Other than the use of clay daub in its construction, Larson's notes did not indicate any additional information as to the above-ground details.

## Structural Design and Level of Effort

The experimental reconstruction described here was planned by drawing on all the lines of evidence summarized above. Archaeological records of small pole structures were the starting point, but ethnohistorical sources served to inform on many details that were less apparent from the archaeology. This was especially important for making decisions about above-ground details and specific building materials. None of these sources gave a precise blueprint for a small pole building, either alone or in combination, but they did allow us to narrow the range of plausible options.

The description of the process that follows emphasizes the hypothesis-testing aspect of the project. Rather than a play-by-play account of the reconstruction, attention is mainly given to the parts of the process that allow for evaluation of the hypotheses set down by Lewis and Kneberg and the few that were formulated separately as the project was planned.

The footprint of the reconstructed building was generally faithful to the Structure 4 evidence from Etowah. The dimensions of the semi-subterranean floor basin, wall trenches, and posts were all derived from this source. Larson's observation regarding the near-certainty of a daub wall was also followed. Working within a staked area corresponding to the dimensions of Structure 4 (6.8 x 4.9 m), a rectangular pit was excavated to about 25 cm below the modern surface, shy of the estimated 40-cm depth of the Etowah example. The side walls of the basin were near vertical and the floor was near level. Wall trenches were then excavated along each side of the floor basin. Specific trench lengths were as follows: north 3.2 m, east 5.6 m, south 3.1 m, and west 5.6 m. Each trench averaged 27-cm wide at the top, ranged from 22- to 25-cm wide at the bottom, and extended an average of 40 cm below the level of the basin floor.

Our next step in the process was assembly of the wall frames, following the hypothesis of Lewis and Kneberg that the walls of small pole buildings were prefabricated prior to setting them in the trenches. Twenty-two poles were selected for the vertical uprights of each long wall after testing them for flexibility and then stripping bark from the lower 45 cm of each. Twelve poles were selected in the same way for the two shorter walls. Based on test bends of individual poles, the uprights were cut to a standard length of about 5.5 m. This length was sufficient to allow each long-wall pole to be bent inward across approximately two-thirds of the floor's width and to maintain an overall maximum roof height 2.5 m above the floor level.

To fabricate the separate wall units, selected poles were placed on the ground, equidistant and parallel to one another, across a space equal to the length of the wall trench. They were also arranged on the ground perpendicular to the trench that would receive them. Next, two or three bracing poles were laid perpendicular across the uprights and lashed to each of them to create a single wall unit. Strips of wet poplar bark were used to lash the horizontal braces to the uprights. The uppermost brace was attached to the vertical poles so that it would be about 1 m above the floor level. We learned that it was important to keep the horizontal braces on the inside of each wall unit, toward the direction the uprights were to be bent. Later, as the poles were being bent to create a framework, it was discovered that three horizontal braces become a hindrance and that it helped to remove the uppermost brace so that the poles could be better manipulated. In the final analysis, the uppermost wall braces need not be placed more than 50 cm above the level of the floor.

Before the prefabricated wall units were placed in the trenches, horizontal "wedges" were placed in the trenches in keeping with observations reported by Lewis and Kneberg. In our reconstruction, a wedge pole in the bottom of the trenches was always placed at the outside edge of the trench, but sometimes a wedge pole was placed on both sides at the bottom. Once the wall trench was partially filled with soil, at least one additional wedge pole was placed near the top along the inside face. In theory, the lower, outside wedge served as a stop to prevent the bottom end of the poles from kicking outward during bending. The upper wedge at the inside face was intended to act both as a fulcrum during bending of the uprights and as a pad to prevent the inner trench wall from collapsing or compressing during the same process.

Prefabricated wall units were erected in the wall trenches by having several people lift the framework to place the lower ends of the uprights into the trenches, and then raising the upper part of the entire structure until the poles were vertical. The position of the wedges described above was maintained as backfilling and thorough tamping proceeded. As poles were bent to form the framework, the hypothesized function of the wedges was confirmed. While it was impossible to directly observe the functioning of the deeply buried lower wedge on the outside of the trench, there is no question that the upper wedge both protected the upper lip of the trench from collapse and enhanced the bending process.

Lewis and Kneberg (1946:51) also hypothesized about the process and sequence of bending the poles to create a rigid frame. Our experiment attempted to follow their suggestions and we discovered in short order that a cautious, deliberate approach was warranted. The systematic, over-under bending sequence that was hypothesized was followed to the extent feasible. The process began by bending the end poles of the two long walls over one or two end poles of a

3.3. The interwoven framework of the experimental structure.

short wall, and securing them at the desired height by binding them together with bark lashing. It was helpful to bend the endmost short wall poles beneath the first long wall poles to bring the roof down to the desired height. In general, the process continued by bending the next long wall poles over short wall poles systematically (Figure 3.3). This alternating sequence of "weaving" allowed us to approximate the building's final form, proceeding from the ends toward the middle. Since the poles in the narrower, end walls were usually too short to span a full half-length of the structure, the alternating weave sequence for uprights was less consistent toward the center. At this part of the frame, opposite long wall poles were sometimes simply lashed together with no overlap from the end poles. The strength and pliability of individual poles had to be judged, too, and these factors affected the way the sequence was followed.

To create a uniform shape, considerable adjustments and adaptations were made along the way. At times it was helpful to unlash vertical uprights from the horizontal wall braces so that the wall poles could be better manipulated during the weaving process. Corresponding poles in opposite long walls could be brought into better alignment by pushing them into the desired position and then interweaving perpendicular, short lengths of pole. These additions served to improve the rigidity of the framework as well as the form, especially near the center. To correct a somewhat saddle-backed roof line, poles in the long walls were unlashed and adjusted to the correct height, short braces were interwoven, and a long, single, unbent ridge pole was woven into the peak from one end to the other.

One design feature was added during project planning based on ethno-

3.4. The experimental structure complete with daub walls and bark roof.

graphic evidence. Since suitable native plant material was not available in abundance, we opted to cover the building with a bark slab roof in the fashion described among Creek Indians of Alabama (Swanton 1946:394). The descriptions of these coverings described how the bark slabs were held in place by the pressure of poles lashed to the underlying framework-like vises.

In the reconstruction, the vise poles were secured across each horizontal row of large bark slabs. We managed success with this method by first lashing one end of a horizontal vise pole to the underlying framework at the end of a wall unit. Overlapping bark slabs were then slid beneath the pole and pressed into position, with the vise pole lashed to the underlying frame through careful cutouts about every 1.5 to 2.0 m and then at the other end. The pole was positioned just below the midline of the slabs. The pressure created by the pole held the bark firmly in place. This process was repeated from bottom to top until the entire roof was covered. The result can be seen in Figure 3.4.

## Level of Effort

The design of this experiment called for keeping a record of the time required to complete specific tasks, with the ultimate goal of providing a set of baseline measurements of the effort involved in construction. To be sure, the record of time that was created probably offers only rough approximations of the actual average effort that might have been required to build a small pole dwelling many centuries ago. The time measures might, however, represent close approximations if lack of experience was offset in some cases by use of modern tools. At the very least, the relative proportions of time devoted to various tasks should prove reasonably informative.

Some comments on the reconstruction process need to be presented in order to allow readers to make their own independent evaluations of the time: task measurements. First, modern hand tools were used in many steps of the process. These included the use of shovels and mattocks to excavate the house basin and wall trenches, the use of saws and steel axes to fell small poles, the use of pruning clippers to cut cane for wattling, the use of draw knives to strip bark from poles, and the use of steel hatchets to detach bark slabs. Second, motorized vehicles were used to transport building material from sources usually measured in tens of kilometers away. Third, all of the labor consisted of inexperienced people. While many had some basic construction and work skills, none had ever attempted to build a structure of this sort. Fourth, the labor consisted of men, women, and children. Fifth, work was carried out intermittently, usually on weekends, since the project was an all-volunteer effort. Sixth, the reconstruction site was on an ancient terrace composed of stiff red clay, as opposed to the lighter arable soils present on the main site area of Etowah. This clay proved very difficult to excavate even with modern hand tools.

The effect of these factors was varied. Modern hand tools and transport potentially reduced the time involved to complete certain tasks. Lack of experience, poor soil, and an erratic work schedule potentially increased the time required. Because transport time using motorized vehicles was not included in the figures, the total effort expended in raw material procurement could well provide a low estimate.

Table 3.1 provides a summary of the time:task breakdown measured in person hours. The application of daub and the procurement of building materials consumed the greatest share of effort, or over 20 percent of the total time each. These two categories of activity were followed by roughly similar expenditures of time to apply the roof covering and to raise the bent pole frame. A host of miscellaneous activities, excavation of the floor basin and wall trenches, and addition of the wattlework to the frame each consumed less than 10 percent of the overall effort. Perhaps most surprising is the time needed to apply daub to the walls. However, considering the estimated 2.3 to 2.7 metric tons (2.5 to 3 tons) of daub mixture that was used, the figures become more comprehensible.

## Results of Experimental Building

Hypotheses formulated from inferences of Lewis and Kneberg (1946) concerning the process of small pole construction were largely affirmed. The bent pole framework proved to be exceptionally strong and relatively uncomplicated to

3.1. Amount of Person Hours and Total Percentage of Time Needed to Complete Experimental Structure.

| Task | Person Hours | Percent |
|---|---|---|
| Daub Application | 161.8 | 28.5 |
| Building Material Procurement | 134.6 | 23.7 |
| Roofing | 86.5 | 15.2 |
| Raise-Assemble Frame | 70.3 | 12.4 |
| Miscellaneous | 48.5 | 8.5 |
| Basin-Trench Excavation | 37.5 | 6.6 |
| Wattlework | 29 | 5.1 |
| Total Person Hours | 568.2 | 100.0% |

execute, particularly when a good working sense of material performance and construction techniques was gained. Prefabrication of individual wall units worked very well and is, perhaps, the only realistically efficient way to erect small poles within wall trenches. Likewise, the "wedges" placed within the wall trenches appeared to perform as hypothesized. This is most apparent for the uppermost, inner wedge that served as both a fulcrum and reinforcement. The suggestion that corner gaps between wall trenches in this type of structure were essentially a function of the bent frame construction was strongly validated. A perfectly sturdy framework can be created without a continuous rank of pliable poles down the full length of the walls. This design feature is ultimately a function of the bending-weaving process that does not require uprights in the corner position. In addition, the alternating bend sequence proposed by Lewis and Kneberg was quite feasible to implement, especially after making allowances for individual pole tolerances, lengths, and so forth. The hypothesized function of pole vises to secure bark roof slabs, derived from ethnohistorical sources, was likewise largely affirmed.

A bark roof over wattle-and-daub walls was determined to be a viable but less than ideal combination. The principal but inherent drawback of small pole architecture is a lack of eaves to protect the exterior daub from weather. As related later, the absence of protection creates significant maintenance problems. Perhaps for the same reason, the semi-subterranean floor often became very wet during rainy periods. Indeed, there was no apparent advantage recognized for the floor basin, although we were not in a good position to evaluate its insulation and other qualities since the performance of the house was not observed by actual occupants.

## Building Material Performance

Choices of building materials and their handling influence the outcome of construction significantly. As already indicated, time allotted for acquisition of materials is a significant component of the overall effort. In addition, the performance of building materials varies widely and is now understood to be among the single most important factors in a successful construction project of this sort.

The first and most important lesson concerns the selection and treatment of the small poles used to create the basic framework. In fact, an initial framing effort had to be abandoned altogether due to selection of unsuitable wood and improper handling. The first batch of poles gathered for the frame was comprised entirely of small-diameter pine trees. Although pliant enough when living, it became painfully clear that this would not carry over to the construction setting. Virtually every one of the pine poles snapped when they were set in wall trenches and bent to create a framework. This is attributed mainly to the relatively brittle nature of the pine wood, especially when it had been cut and inadvertently air-dried. It is highly probable that the drying was hastened by removal of all the bark from these poles, and leaving them unused in the open for a week afterward.

To recover, we took more seriously the numerous accounts that described use of hardwood poles, especially hickory, walnut, or oak. The next set of uprights we gathered consisted mainly of hickory but a few other deciduous types like oak, maple, and hornbeam were included for comparative purposes. Bark was only removed from the lower ends of these poles, and as an extra precaution against drying they were cached in the river until ready for use. As indicated in the preceding section, this choice of poles was far superior as only one or two of them were strained to the breaking point.

Bark for roofing slabs was, from the start, chosen in closer accordance with the ethnohistorical accounts. Still, there were lessons to be learned. Local sawmills were more than happy for us to remove bark from large poplar and sweet gum logs, and the availability of species at the mills strongly influenced our choices. Poplar was the most common species at our disposal. Because most of the trees we stripped of bark had been felled in the spring or early summer, we discovered that the bark was fairly easy to remove. The lumbermen and the mill workers commented, in fact, that we would have had a much tougher time of it if the trees had been cut in seasons when the "sap wasn't running."

Bark slabs were applied to the experimental structure while they were still somewhat green, and the result was rather severe curling that created numerous openings in the once sound roof. Through this experience, we recognized that, unlike the framing poles, it would have been best to stack and press the slabs until they had dried. It was also observed that the thicker bark of poplar trees curled more severely on average than the thinner bark of sweet gum trees.

A great deal of insight was gained from the daubing process. Attention to clay quality, temper density, wetness, and method of application all had significant bearing on the outcome. Because of the very high labor investment that daub application in this experiment represents—the lessons that we learned by trial and error—the process was probably taken seriously by Native people. In short, it seems abundantly clear from this experiment that successful daub application occurs within a rather narrow range of parameters.

The quality of the clay used for daub in this experiment was, in hindsight, probably not of the optimal variety. This is, however, very much a subjective view that only careful performance comparisons will eventually confirm or refute. For the sake of the following discussion clay quality will not be addressed and it will be assumed that the lessons learned would apply to any reasonable daubing clay. It is worth adding that our learning rate increased exponentially by virtue of some unsolicited input from a visiting concrete foreman. His professional experience taming wet mixtures translated well, it seems, to daub wall construction, and much about the daubing process was based on his advice.

Lesson one from the daub application process was to minimize the water content of the mixture. The first advantage afforded by reducing moisture is a gain in plasticity or workability. If the mixture is too wet, the daub simply does not adhere to other daub or to the wattlework. The second advantage is a reduction in cracking during the drying process. Less water generally means fewer and thinner cracks in the finished wall since shrinkage from water loss is the principal source of cracking.

The second lesson was to maximize the quantity of temper in the mixture. Vegetable material in particular was an effective binding agent that helps to strengthen the clay walls. In theory, the added fiber serves to offset weakening from cracks. In this case, we took advantage of discarded cane leaves for temper but any relatively thin, narrow, or stringy material would probably serve well.

It was also learned that application of the daub in manageable sections and layers is advisable. Working from the bottom up was understandably very important, so as to create a sound base for new daub. By working in small sections it is also easier to concentrate on thoroughly packing the daub onto the wattlework to give it the best shape or form.

## Structure Maintenance Requirements

Beyond evaluation of hypothesized design elements, the project was extended to include consideration of the maintenance demands of a small pole structure. This part of the project involved monitoring the condition of the building with periodic inspections for one year after the construction phase ended. A standardized form was created to collect consistent information, and the building's condition was occasionally documented with photographs.

Daub was obviously the least durable of all the structural components. Failure of the daub can be attributed to multiple factors, including, but not limited to, lack of protection from elements, poor quality clay, and differential drying. No sooner than the daub dried it began to exhibit shrinking cracks, and within two months open holes in the walls were noted. Monthly observations document steady loss of daub, characterized by mass wastage on the interior walls and less severe but steady erosion outside.

As noted, several factors appear to have contributed to the rapid progression of daub failure. It is suggested that the leading cause of daub deterioration on the exterior walls was severe weathering, most obviously from the effects of rain wash but freeze and thaw seemed to cause small-scale crumbling. A bent pole design necessarily eliminates good options for extending roof members to create protective eaves above the walls. This is not to say that eaves could not be added, but to do so would considerably complicate the framing and roofing process, and ethnohistorical accounts do not describe this additional feature on small pole buildings. Without protection provided by eaves, the daub walls were exposed to frequent episodes of wetting by rain and rapid drying from sun, creating a highly changeable environment that clearly weakened the wall covering.

Moisture in the daub walls also appeared to have been uneven due to wicking of ground water. At every inspection it was noted that the lower section of the walls was always damp compared to the upper sections. It is suggested that this is due mainly to contact with the ground surface but it is possible that it also represents a general accumulation of moisture toward the bottom of the walls. In any event, one can surmise that the inconsistent clay condition contributed to its vulnerability to failure. The quality of the clay used for daub in this structure also potentially accounts for the rapid rate of deterioration, although comparative performance tests will ultimately be necessary to confirm the suspicion.

Finally, the slight incline of the bent pole frame appears to have accelerated loss of daub on the interior walls. It was observed that larger pieces of daub became detached from the interior more readily than they did on the exterior. The immediate suggestion is that the simple effect of gravity on the insloping walls was the principal cause. However, it is also probable that visitors were taking advantage of the concealed space to pry chunks of the daub from the interior walls. Regardless, the loss of large pieces on the interior quickly weakened those sections of daub, and they were usually the first to become open holes.

The second major problem that would present maintenance challenges was curling and slippage of the bark roof slabs. As already described, the green bark was prone to curl severely in many instances, thereby opening many gaps in the roof covering. This curling began almost immediately, as did the initial cracking of daub. At a more gradual rate, drying of bark slabs and the lashing that held the vise poles in place caused some of the slabs to loosen and shift. Obviously, these issues exposed the interior to weathering. Advance drying of roof slabs and addition of a second layer of roof covering, such as mats, would significantly improve the level of protection inside.

## Evaluation of Archaeological Method

The final phase of the experimental project involved a blind test of archaeological method and reasoning. The test involved a controlled excavation of the experimental site by individuals who had no direct knowledge of the construction phase, following a period of ten years after intentional burning of the building and burial of its remains. This team of volunteer excavators, who worked under the professional supervision of the second author, had no information regarding the design or size of the building, the materials used, or the circumstances of its destruction. The primary objective of this exercise was to determine how thoroughly standard excavation practices would record evidence of the structure after it had been buried for a decade, and how accurately inferences would be made from the recovered evidence concerning the design and appearance of the building. In the final analysis, interpretation of findings from the excavation phase was found to be very accurate. Indeed, the exercise can serve as a restorative to failing confidence in the fundamental archaeological process.

Inferences about the nature of the building made from the excavation evidence were so accurate and thorough that it serves best here to focus on the features of the structure that were not readily apparent. But before addressing these aspects the positive interpretations deserve at least some attention. Considering all the evidence and with a series of deductions, everything from the dimensions of the building to the location of the entryway to bent pole design features was determined. For example, the following conclusions were drawn in the excavation report (Gresham and Simpkins n.d.):

The structure had a semi-subterranean floor
The northeast corner of the building served as the entrance
A basin-shaped hearth was present at the center of the floor
Small flexible poles were used to create a continuous framework, negating the need for internal roof supports
Framing poles were set in wall trenches that contained horizontal braces
Hickory and white oak were common woods used for vertical framing members
The walls were of wattle-and-daub construction

The excavators were challenged in some expected and unexpected ways, too. First and unexpectedly, the wall trench features were not readily apparent at all since the local clay used to fill them did not create an obvious contrast with the undisturbed soil in the house basin. It was only when preserved ends of wall poles were removed or very closely examined that the trenches became evident.

More predictably, the feature of the structure that most eluded interpretation was the type of roof covering. Apparently, no traces of the bark slabs survived the fire, at least in recognizable form. This lack of direct evidence left the experimental excavators in the same position as Larson in describing the Etowah model that was used (Structure 4). He was reasonably confident in describing the basic nature of the structure up to the level of the roof but acknowledged that the type of covering was undetermined.

## Closing Observations

An experimental investigation of prehistoric architectural design and performance is the only means of collecting certain kinds of information on the subject. This is certainly true of issues like building material performance and task:time figures that are not readily modeled without a basis in empirical testing. In the foregoing sections, we have attempted to describe the most basic kinds of new information of this sort. There are, however, a number of less direct lines of reasoning that can be pursued from the same evidence, and it is these inferences that will be offered in this closing discussion. The leading goal of this final section is to outline topics that might be profitably pursued in future studies, experimental or otherwise.

With the advantage of hindsight, a number of benefits associated with the small pole building design seem apparent. Structurally speaking the bent pole framing method eliminates a potential weak link inherent to designs that join rafters to sturdy uprights and plates. As with small pole buildings, the "studs" and rafters are continuous elements. Overall, the creation of a flexible frame is probably a less complex process than assembly of a large pole raftered building. There are fewer individual framing elements in a small pole building and they require only the barest degree of custom treatment. Small pliant poles would also have been far easier to fell and transport than large poles. With respect to interior space, small pole structures would have provided freer movement since obstructions created by interior roof supports are eliminated.

Reflection on the experience also leads to consideration of the optimal timing of new construction, and there are numerous indications that it may have been most practical during warm seasons. First, small poles are most easily manipulated during the growing season when plant tissue is active and "green." Not only do small trees bend well during the spring and summer but their bark is also easily removed then. In addition, daub would not be exposed to the hazard of freeze-thaw cycles, especially during the vulnerable time before it thoroughly dried. Finally, springtime preparation of fallowed fields might have offered an opportune time to cut young growth eminently suitable for use in a small pole building.

The final comments apply to the organization of experimental projects. It is clear from this case that better results could be achieved by designing the work around a series of discrete, problem-oriented tests as opposed to launching into a complete reconstruction. Such an approach takes into account a very real and steep learning curve associated with these undertakings. For example, it would likely be as useful to replicate only full-scale sections of daub walls or, perhaps, only one-half of a scale structure. A carefully designed experimental strategy of this sort would not only be more practical to execute but, arguably, it may be more conducive to closer controls. Complete reconstruction would, therefore, best mark the culmination of an extended series of particularistic experiments designed to narrow the range of feasible options for different structural components.

## Acknowledgments

The authors wish to recognize the Society for Georgia Archaeology and the Georgia Department of Natural Resources for their assistance and cooperation. Very special thanks are due to the dozens of volunteers whose generous efforts made this project possible.

# 4
# Typology, Chronology, and Technological Changes of Mississippian Domestic Architecture in West-Central Alabama

*Cameron H. Lacquement*

Archaeological studies of Mississippian houses in the southeastern United States have revealed several forms of domestic floor plans. The two most common floor plans are a design utilizing small poles, which are set relatively close together and typically inserted in a wall trench, and a design employing large posts spaced relatively far apart and set in individual postholes (see Figure 1.2). These two layouts of domestic houses are also apparent at Moundville and the surrounding areas in west-central Alabama. The purpose of this research was to first, statistically test the idea that these two forms of domestic floor plans are distinct and not a continuum of the same floor plan. Early southeastern archaeologists such as David DeJarnette (Jones and DeJarnette 1936), Thomas Lewis (1937), and William Webb (1938) believed that these layouts were indeed two distinct designs, each representing a distinct form of architecture. If this assumption can be statistically supported, it would provide additional evidence for the existence of two distinct above-ground architectural forms. Second, this research seeks to provide a chronology of all Mississippian domestic house types in west-central Alabama. The diagnostic components and chronology of each house form are presented based on a sample of 73 Mississippian structures from six sites in west-central Alabama, including Moundville, Lubbub Creek, Bessemer, Big Sandy Farms, the Pride Place site, and the Powers site (Figure 4.1). Concluding the discussion of the results, a typology and chronology of house types from the six Mississippian sites is presented, focusing on both archaeological characteristics and inferred above-ground architecture. Assuming that there is an architectural shift, reasons for this transition will also be explored.

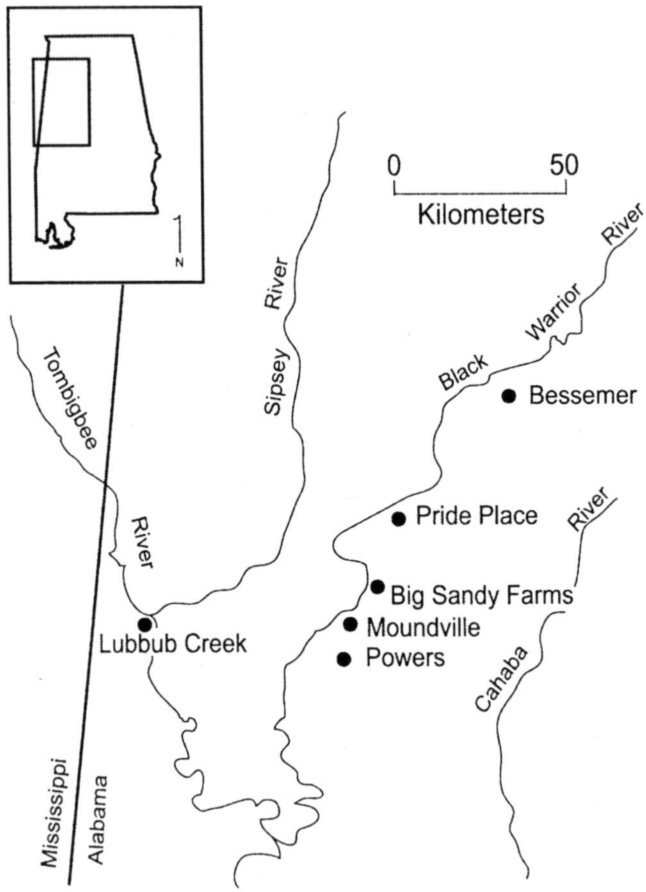


4.1. Map of Moundville and surrounding areas.

## Study Specifications and Research Sample

This study will be focused specifically on Mississippian (A.D. 1000–1550) domestic architecture. For this purpose, "structure" will be defined as a building that possessed wall posts and a roof. Therefore, palisades and stockades are excluded from this research. The examination also will be focusing on domestic housing rather than public or ceremonial buildings. For the purposes of this study, "domestic" will be defined in terms of size, location, and internal features within the structure. Only structures that are less than 37 $m^2$ (400 $ft^2$) of roofed space, and which are neither located on earthworks nor in the possession of specialized internal features such as clay seats or specially prepared clay floors will be considered domestic buildings (Lewis and Kneberg 1946).

Because the focus of the study is Moundville, the architecture examined will be only that of square and rectangular structures, omitting consideration of ones that possessed a circular or oval foundation shape. Many Mississippian societies and historic southeastern tribes used circular structures, and there is no evidence to suggest that these structures were limited to one specific building technique. However, no evidence of circular structures has been found at the Moundville ceremonial center and they are of rare occurrence at Mississippian sites in the surrounding areas. In the immediate region, they are found only at the Bessemer site (DeJarnette and Wimberly 1941), in the Pickwick Basin of the Tennessee River in northern Alabama (Webb and DeJarnette 1942), and on the Mississippi side of the Tombigbee River (Blitz 1993).

### *Moundville*

Moundville is a Mississippian mound site on the banks of the Black Warrior River in west-central Alabama. The civic-ceremonial center, including at least 29 earthen mounds situated around a central plaza, was initially excavated by Thomas Maxwell and Nathaniel Lupton during the mid-nineteenth century (Knight and Steponaitis 1998). The largest excavations at Moundville occurred in the 1930s and early 1940s by geologist Walter B. Jones and the Alabama Museum of Natural History, in which the Museum used Civilian Conservation Corps (CCC) federal relief labor for a number of archaeologically related projects. One of these projects of the CCC was to construct a road that encircled the site. The excavations undertaken to complete this project are referred to as the Roadway excavations.

McKenzie (1964) described the characteristics of 22 of these Roadway structures, 21 of which were constructed with wall trenches and one with individually placed posts. Nineteen of these structures were used in the sample of this study, as the other three exceeded the dimensions for typical domestic structures. Also included in this study were 17 structures of domestic size, that McKenzie did not use in his study, that were taken directly from unpublished field drawings of the Alabama Museum of Natural History Roadway excavations. These additional structures from the Roadway excavations consisted of individually set, wall trench, and individually set and wall trench combination forms. All three techniques were also found on the Northwest Riverbank of Moundville during excavations in 1992 (Scarry 1995, 1998). Twelve structures were located at the Northwest Riverbank, four of which had been rebuilt, for a total of 16 cases included in the sample. These 16 structures from the Northwest Riverbank, along with the 36 structures from the Roadway excavations, comprise the 52 Moundville structures for the sample.

### *Lubbub Creek Site*

The Lubbub Creek site is a Mississippian mound site in the Central Tombigbee River Valley of western Alabama, approximately 53 km from Moundville (Blitz 1993). The site was excavated by Christopher S. Peebles (1983) in 1978 and 1979. The site possessed several varieties of domestic structures, including small closely set pole structures constructed either using a wall trench or individually set postholes, as well as several large widely spaced post architectural forms with four internal roof supports. The small pole structures of the Lubbub Creek site appear to be characteristic of the Summerville I phase (roughly equivalent to Moundville I phase), while the large widely spaced post structures occurred later in the Summerville II/III and IV phases (roughly equivalent to Moundville II through Early Moundville III and Late Moundville III and Moundville IV, respectively). Many of the Lubbub Creek structures were too large for inclusion in the sample; however, five structures dating to the Summerville I were included, as well as three from Summerville II/III, and three from Summerville IV for a total of 11 houses that met the study's criteria. It should be noted that three of the Lubbub structures were described as oval in foundation (Blitz 1980; Peebles 1983); however, I believe that these structures were rectangular with rounded corners and bowed walls.

### *Bessemer*

The Bessemer site lies approximately 48 km north of Moundville in west-central Alabama. The site was first recorded in 1890 by Cyrus Thomas, the man indirectly responsible for ending the mound-builder race theory while at the same time compiling a great deal of information concerning sites throughout the eastern United States. The Bessemer site, which consists of three mounds—a ceremonial, a domiciliary, and a burial mound—was extensively excavated in the late 1930s by DeJarnette and Wimberly (1941) (also see Welch 1994). Four structures, including three wall trench structures and a single set pole structure, were found under and around the ceremonial mound. However, Structure 1 contained an elevated clay seat, and was therefore eliminated from this study, as the building was possibly public or ceremonial in nature. Seven structures were found on top of the domiciliary mound and were thus excluded from this study as well. There were also 17 structures found under and around the domiciliary mound. However, only one of these structures was added to the sample, as three were circular, and the other 13 exceeded the size threshold for a domestic house and were therefore excluded. Altogether, four structures from the Bessemer site met the criteria laid out for this study.

*Pride Place*

The Pride Place site is located in Tuscaloosa on the banks of the Black Warrior River. It was first partially excavated by David L. DeJarnette and geologist Walter B. Jones in January of 1933. Johnson (1999, 2001) conducted the data recovery for a cultural resource management project there in 1998. Two individually set post structures were located, which utilized both large and small post wall members. Based on the ceramic analysis, Johnson inferred that the site was a Moundville III phase farmstead. In his original presentation, Johnson (1999) stated that both of these structures were constructed in a flexed pole form that possessed central roof supports. However, in his later presentation, Johnson (2001) stated that it was unclear as to whether these houses were flexed or rigid.

*Big Sandy Farms*

The Big Sandy Farms site was located and excavated in 1990 during a pipeline survey project. This Mississippian site lies 3 km north of Moundville, in the area near where Big Sandy Creek flows into the Black Warrior River. Ensor (1993) discussed four structures, one complete semi-subterranean structure, and three other partial structures that were located at the site. Only the semi-subterranean structure, Structure 1, and Structure 2 are included in the sample, as the other two are not convincingly identified as structures.

*Powers Site*

The Powers site is located 5 km southwest of Moundville within the vicinity of Elliotts Creek. The site was recorded by Walter B. Jones in the early 1930s. Excavations were conducted by Richard Krause and University of Alabama field schools in 1981, 1988, and 1991 (Welch 1998). During his excavations, Krause uncovered three individually set post structures. Two of these structures were included in the sample (Structure 1 and Structure 2). The remaining structure (Structure 3) was excluded based on its large size. All three houses Krause excavated date to approximately A.D. 1400, the estimated beginning of the Moundville III phase. Redwine (2002) has proposed that all three houses consisted of rigid post architecture, even though Structure 1 possessed four internal roof supports and large quantities of daub, while Structure 2 only possessed one roof support and very little daub.

## Methods

Seventy-three complete or partial structures from six sites in the west-central Alabama region met the criteria for this study. The focus of the remaining pages of this chapter is first, to statistically compare characteristics of the structures located at these six sites, followed by an explanation for the transitions in house form. In order to record variables such as posthole diameter, post spacing, floor area, and the presence or absence of wall trenches and roof supports, plan view representations of all the houses in the sample were collected. The dichotomous variables such as the presence or absence of wall trenches or roof supports were recorded simply by examining the text and/or the accompanying diagrams. If there was any indication of a wall trench in any part of the structure, with the exception of entry wall trenches, the structure was recorded as possessing wall trenches.

It should be noted that the terms posthole and post mold are sometimes used interchangeably. However, for accurate analysis the two need to be distinguished. The difference is that postholes are the actual holes that were dug in the ground in order to plant the post. Post molds are the stains within the postholes, only occasionally present, that provide data on the actual size of the post. In measuring post diameters, postholes, not post molds, were recorded for this study. The reason is that post molds are not as clearly identifiable as postholes and as a result, postholes are more frequently recorded than post molds. The measurement of postholes reflects the maximum diameter of the wall member. However, comparisons of posthole to post mold size at the Toqua site in eastern Tennessee reveal that post molds are typically 25 to 50 percent smaller than postholes, so the values given for this variable are no doubt slightly larger than the size of the wall posts used (Polhemus 1985:18).

Mean post spacing was a slightly more difficult variable to record. This measurement was absent from many of the published works from which structures were taken, or in some cases was over-generalized. Therefore, in almost every case, post spacing was manually remeasured. In order to limit posthole/post mold size discrepancies, spacing was measured between the centers of postholes, not at the edges. The scale provided with the illustration was used to measure a span of posts judged as average for the structure. This distance was divided by the number of spaces within the selected span. For example, if five postholes, from the center of the first to the center of the last, were found in a span of 1 m, this distance would be divided by four, as there are four spaces between five posts when measured in this manner. The average spacing would then be calculated as 25 cm.

Determining the presence of roof supports required a different method. Not only did interior postholes have to be present to be considered roof supports, but they also needed to be positioned in a particular location within the floor plan. There are typically several scattered postholes throughout the floor area of any given structure. However, only cases where (a) one large roof support is in the middle of the structure, (b) two or more large central postholes are parallel to the long axis of the house, or (c) four large postholes form a square in the center of the structure, would the structure be considered to possess roof supports. Floor area and posthole size, if not specifically provided in the text that accompanied the drawings, were measured using the appropriate scale, manually gauged as accurately as possible with a ruler and calculator. This method does introduce a small degree of error; however, if there were indeed two very distinct floor plans, the degree of error should be negligible.

In addition, close attention should be given to the terminology used in describing architectural forms. Structures possessing relatively small postholes, averaging less than 20 cm (8 in) in diameter, are referred to as small "pole" buildings, whereas structures with postholes averaging larger than 20 cm are referred to as large "post" buildings. This categorization of structures based on wood size was loosely adopted from the field of structural engineering in their distinction between Structural Light Framing (SLF) such as studs, and Post and Timber (P&T) (Breyer et al. 2003). Applying this division archaeologically enables one to distinguish between houses based on post size instead of or in combination with insertion methods.

## Results

The results of the comparison of structures from the six Mississippian sites indicated that the floor plans clustered into distinct groups based on both post diameter and post spacing when separated by the method of insertion. By graphing the frequency of posthole diameters divided by the presence or absence of wall trenches (Figure 4.2), it is clearly shown that this sample of structures supports the idea that there were two distinct sizes of Mississippian construction materials, a small "pole" and a larger "post" size.

The pole diameter of houses constructed in wall trenches ranged from 8.0 to 15.0 cm ($\bar{x}$ = 10.69, $s$ = 1.63, $n$ = 24) while the individually set poles and posts ranged from 10.0 to 30.0 cm ($\bar{x}$ = 17.63, $s$ = 6.343, $n$ = 26). It should be noted that the mean diameter for individually set wall posts is very conservative, as the smaller and larger diameter, individually set postholes were grouped together even though they are believed to represent different archi-

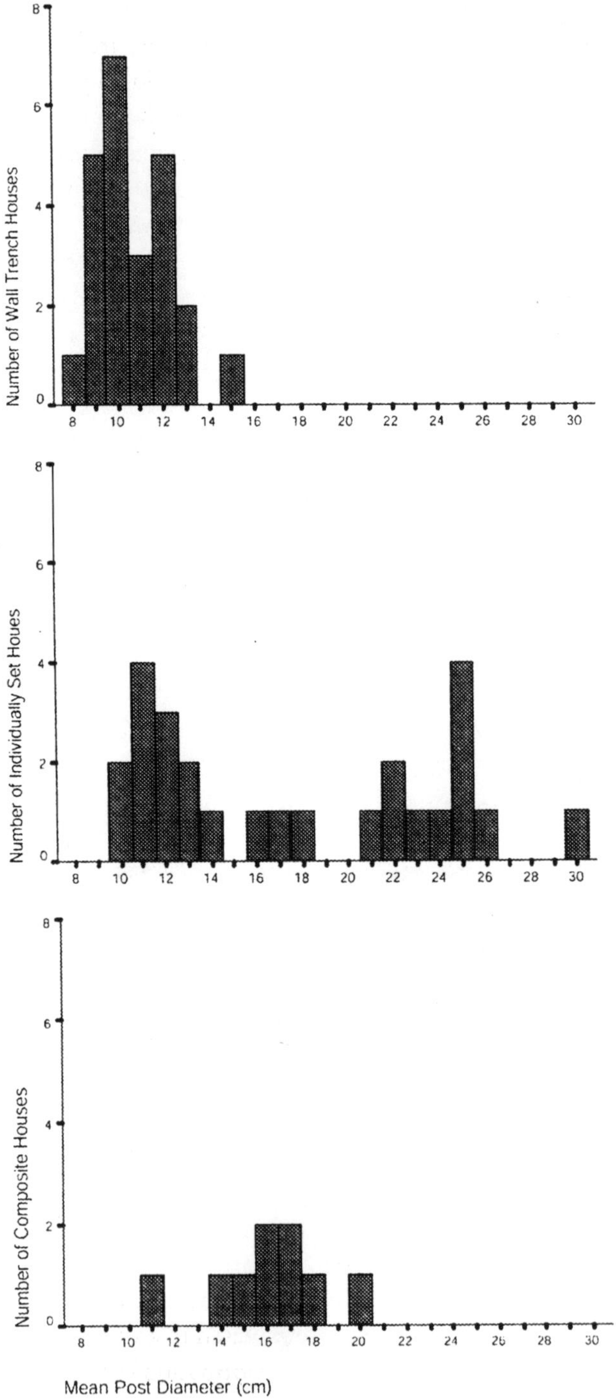


4.2. Histogram of post diameter with cases labeled by method of insertion.

tectural floor plans. If the individually set postholes are divided between 18 and 20 cm, the evidence reveals that the small individually set pole structures, with a mean of 12.7 cm ($s = 2.419$, $n = 15$), and the large individually set post structures, with a mean of 24.36 ($s = 2.461$, $n = 11$), are significantly distinct ($t = -12.061$, $df = 24$, $p = .001$). Statistical testing in the form of independent $t$-tests also suggested that there was no distinction between the mean size of the wall trench postholes and the small individually set postholes ($t = -2.825$, $df = 37$; $p = .004$). The larger individually set poles of the composite form clustered between the small diameter and large diameter distributions ($\bar{x} = 16.6$, $s = 3.245$, $n = 9$). The small wall trench poles of the composite houses were not included in this part of the statistical analysis, as they appear virtually indistinguishable from the small poles of houses utilizing only wall trenches.

Post spacing, when similarly graphed (Figure 4.3), shows two distinct clusters—closely spaced and widely spaced wall members. When these data are broken down into groups based on the presence or absence of a wall trench, the histograms show that the post spacing of all wall trench houses is concentrated in the area of the graph that represents closely spaced wall poles ($\bar{x} = 16.72$ cm, $s = 3.71$, $n = 22$). In other words, widely spaced postholes are not found in wall trenches. The post spacing of individually set posthole houses is bimodal, representing both a small closely spaced individually set method ($\bar{x} = 21.88$, $s = 4.7$, $n = 15$) and a large widely spaced individually set method ($\bar{x} = 71.52$ cm, $s = 10.19$, $n = 11$). Statistical evidence in the form of independent $t$-tests also indicated that there was a significant distinction between the means of the proposed two groups of individually set spacing techniques based on post size ($t = -16.69$, $df = 24$, $p = .001$), and between the means of the small poles both individually set and wall trench compared to large individually set posts ($t = -24.034$, $df = 46$, $p = .001$). However, statistical evidence does not confirm a distinction between the spacing of small individually set poles and wall trench poles ($t = -3.567$, $df = 34$, $p = .001$). The spacing of the larger individually set posts of the composite construction houses distributes in the high end of the closely spaced distribution ($\bar{x} = 26.94$, $s = 4.00$, $n = 7$).

The correlation between post diameter and post spacing was calculated, indicating a strong positive relationship ($r = .890$ $p = .001$) (Figure 4.4). In other words, as post size increases, so does the spacing of the posts. The scatterplot also shows that there are two distinct building techniques, (a) a small pole, closely set technique, usually in a wall trench but not always; and (b) a large post, widely spaced technique, never constructed in a wall trench.

For the purpose of having quantifiable information to build the chronology, the presence or absence of wall trenches was used in examining the frequency of forms from each of the phases in the Moundville-Summerville phase se-

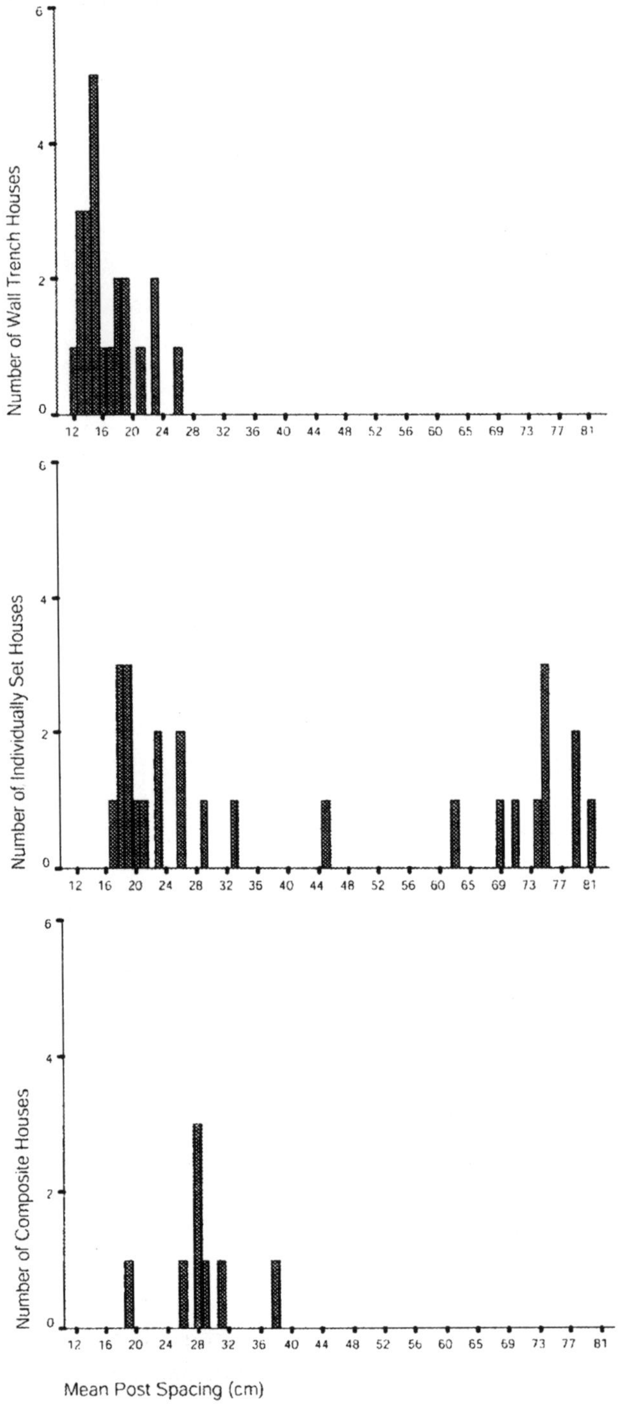


4.3. Histogram of post spacing with cases labeled by method of insertion.

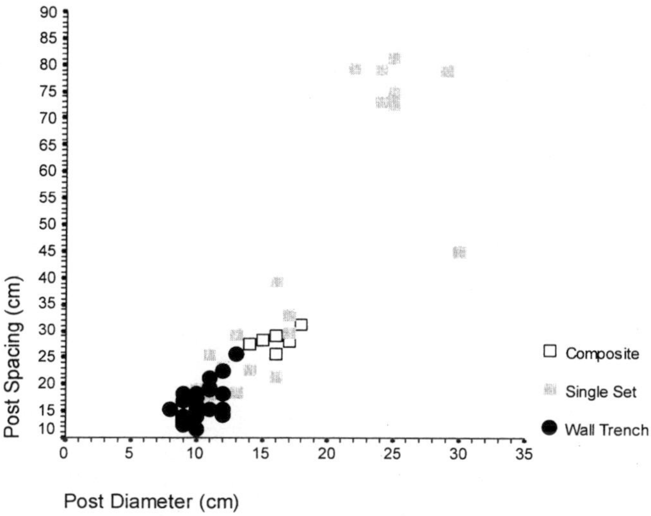


4.4. Scatterplot of post diameter and post spacing with cases labeled by method of insertion.

quence (Figure 4.5). This graph shows that individually set pole houses are the primary form in the Early Moundville I phase.

These Early Moundville I phase houses tend to possess small individually set poles, while the houses of the Late Moundville I phase are almost exclusively constructed in a wall trench. However, the importance of the wall trench as an architectural characteristic declines in the Moundville II phase, and completely disappears by the Moundville III phase. Houses late in the Moundville and Summerville sequences are entirely constructed of individually set posts. More information concerning these data can be provided by a proposed chronology of these house forms.

## Typology

There are five types of floor plans represented in the Mississippian archaeological record in west-central Alabama: (I) a composite construction form, which combines small wall trench poles and slightly larger individually set poles; (II) a small pole individually set form; (III) a small pole wall trench form; (IV) a large post individually set form; and (V) an amorphous post daubed form (Figure 4.6). This last form was omitted from the statistical analysis, as little is known or can be identified regarding its above-ground architecture, and patterns of posts are difficult to distinguish in the archaeological record of these structures.

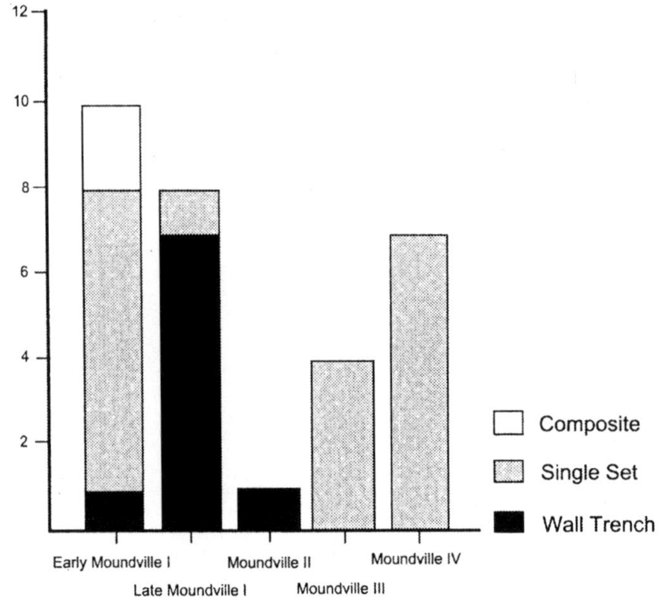


4.5. Bar graph showing the frequency of post insertion techniques by phase in the Moundville/Summerville sequence.

Type I. *Composite Construction Form.* Nine examples of this form are in the sample, eight of which occur at Moundville and one at the Big Sandy Farms site. This form employs both individually set and wall trench techniques simultaneously. Two of the nine were constructed in a semi-subterranean basin: Structure 3 from the Northwest Riverbank at Moundville and Structure 1 from the Big Sandy Farms. The composite construction form in general is characterized by small, closely spaced poles placed in wall trenches on two opposing walls, together with slightly larger wall poles spaced a little farther apart on the remaining two walls. In eight of the nine cases the structures were rectangular, with the larger individually set poles positioned on the short sides of the building and the small wall trench poles placed on the long sides of the structure. In the other example, the layout is square, created with two equal opposing sides of wall trenches and individually set poles. There are no indications of internal roof supports in any of these structures.

Based on the two sizes of wall member diameters and spacing, this composite form probably consisted of two bent pole sides and two rigid sides, resembling the historic architecture of the Algonquin tribes of the Atlantic coast. The structure type may or may not have had longitudinally running ridge poles

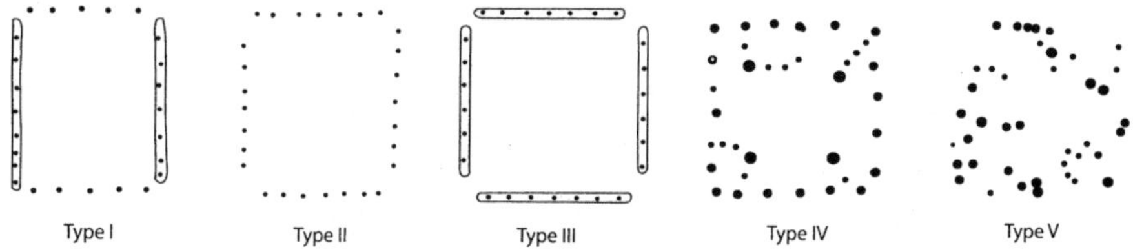


4.6. Illustration of five distinct floor plans of Mississippian houses in west-central Alabama.

that were used to connect the two bent sides, which could have been propped up on the large posts of the shorter sides (see Figure 6.6, same form different floor plan). It is very unlikely that this house form was originally created with individually set poles and later repaired in the wall trench method, as suggested by Jenkins (1982:109), Scarry (1998:91), and Wilson (2005:80). The post sizes of the individually set postholes of these composite houses are slightly larger and spaced farther apart than those structures that are constructed completely with small individually set poles (Type II). The consistent nature of this form, with opposing pairs of wall trench and individually set pole walls, indicates this type to be a distinctive kind of construction technique. Radiocarbon dates place this form at the beginning of the Moundville chronology, contemporary with the earliest wall trench and small individually set pole forms.

Based on the calibrated average of radiocarbon dates from Structure 3 (A.D. 1030–1146 at 1σ) of the Northwest Riverbank excavations at Moundville, and the ceramic analysis of Structure 1 from the Big Sandy Farms site, this composite construction form was most likely constructed within the Early Moundville I phase. There is also a perfect example of a rebuilding episode that can provide chronological evidence. House 23 of the Roadway excavation was a composite construction structure utilizing both individually set posts and wall trenches, which was rebuilt twice, once in the same composite form, and the second time completely in the wall trench fashion, which may indicate a fairly rapid transition. There are no dateable cases of this form in any other phase, which suggests that perhaps this architectural form was no longer being utilized after Early Moundville I.

Type II. *Small Pole Individually Set Form.* This small pole individually set form, represented by 15 structures in the sample, was constructed with small poles that were positioned closely together. Examples of this architectural form occur at the Lubbub Creek site, the Big Sandy Farms site, the Bessemer site, and Moundville. The majority of these structures were rectangular in plan.

There is no indication of central roof supports, and interestingly, no indication of significant amounts of clay daub in these structures, suggesting that the walls were not covered in clay daub. Daub may have been used sparingly as a plaster to cover gaps and holes. However, the CCC excavated the majority of the houses at Moundville, and the reports from this time do not address which buildings were burned and which ones were not. Therefore, it may be reasonable to assume that the lack of daub was the result of few structures being destroyed by fire.

Based on the statistical evidence previously discussed, there does not seem to be a continuum in size or spacing between the small individually set pole form and larger individually set post form. It appears that these small individually set postholes are more closely related with the small poles used in wall trench construction. Therefore, it is likely that these small pole structures are constructed in the same fashion as those using a wall trench, representing a variant of the same above-ground architectural form.

It should also be noted that wall trenches are sometimes difficult to discern archaeologically. Wall trenches are usually only visible when more than one stratum of soil is disturbed in their creation. In investigating a burned experimental structure 10 years after its destruction, Blanton and Gresham (this volume:47) mention this exact problem, where wall trenches were basically invisible. The same problem was encountered when the author excavated his experimental wall trench structure at Moundville (Lacquement 2004, 2005) one year after its destruction. In this case, wall trenches in some areas of the structure were well defined but invisible in others, giving the entire floor plan a patchy appearance, presenting the impression that both individually set and wall trench methods were utilized in a single wall of a structure. Therefore, it may be reasonable to believe that many of these early Mississippian small individually set pole structures may have been constructed in a wall trench fashion, but that the wall trenches themselves are no longer visible.

In the Northwest Riverbank excavations, Scarry (1998:91) determined that the small individually set pole structures (Type II) and the composite construction structures (Type I) were older than the wall trench structures (Type III). The composite construction form, Structure 3 of the PA tract, produced an average calibrated date of A.D. 1030–1146 at 1σ, while the other small individually set pole structures (Structures 1, 2, and 6) produced a calibrated date of A.D. 1044–1151 at 1σ. Of the wall trench structures, Structure 4 of ECB excavations has a calibrated date of A.D. 1214–1393 at 1σ, while Structure 5 at the PA tract excavations has a calibrated date of A.D. 1221–1256 at 1σ (Scarry 1998:69). This evidence indicates that the small individually set pole form was contemporaneous or slightly more recent than the composite construction form, but appears to predate the wall trench method.

Figure 4.5 shows that the small individually set pole method was a dominant form during the Early Moundville I phase. The frequency of this form declined considerably in the Late Moundville I phase, and disappeared or became very uncommon by Moundville II, being replaced by the wall trench form (Type III). There is some evidence to suggest that the small individually set pole form was used sparingly throughout the Moundville II phase along with the more prominent wall trench form, as indicated by a small individually set pole structure (Structure 2) at the Powers site. However, this particular structure seems to be an outlier between the two means in both post size and post spacing, and may therefore represent what Nash (1968) identified as an intermediate form between the small closely set pole and large widely spaced post techniques. Radiocarbon dating of Structure 2, which may have been misidentified as a rigid post structure, has produced a calibrated date with an intercept of A.D. 1360 ± 50 at 2$\sigma$ (Redwine 2002). This structure was in possession of one centralized roof support and lacked large quantities of daub. However, it has been shown through ethnographic analogy that flexed pole houses were occasionally constructed with one or two centralized roof supports, as in the larger Sidamo houses of Ethiopia (Gebremedhin 1971:123). There is also the possibility that this centralized internal support was the remains of a scaffolding system, which was removed after construction was complete.

Type III. *Wall Trench Form.* Thirty-eight examples of the wall trench form are in the sample. These structures appear at Lubbub Creek, Bessemer, and Moundville. All cases of this form were constructed with small, closely spaced poles, and with the exception of Structure 5b of the Northwest Riverbank excavations, there were no indications of internal roof supports. Structure 5b has one support post sunk in the center of the floor (Scarry 1995:154). Regardless, this single roof support is insufficient evidence that the structure had a separate roof component considering the use of small wall poles and an open corner. More than likely, this post represents some form of scaffolding.

Notably, none of these wall trench structures possessed substantial amounts of clay daub. This evidence is contrary to the general belief that early Mississippian houses in west-central Alabama were usually created with daubed walls. Using clay daub would require a large amount of labor with very little benefit, as there were no eaves in this architectural form to protect the daub from rain runoff, a problem experienced in the construction of an experimental flexed pole house at Etowah in 1981 (Blanton and Gresham this volume).

Like the architecture of the small individually set pole form, the wall trench form probably was constructed using a basketlike method consisting of a single wall roof component (Blanton and Gresham this volume; Polhemus 1985; Reed this volume; Scarry 1998; for opposing views see Brennan this volume and McConaughy this volume). None of these structures possessed horizontal trench wedges, so it is presumed that the vertical wall poles were stabilized through the use of a horizontal support placed above ground. The wall trenches were constructed in a number of ways. The majority of the wall trenches were constructed with open corners, but a few possessed closed corners forming a continuous wall trench around the entire perimeter of the house. It is usually assumed that the doors of this architectural form were typically positioned in the corners of the structure. This assumption comes from the fact that the corners are usually open, a misunderstanding of what the open corners are all about (see Reed this volume). However, it is not doubted that the door could have been placed anywhere along the wall, as was the case with a few structures at Lubbub Creek in which the entryway was marked with wall trenches that lead to the center of a wall, not a corner.

As stated previously, Scarry (1998:69) determined that the composite forms (Type I) and the small individually set pole forms (Type II) were slightly older than the wall trench form (Type III) at the Northwest Riverbank. Wall trench Structures 4 and 5 date to the Late Moundville I to Moundville II phase. Based on the chronological results, I believe that a majority of the Roadway structures, which are not independently dated, represent forms associated with Late Moundville I through Moundville II. However, based on a radiocarbon date of A.D. 1070 ± 55 from a charred wall post from a wall trench in Structure 3 from the Bessemer site, there is reason to believe that wall trench architecture (Walthall and Wimberly 1978), may have been contemporaneous with small individually set pole and composite architectural forms. There is also evidence to suggest that this change from wall trench architecture (Type III) to large individually set posts (Type IV) occurred fairly rapidly, in the form of large post floor plans immediately superimposed on previously wall trench buildings. Examples of this superposition occur at Lubbub Creek (Blitz 1980; Peebles 1983), the Angel site in southern Indiana (Black 1944, 1967), and the Jonathan Creek site in western Kentucky (Webb 1952).

Type IV. *Large Individually Set Post Form.* This building technique, represented by 11 structures in the sample, appears to be prevalent only during the later phases at the Lubbub Creek site and among the Moundville farmsteads. There is also one case of a large individually set post structure at Moundville, House 15 (McKenzie 1964:239). The existence of this case indicates that the Type IV form was probably becoming more popular around the same time the chiefdom was being reorganized and individuals previously living at Moundville spread out up and down the Black Warrior River Valley (Knight and Steponaitis 1998). The large individually set post form is the predominant architecture found at the excavated Moundville farmsteads, with all of the excavated examples occurring late in the Moundville sequence.

This architectural form is characterized by large, widely spaced, individually set wall posts. There is a clear indication of internal roof supports in many of these houses, such as in Structure 1 at the Powers site (Welch 1998:146) and in structures USN 6422, 7470, 3880, and 8168 at Lubbub Creek (Peebles 1983), whereas there are no clearly distinguishable internal supports in either of the Pride Place houses (Johnson 1999, 2001). These houses were commonly constructed with large quantities of clay daub (also see Gougeon this volume for more information about Late Mississippian housing).

Based on the ethnohistoric and ethnographic data (Adair 2005; Lacquement 2004; Reed this volume; Wauchope 1938), Type IV houses were constructed with a hipped or gabled roof. Several large, widely spaced wall posts were planted in the ground in order to support a wall plate. The wall plate supported the basal ends of the rafters. The upper portions of the rafters were supported by a roof plate or ridge pole, which was propped up by the internal roof supports. According to the chronological data, this large widely spaced post structural form was not adopted in west-central Alabama until around A.D. 1400, the end of the Moundville II phase. From that point on, the large widely spaced post form was the predominant architectural form lasting into the Protohistoric period.

Type V. *Amorphous Post Daubed Form.* This amorphous structural form is characterized by large, widely scattered, individually set posts that do not indicate any clearly identifiable posthole pattern. The Type V form is also marked by large quantities of daub. This protohistoric house style has been coined the "Blob" type, due to its irregularly placed posts, lack of clear wall alignment, and amorphous shape, creating typological blueprints that have often plagued archaeologists. Based on the large individually set and widely spaced posts, this form was probably constructed with vertical walls, using a rigid architectural fashion consisting of wattled walls, and large amounts of clay daub that was typically tempered with Spanish moss. There were no examples of this form in the statistical analysis of the sample, but this house style has been identified at sites in west-central and southern Alabama, including Mound E at Moundville (Vernon J. Knight personal communication 2005, in preparation), Lubbub Creek (Peebles 1983), the Camden site (Regnier 2006), the Furman site (Curren 1984), and the Moody Slough site (Curren 1984). Based on ceramic

4.1. Architectural and Ceramic Comparison at Moundville.

| Time Period | Floor Plans | |
|---|---|---|
| A.D. 1050–1150 | Early Moundville I | Type I, II, and III |
| A.D. 1150–1250 | Late Moundville I | Type II and III |
| A.D. 1250–1400 | Moundville II | Type III |
| A.D. 1400–1550 | Moundville III | Type IV |
| A.D. 1550–1650+ | Moundville IV (Protohistoric) | Type IV and V |

analysis, this type of structure dates to the Protohistoric period corresponding to Moundville IV and Summerville IV (Curren 1984; Regnier 2006).

## Discussion

According to the most recent ceramic chronology (Knight and Steponaitis 1998) (Table 4.1), Type I, the composite construction form, which combines both small pole wall trench and larger individually set posts, and Type II, the small individually set pole structures, existed during the Early Moundville I subphase (A.D. 1050–1150). Both Type I and Type II houses were constructed in a flexed pole manner. However, whereas Type I had two flexed sides, Type II had four flexed sides.

Type I architecture was a short-lived form in this region, only existing in the Early Moundville I subphase. Type II houses, individually set small pole structures that characterized the Early Moundville I subphase, may have persisted as late as the end of Moundville II, as indicated by the structures excavated at the Powers site. However, Type II was probably replaced by the wall trench method (Type III) by the beginning of the Moundville II phase. It is also possible that this form was constructed in wall trenches that were not discernible in archaeological excavations.

Type III, the subsequent wall trench form, existed during the early and late Moundville I (A.D. 1150–1250) and Moundville II (A.D. 1250–1400) phases. However, according to the data, this form occurred much more frequently in the latter half of the Moundville I subphase than in the earlier portion of the subphase. This form, like Type II, was constructed in a flexed pole fashion with four flexed sides and without internal roof supports. This method was overwhelmingly popular during this period but was quickly replaced by Type IV architecture by A.D. 1400, becoming characterized by large individually set posts, typically with four internal roof supports.

During the Moundville III and Moundville IV phases, Type IV houses, large individually set rigid post structures, were the dominant form. An example of this construction technique is located at the Powers site, in the form of a large post single set structure with four central roof supports (Redwine 2002; Welch 1998). The transition from various methods of flexed pole construction to that of rigid posts with central roof supports also has been observed in east Tennessee (Lewis and Kneberg 1946; Polhemus 1985; Webb 1938), and central and west Tennessee (Nash 1968). Large post houses in western North Carolina have been dated as early as A.D. 1200 (Dickens 1976), and those along the Upper Savannah River as early as A.D. 1400 (Anderson and Schuldenrien 1985). Generally, this rigid post building technique was common during the late Mississippian/early Protohistoric period, and in some areas persisted into the Historic period (Hally 2002). In the Moundville area, Type IV, the large individually set post form with four internal roof supports, was succeeded by another form of large post construction method during the Protohistoric period—Type V. This presently enigmatic structural form demonstrates no clear wall post patterns, marked only by heavy daub concentrations, and randomly distributed postholes (Curren 1984:84).

## Technological Change in Architecture

It has been established that there is a high probability that at least two forms of domestic architecture existed in west-central Alabama during the Mississippian stage. Using the established chronology, it is possible to determine that there appears to be a sudden, dramatic change in the architecture during the latter half of the Mississippian stage. It should be stated that the motivation for these technological changes from small closely spaced pole houses to large widely spaced post houses is not a primary concern of this study, but certainly, the topic needs to be examined. Several possibilities for the transition in architecture will be explored, including sociocultural and environmental change, material variability, and resource availability.

It also should be noted that the transition from pole to post architecture did not occur everywhere simultaneously, but it seems to occur rather abruptly in each local area. Terminal Woodland tribes such as the Iroquois of New York (Fenton 1978) or the Powhatan of the Virginia coastal plains (Callahan 1981, 1985) used flexed pole architecture in the creation of longhouses until European contact. However, in the Southeast, evidence demonstrates that Mississippian cultures made use of a rigid post form as early as the thirteenth century in western North Carolina and eastern Tennessee (Dickens 1976; Nash 1968; Polhemus 1985), yet Le Page du Pratz witnessed a flexed pole house construction in the Lower Mississippi Valley during the eighteenth century (Swanton 1911, 1946). In west-central Alabama, this transition began around the beginning of the fifteenth century, according to the chronology that has been established in this study. The question therefore remains as to what caused this architectural transition, and why it became so widespread in the southeastern United States.

In order to determine if in fact it was social circumstances that led to these changes in architecture, the floor areas of each house were recorded and compared to the corresponding type of architecture. According to Trigger (1968), the arrangement of a domestic structure reflects the social organization of the family unit. A large change in domestic floor area, whether positive or negative, would indicate an alteration in social conditions. For instance, if the floor size of a domestic house doubles, then one might assume that the structure is housing twice as many members.

The average floor area of small pole structures ranged from 6.9 m$^2$ to 37.18 m$^2$ ($\bar{x}$ = 19.61, $s$ = 7.85, $n$ = 56), while the large post dwellings ranged from 8.84 m$^2$ to 37.00 m$^2$ ($\bar{x}$ = 29.59, $s$ = 9.79, $n$ = 8) (Figure 4.7). As a result, an independent two-tailed $t$-test was calculated to test the null hypothesis ($x1 = x2$) that the difference in the mean floor area of the two architectural types is not statistically significant. The results of the test indicated otherwise, that there is sufficient evidence to reject the null hypothesis ($t$ = -3.262, $df$ = 62, $p$ = .002). The confidence interval generated also supported the rejecting of the null hypothesis, in that the mean of small pole houses was 3.9 to 16.1 m$^2$ smaller than the mean of the large post houses. In other words, there is statistical evidence to assume that the average small closely spaced pole houses were smaller than the average large widely spaced post houses, and therefore it appears there was an increase in floor area corresponding with the change in architecture.

With 50 percent more floor area resulting from the transition between flexed pole architecture and rigid post architecture in the sample from west-central Alabama, it is possible to suggest an increase in the number of occupants. The addition of more people living under the same roof may have been related to the architectural transition. A counter point to this argument is that there are public structures constructed with wall trenches that exceed the size of the average domestic rigid post house at several sites such as Cahokia (Milner 1998), Moundville (McKenzie 1964; field notes on file, Alabama Museum of Natural History), and Hiwassee Island (Lewis and Kneberg 1946).

Another possibility for the increased floor area is more emphasis on household identity. In southeastern Tennessee and northern Georgia, there are few subfloor burials in early Mississippian houses (Hally and Kelly 1998; Polhemus

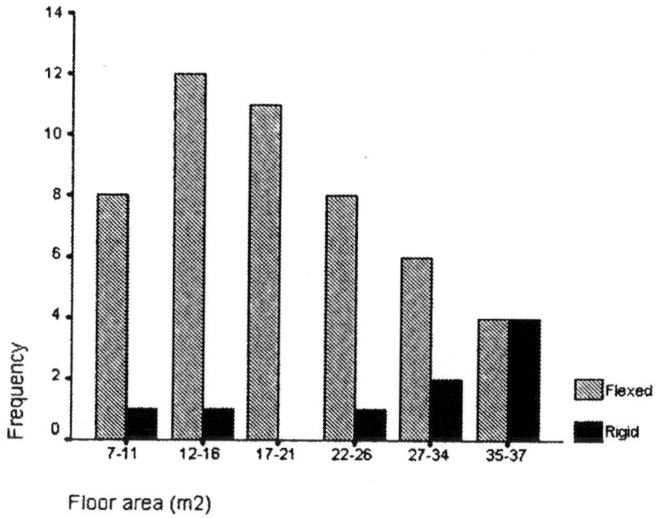


4.7. Bar graph illustrating floor area by architectural type.

1987; Sullivan 1987). However, in later Mississippian times, it is very common to find burials on the interior of house structures. Perhaps the house dimensions increased as a result of people wanting to be buried with other family members of the same household. This argument also has its flaws. First, there are several public structures constructed with wall trenches at Moundville that possess several burials, including House 16 (McKenzie 1964:239, 241), which has at least 25 burials, and Structure 16, which has at least 10 (field notes on file, Alabama Museum of Natural History). It is difficult to determine whether these burials are contemporaneous with house structures, or were deposited after Moundville became a necropolis. The other point in opposition to this argument was mentioned previously, that public houses constructed with wall trenches exceed the average size of rigid post houses for this study. If public buildings were constructed to this size, it is reasonable to assume that domestic houses could have been too.

According to Grove (1988), Jones et al. (1998), and Mann et al. (1998), the 15th to 19th centuries marked a global cooling episode over the Northern Hemisphere referred to as the Little Ice Age (LIA), which preceded a period of gradual warming referred to as the Medieval Warm Period of A.D. 900 to 1400 (also see Little 2000). The duration and geographical extent of the Little Ice Age has been debated (Bradley and Jones 1992, 1993; Crowley 2000; Hughes and Diaz 1994). However, it is reasonable to assume that climatic change influenced the architecture of the Mississippian stage. As temperatures began to cool, large post rigid architecture, and therefore eaves, may have become necessary to protect the clay daub that was used as insulation—a more suitable material than grass or bark. Hally (2002:91) claims that the interior roofs of the rigid post houses in Georgia were also daubed, which would have produced a very heavily insulated building overall. If the climate did influence architecture in the Southeast, it is odd that it did not have any effect on the Terminal Woodland tribes of the Atlantic Coast and the Northeast and the Mississippians of the American Bottom and Lower Illinois Valley. The Natives of these areas lived in more extreme cold conditions without rigid post architecture or the use of daub throughout the Little Ice Age. Climate may have been a strong influencing factor, but is probably not the main cause of the architectural transition. Nevertheless, it is difficult to ignore the fact that the Little Ice Age begins at the same time as the appearance of rigid post structures in the Southeast.

Polhemus (1985) suggested one possibility for this transition—changes in resource variability. The earlier flexed pole method, with its single wall roof component, required that much of the construction material meet rather rigorous specifications. The wood would have to be flexible, strong, uniform, decay resistant, and most of all, readily available. Based on the wood technology data, Polhemus stated that the wood that met the flexibility, strength, and uniformity requirements was usually not the most decay resistant (Polhemus 1985:99). This makes the process of choosing suitable woods more selective in flexed pole construction than in rigid post construction. The larger diameter wall members of the rigid post houses would have resisted decay longer than smaller poles. In addition, several different types of wood could easily be used for different tasks in the construction process of rigid post architecture. For instance, wood science technology has indicated that pine is a poor material to create a flexed pole house, but due to the exceptionally high crushing strength, pine would have made an ideal wood type for center roof supports in a rigid post house (Blanton and Gresham this volume; Lacquement 2004; U.S. Department of Agriculture 1987). Rigid post architecture allows for the use of different woods in different parts of the structure. For instance, woods that are more decay resistant could be placed in the ground, while the more flexible types could be used as roof framework (Polhemus 1985:100). Therefore, a reliance on a variety of wood resources made rigid post house construction less problematic than flexed pole house construction.

Another possibility for the transition in architecture is a decrease in the availability of suitable materials. Small trees for flexed pole construction needed to meet the strict qualifications of being slender, long, and free of deformities. The longest, most flexible trees would be those located in a heavily canopied forest, the trees of which would have grown long and thin in order to compete for sunlight. Clearing land for agricultural, domestic, and ceremonial purposes decreases the canopy, promoting the growth of pine trees that thrive in disturbed environments. These long and slender hardwood trees would have been exploited quickly, leaving only larger trees and softwoods to choose from. Climate may have influenced this process slightly. Colder temperatures would slow the reproduction and growth of the hardwood trees, which seem to be the most viable option for flexed pole houses. Larger trees obviously cannot be bent, therefore, rigid post architecture may have arisen in order to provide shelter to those who had increasingly limited access to suitable small and/or hardwood poles.

The lack of available materials may have been due to the large palisades that typically encompassed Mississippian mound sites. Especially during the Moundville I stage, there was a huge demand for large posts to build and rebuild the palisade. Palisade construction may have depleted the stock of large posts for house construction, leaving only the young pliable saplings as construction materials.

It has been estimated that Moundville would have been occupied by approximately 1,050 to 1,680 people at any given time during the Moundville I phase based on the average density of houses from the Northwest Riverbank excavations (Steponaitis 1998:42). According to this estimation of the number of people and assuming that there were roughly 5 to 8 people per residence (Swanton 1911:43), Steponaitis estimated that there were approximately 210 houses. If the building techniques utilized in one experimental structure (Lacquement 2004, 2005) were accurate, then it would take at least fifty poles to create a flexed pole dwelling. Therefore, roughly 10,500 wooden poles would have been needed to house the Moundville inhabitants at any given time during Moundville I. The average house life expectancy for the wooden framework of a house has been estimated at 10 years (Pauketat 2003; Warrick 1988). Therefore it would have taken an estimated 210,000 thin, flexible, wooden poles to house the Moundville inhabitants for the entire 200 years of the Moundville I phase, assuming there were no large changes in population.

Upon examining all the possibilities for the architectural shift, it is difficult to state that one explanation is more accurate than another. There were probably several reasons for this shift. First, evidence suggests that there was a change in floor area with the transition in architecture. This may be due to a change in the social unit of the family or perhaps due to a change in household identity. With the appearance of rigid post architecture, an increased segregation between work and personal space is surmised. This division was created by using rows of posts that extended from each corner to the corresponding roof support (Polhemus 1985:95). This can be seen in several of the rigid post structures in this sample, including Structure 1 from the Powers site and Structures USN 8168, USN 3880, and USN 2317 from the Lubbub Creek site.

Second, climate also may have influenced the transition of house forms. Rigid post architecture appears at the very beginning of the Little Ice Age. With eaves to protect daub, rigid post houses may have been better suited for colder temperatures. However, the majority of rigid post structures in eastern Tennessee and western North Carolina (Dallas, Pisgah, and Mouse Creek phases) do not have wall daub. Daub is restricted to the interior partitions and, more consistently, to the underside of the roof component—from the main roof supports to the center of the structure. There is no daub on the outer portions or on the roof interior (Polhemus 1987). Third, these later rigid post houses also could have been constructed with several different wood types with a wide array of physical qualities, and could have been placed in positions that would have increased the life of the structure. The wood selected for the construction of these rigid post dwellings did not have to meet the stringent criteria necessary for flexed pole houses, therefore expanding the range of wood that could be used. The reliance on a variety of wood types may have been necessary due to the exhaustion of the particular type of saplings needed for flexed pole construction.

## Conclusions

In conclusion, it appears that there are at least two building techniques represented in the archaeological record of the Mississippian stage—a small closely set pole design and a large widely spaced post design. This statement would have come as no surprise to early southeastern archaeologists such as DeJarnette, Lewis, Kneberg, and Webb. The evidence from this study also suggests that there may have been additional building techniques, including a composite construction form and large post amorphous shape design.

Based on the typology and chronology created in this study, it is possible to date the transition between flexed pole and rigid post architecture in west-central Alabama to approximately A.D. 1400. However, there does not appear to be a single factor that influenced this change in building form, but rather several distinct yet possibly interrelated factors that have may contributed to a change in southeastern architecture.

# 5
# In-Ground Evidence of Above-Ground Architecture at Kincaid Mounds

*Tamira K. Brennan*

> These [primitive] houses, being the *direct* expression of changing values, images, perceptions, and ways of life, as well as of certain constancies, become a very fruitful topic for study.
>
> Rapoport (1969:12)

## Introduction

"Primitive architecture" as defined by Rapoport (1969:2–3) is a type of architecture that exhibits homogeneity as a direct result of the cooperative construction of the community, wherein there are no specialists. Depictions of primitive architecture ranging from Native American houses and temples to entire village complexes can be readily found in standard references such as site reports and in less typical sources like the colorful mural of a Mississippian mound center painted on the Paducah, Kentucky, floodwall. In many instances, these portrayals of "Indian towns" are based upon contact period accounts, while others remain the product of an archaeologist's educated guess. Unfortunately, neither ethnographic literature nor the speculation of researchers alone can provide the empirical basis that accurate interpretation of precontact architecture demands.

Divergence within Native architecture is understandable given the geographic variability of material and technological resources. While available resources place limitations on or restrict certain forms, a wider range of architectural possibilities exists than is realized among primitive societies. We must ask then, why does primitive architecture appear so stylistically homogenous? I believe that beyond engineering and material constraints, deviations within primitive architecture are reined in by social and cultural variables that dictate form. For this reason, understanding primitive architecture is a significant step toward understanding the society that built it.

This study provides a means for in-the-ground identification of several architectural styles commonly found across the Mississippian Southeast. Both

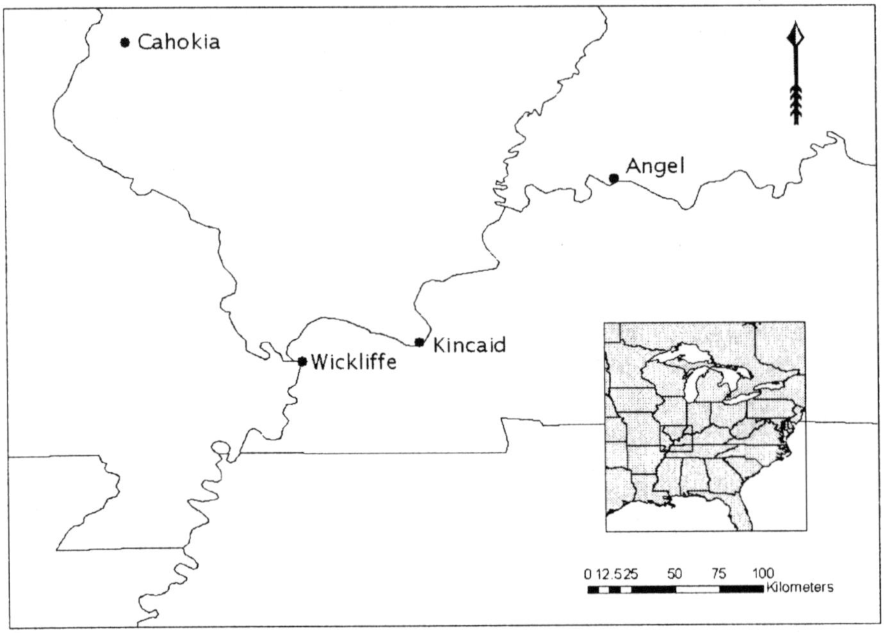


5.1. Location of the Kincaid Mounds site and nearby mound centers.

rigid and flexed pole construction techniques as well as hipped and gabled roof styles will be discussed in an effort to clarify or correct previous interpretations of building form and to furnish future research efforts with an empirical basis from which to draw conclusions. Field records concerning the Mississippian component at the Kincaid Mounds site of southern Illinois (Figure 5.1) will be used to illustrate how uniting architectural principles and archaeological interpretation aids in eliciting new architectural data from old records.

## Construction Techniques

Neither the technological nor the material resources of a society can be exceeded in any architectural endeavor. Likewise, the general principles of architecture cannot be broken. Therefore, the following three questions should be addressed when assessing building form and style: (1) what were the locally available construction materials, (2) which materials have actually been recovered from archaeological contexts, and (3) what are the physical properties of those materials (i.e., how much stress can a flexed pole of oak 6 cm in diameter withstand, what distance can a horizontal beam of rigid cedar span before it needs additional support, and so on)? The answers to these questions will set the limits as to what architectural forms are physically feasible.

Contact period accounts and ethnographic studies provide an excellent starting point when considering prehistoric structures. As has been repeatedly cautioned, however, analogies are often inappropriately used and cannot safely be drawn backward in time as if on a continuum (Wobst 1978; Wylie 1985), nor can ethnographic accounts be taken as wholly accurate reports or safely associated with peoples of a different time and region. They do, however, provide a useful framework for the possibilities. Such a framework has been successfully supplemented in many instances through multidisciplinary collaboration in the fields of architecture, wood science, and experimental reconstruction (Blanton and Gresham this volume; Brennan 2005; Harn 1972; Heilman et al. 1988; Iseminger and Williams 1998; Lacquement 2004, 2005; Litchford 2002; Reed this volume).

## Construction Style

The most prevalent interpretations of standard building forms among the Mississippian peoples are of two kinds: rigid pole and flexed pole (also known as arbor or curved roof) construction (Figure 5.2). In the former style, the roof is a separate and peaked element supported by vertical walls of rigid poles that are either set in individual postholes or placed in wall trenches. The latter style consists of more slender poles flexed inward to create a domed or barrel shaped roof contiguous with the walls. The bases of these poles are usually set in wall trenches, often accompanied by a horizontal pole laid at the base along the outside edge of the wall trench. This bracing technique is occasionally supplemented by an additional horizontal pole near the top of the trench along the inside of the wall (Blanton and Gresham this volume: Lewis et al.). Both styles may have interior post molds that indicate either a load bearing function such as carrying the weight of a roof, or a nonstructural role as is the case with interior benches and partitions.

Webb (1938) associated these two architectural styles with different cultural traditions in the Norris Basin of Tennessee, referring to them as "small log" (flexed) and "large log" (rigid). Lewis and Kneberg (1946; Lewis et al. 1995) report similar findings in the Chickamauga Basin and determine that these differences were a result of major occupations of different time periods based on their exclusivity in distinct stratigraphic levels, the small log chronologically preceding large log style. Currently, no evidence supports the coexistence

5.2. Examples of flexed (top) and rigid pole (bottom) construction styles showing a cutaway to reveal possible construction technique.

of these two styles at the same site in either the Norris or the Chickamauga Basins. Farther north, however, at the Angel site of southern Indiana and at the Rench site in central Illinois, it appears that these styles were indeed contemporaneous, perhaps as paired summer and winter dwellings (Black 1967; McConaughy et al. 1985:178).

Both construction styles may have either opened or closed corners or a combination of both. However, opened corners (the absence of corner posts) are often posited as a defining attribute of flexed pole architecture (Lewis and Kneberg 1946; Lewis et al.; Reed this volume) and thus it is central to the rigid/flexed debate. Structural deficiencies caused by the weight of a separate roof element on narrow-poled rigid walls may indeed make an opened-corner design illogical in many cases. An experimental structure built in this manner at Cahokia (Iseminger and Williams 1998:33) exhibited the very problems with this design that Reed (this volume) discusses. However, these problems were quickly remedied through the addition of horizontal tie beams connecting opposing wall plates, acting to counter the outward forces placed on the walls by the heavy roof. This is only one example of several techniques rendering an open-cornered design and narrow wall poles feasible. I will later discuss how certain notching techniques, the addition of a wall plate, proper lashing of the roof to the walls, tight wattling, and exterior wall embankments or semi-subterranean basins may all be used in conjunction or alone in order to counter the potential problems with a separate roof element on such a structure.

*Rigid Walls*

Experimental reconstructions, ethnographic literature, and burned debris recovered archaeologically all indicate that the walls of rigid structures were stabilized in one or more of the following manners. One manner is wattling, wherein flexible materials such as young willow or cane are woven in and out of the wall posts and wrapped around the corners. While the use of wattle in the Southeast is a widely accepted assumption, see Knight's note (this volume) concerning the paucity of archaeological evidence for such. Accompanying this technique across much of the Southeast is daubing. This process involves tempering mud and clays with natural fibers and plastering it over one or both sides of the walls. Daubing is typically followed by smoothing and, in some cases, finishing with a wash or paint (Black 1967:498; notes on file SIUC; Wesler 2001:151). According to Robert Swenson, associate professor of architecture at Southern Illinois University–Carbondale (SIUC) (personal communication 2006), both the wattle-and-daub techniques will add greatly to the stability of a wall and furthermore allow for the use of more slender poles in a rigid frame structures.

The practice of daubing walls is notably absent among excavated structures at Cahokia and the surrounding region (Collins 1990:68; McConaughy this volume; Pauketat 1986:52). However, the ubiquity of semi-subterranean house basins, or "pit houses," is much greater here than elsewhere in the southeast (Dalan et al. 2003:71) until late in the Mississippian sequence. Semi-subterranean basins are created by excavating an area slightly larger than the expected floor of the building inside of which wall poles are set, penetrating the floor of the basin. The excavated fill is then piled against the walls, functioning structurally to strengthen them in a manner similar to daub (also see Blanton and Gresham this volume).

The purpose of a semi-subterranean house has not been firmly established, although it may be related to climate control. A house set within a basin will remain temperate in the blistering summers and warmer in the wintertime due to the insulation that the soil provides (Hargrave 1991:148). Webb (1952:51) explains the presence "pit houses" (type A) at the Jonathan Creek site in Kentucky as seasonal structures most likely employed only during cold weather. This seasonal assessment may be further supported by the fact that the water table is very near to the ground surface in bottomland areas, proving subterranean foundations disadvantageous during the flood season (warm seasons) in these areas (Hargrave 1991:156).

Following the previous steps, a separate roof element is erected, likely set atop a wall plate. Both contact period accounts and burned debris found lying above wall refuse indicate that these roofs were covered with bundles of thatch or bark, often treated in some manner to prevent highly flammable grasses from catching a spark. This treatment could include a thin layer of daub lining the insides of the roof and perhaps the outer sides as well. A more lightweight option is tightly woven cane mats, which may be easier to repair and longer lasting than a daub treatment. Inner walls were also covered with cane or woven fiber mats, as were interior features such as benches and sleeping platforms (notes on file SIUC).

The wall poles used in a rigid construction style may reach great proportions as the building size increases. It seems that the upper range for post diameter is limited only by available timber and the willingness of the builders to fell and transport it. A more important measure is the minimum allowable diameter of wall poles. This data can provide a cut-off point between rigid and flexed pole designs. Unfortunately, a minimum allowable diameter has never been established and would require considerable knowledge about a particular structure in order to do so. Many of the necessary details such as wood type and wall height, for example, are unavailable via archaeological evidence, although reasonable estimates may be made in some cases.

One step toward determining minimum allowable diameter is by calculating the slenderness ratio (length divided by diameter), a simple formula that determines the load that a pole of a certain diameter and height can support. In order to apply this calculation to minimum allowable post diameter, however, other variables must be accounted for as well, such as the total number of posts in a wall, the roof load (weight), the manner in which this load is distributed across the walls, whether or not interior posts carried part of this load, the spacing of the wall posts, and so on. Because it is not likely that all of these variables can ever be accounted for simultaneously in an archaeological example, experimental archaeology may be the best avenue through which to explore this problem.

Several researchers have attempted to estimate the range of diameters for rigid walls based on the houses examined in their studies. Lewis et al. (1995:55) classify "large log" structures as those with post molds ranging from 15.2 to

30.5 cm (6 to 12 in) in diameter, spaced at an interval of 30.5 cm (12 in) or greater. Webb's (1938:191–192) limits for the same type of structure fall within a much higher range at 25.4 to 35.6 cm (10 to 14 in) for pole diameter, spaced .76 to 1.2 m (2.5 to 4 ft) apart. Although these criteria do not exactly match, they do reveal a rough correlation between the diameter of posts in a structure and the expected distance between them. This finding is supported by statistical tests on individually set post structures from Moundville, showing a high positive correlation between the diameter and spacing of poles (Lacquement this volume). Such is not the case throughout the entire Southeast, however. Welch (2006:139) found a much larger spacing of 30 cm between posts averaging 5 to 8 cm among flexed pole structures at the Shiloh Mound site of southwestern Tennessee. These data indicate that the correlation between narrow pole diameter and close spacing may be a widespread but regionally articulated phenomenon.

### *Flexed Walls*

The flexed pole construction style employs slender, often closely spaced poles of pliable woods such as young oak, hickory, and locust (Lacquement 2004:75; Polhemus 1985). In this architectural style, one wall is flexed inward across the floor and affixed to the opposing wall, creating a single roof/wall element. All four walls may be interwoven to form a basketlike latticework (Lewis et al. 1995:58) or bound near their peaks in a simpler manner. Stabilization of flexed pole structures is achieved by lashing horizontal poles to the vertical wall supports. The whole structure is then covered with some combination of thatch, bark, and cane in a manner similar to that of the roof of a rigid pole structure and sometimes coated with a relatively thin layer of daub (Le Page du Pratz [in Swanton 1911]).

Excavations at several sites (Lewis and Kneberg 1946; Lewis et al. 1995; Webb 1938) indicate that the placement of a horizontal pole along the exterior side of a wall trench was a relatively common practice in some regions of the Southeast. More rare are double horizontal trench supports, wherein an additional log is laid within the wall trench on the inner side of the wall, positioned slightly higher than the outer log. The function of the exterior logs is presumably to counter the outward force created as these poles were flexed inward, which perhaps served to stabilize walls placed in loose soils such as mound fill. The presence of exterior horizontal bracing in trenches appears to be unique to flexed pole architecture, whereas interior bracing occurs in several instances of rigid construction as well (Pauketat and Woods 1986:111; Price 1969). Rather than serving to counter architectural stresses, Pauketat and Woods have suggested that this feature may indicate a new construction technique wherein walls were prefabricated before being set into trenches.

The maximum allowable diameter of timber selected for flexed pole architecture must necessarily be more slender than the maximum allowable diameter of timbers employed in rigid frames due to the fact that arbor roofs are bent inward by hand when connected to the opposing wall. Determining exactly what post diameters represent a flexed pole frame is an important yet challenging task. According to Lewis et al. (1995:55) a range of 9.1 to 15.2 cm (.3 to .5 ft) is given for post molds that represent flexed ("small log") structures, reportedly spaced at intervals approximately 15.2 cm apart. In his Norris Basin report, Webb (1938:191–192) considers poles less than or equal to 10.2 cm in diameter (4 in) to be small log, and indicates no average spacing. There is a considerable and unaccounted for gap of 15.2 cm (6 in), however, between his limits for small log and large log post mold diameters.

Lacquement's (2004) experimental strength tests on young hickory and white oak provide a more reliable measure of the acceptable range of post diameter than do previous field observations. He reports suitable diameters as those ranging from 5 to 7 cm (2 to 3 in), noting that poles with a diameter greater than 7.6 cm were no longer bendable by hand. The stresses exerted by a tree with a basal diameter falling within this upper limit will inhibit the retention of a dome form without interior horizontal bracing between opposing walls (Swenson personal communication 2006). Therefore, it is less likely that flexed pole structures would actually employ trees approaching 7.6 cm in diameter.

### *Discerning the Differences*

Ethnographic accounts of both styles of architecture among Southeastern tribes exist (Adair 2005; Le Page du Pratz [in Swanton 1911, 1946]), as does legitimate in-the-ground evidence for each (Brennan 2005; Lewis and Kneberg 1946; Lewis et al. 1995; McConaughy et al. 1985; Pauketat and Woods 1986). However, the technological and material constraints associated with the construction of each type have seldom been included in previous architectural assessments. This oversight has historically led to interpretive "trends" subject to change over time among reconstructions, museum depictions, and artistic renderings (Lacquement 2004:29) as well as archaeological reports. The following list will provide several means to assist in making determinations of construction style (Table 5.1). Although each factor can be assessed independently, the most convincing arguments for construction style will incorporate as many as possible. While wall trench vs. single pole structures may reveal construction

5.1. Structural Attributes Useful for Determining Construction Style.

| Indications of Construction Style | | | Flexed Pole | Rigid Pole |
|---|---|---|---|---|
| wall posts | | | | |
| | < 7.6 cm diameter | | B | B |
| | > or = 7.6 cm diameter | | | X |
| | angled inward | | X | |
| | angled outward | | | X |
| | exterior horizontal brace in trench | | X | |
| | interior horizontal log in wall trench sill | | | X |
| | notched to receive wall plate | | | X |
| | close spacing of posts | | X | |
| | wide spacing of posts | | | X |
| | curved | | X | |
| interior posts | | | | |
| | patterned | | | |
| | | substantial width | | X |
| | | substantial depth | | X |
| | | small diameter | B | B |
| | | shallow depth | B | B |
| | random | | B | B |
| daub | | | | |
| | heavy (> 4 in thick) | | | X |
| | light (< 4 in thick) | | B | B |
| roof | | | | |
| | bird's mouth notch | | | X |
| | perpendicular elements bound together | | | X |
| | interwoven construction | | X | |
| | tie beams | | | X |
| thatch | | | | |
| | green wood/accidental burn | | | X |
| | old wood/intentional burn | | B | B |
| corners | | | | |
| | opened | | B | B |
| | closed | | B | B |
| wood type | | | | |
| | hickory, ash, oak | | B | B |
| | cedar, cypress | | | X |

style at a regional level, these factors are not definitive of rigid or flexed pole structures and are thus not considered in this table.

One of the most useful, yet potentially problematic, manners of determining superstructure is a close examination of post molds. Several factors often confound post mold analyses. In the instance of wall trench structures, little to no distinction between trench fill and post fill hinders determination of the true size and location of posts. Another problem arises when one considers post molds vs. postholes. Post mold indicates the original dimensions of the post-in-ground, whereas posthole refers to the hole that received the post. A post mold may be 25 to 50 percent smaller than a posthole (Polhemus 1985:18) depending on whether the hole receiving the post was excavated to be larger than the post itself, whether this post was pushed outward or pulled inward by architectural stresses, and finally whether it was removed at the end of the structure's use-life or rotted in place. Even when the charred post itself is recovered within a structure, its original size may be reduced due to shrinkage or decay (Pauketat and Woods 1986:111). The possibility that post width and depth may not have been recorded at the uppermost elevation further complicates analysis.

In the case that reliable data on posts is available, post mold diameter may easily be used to exclude flexed pole structures in instances where they measure greater than 7.6 cm in diameter. As mentioned above, wood science studies have shown that the types of wood appropriate for flexed pole structures (flexible enough to bend without breaking but strong enough to carry a roof load) could no longer be flexed by hand at this width. Wood type should also be considered whenever possible, as certain wood types are more or less likely to be employed in a flexed frame based on their structural qualities. For example, locust is a very strong wood but not very flexible, whereas willow, while quite flexible, has a low strength (U.S. Department of Agriculture 1987).

As mentioned previously, smaller, closely spaced poles are suggested to indicate a flexed frame, while larger, widely spaced poles indicate a rigid frame (Lacquement this volume; Lewis and Kneberg 1946; Lewis et al. 1995; Polhemus 1985; Reed this volume; Webb 1938). While a comparison of floor plans and their proposed superstructures does exemplify this trend (excepting the previously mentioned Shiloh example), closely spaced post molds should not alone be used to determine frame type. While it is possible for rigid walled structures to support a roof with only several large supporting wall poles, there are several reasons why many smaller poles might be preferred for the frame of a structure. One of the most basic explanations for numerous wall supports among Mississippian architecture would be to provide a medium for wattling the walls. More, closely spaced posts would allow for a tighter weave, leading to a more weather-tight structure, adding stability to the wall, and providing a framework for applying the daub.

Interior posts can also be very useful in determining superstructure when considered in the appropriate manner. Not all interior post molds represent structural elements, and it is possible that both rigid and flexed pole structures will evidence interior posts as a result of features such as partitions and benches. Therefore, the presence or absence of less substantial interior post molds should not in isolation lead to the assumption that the roof is of one type or the other. Rather, post function needs to be considered. Posts with a weight-bearing function will generally be as substantial as, or more so than, wall poles and will penetrate the floor to a similar or more substantial depth. Signs of soil compression and insertion/extraction ramps may be good indications of this function. The placement of these posts is also telling of their purpose. Preplanned support posts (see, for example Black 1967:197; Cole et al. 1951:64, 77, 82; Lewis et al. 1995:68) will be regularly placed along the line of the ridge pole or following tie beams. If added to later remedy particular structural problems, their placement may be more random.

It should also be noted that several other means could be employed to support a separate roof element, precluding the need for interior supports. These are the same techniques outlined above for overcoming the potential engineering problems of open-cornered floor plans. Among these are a number of techniques that either strengthen the outer walls or act to divert or spread pressure caused by the roof across other structural members (Figure 5.3). For example, the use of a small triangular notch in the vertical roof beams, referred to as a bird's mouth notch, would divert outward force into downward force (Figure 5.4). A semi-subterranean basin, in addition to its insulating properties, is another means of overcoming load problems. As the height of a wall increases, it becomes less capable of withstanding outward forces created by the weight of a separate roof. Setting posts immediately adjacent to a vertical basin wall effectively reduces their height, reducing the slenderness ratio of the wall and thus increasing its load capacity (Robert Swenson, personal communication 2006). Therefore, progressively smaller poles could be used as the depth of the basin increases or additionally, as an earthen banking against the outer wall increases in height. Tie beams connecting the wall plates would also allow for smaller poles to support a separate roof. Tie beams are horizontal beams used to prevent two other structural members from spreading apart. Their employment may be especially useful in houses without interior support posts, although they serve another purpose as well. In a structure without tie beams,

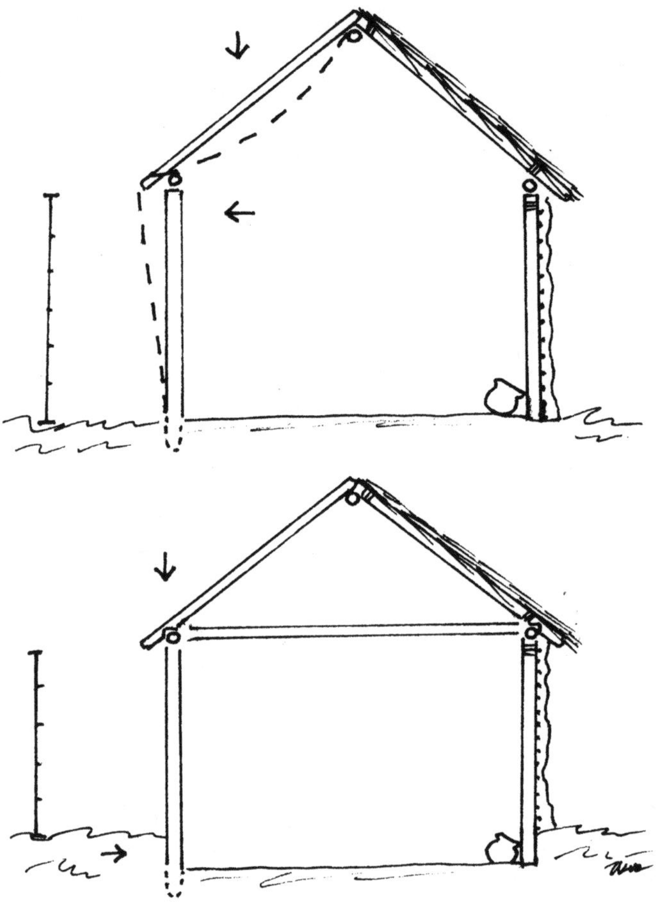

5.3. Arrows in the top illustration indicate possible forces created by the roof load in a rigid wall structure. The bottom illustration shows how outward force can be converted into downward force with the use of a bird's mouth notch (see Figure 5.4) and further countered with the addition of horizontal beams. By setting the structure in a basin, the walls are effectively "shortened," allowing for more slender poles in wall construction.

interior supports must be equal to the height of the structure from the floor to the ridge pole. When tie beams are utilized, the interior supports must only equal the distance from the floor to the tie beam itself in order to accept the weight of the roof, thus reducing their height to that of the wall plates. This technique would be especially useful in very large structures such as that illustrated in the top portion of Figure 5.5, a building with over three times the

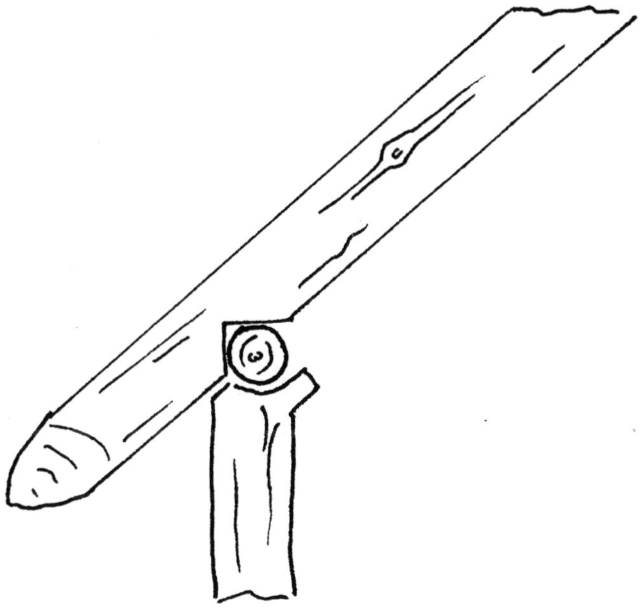

5.4. Example of a bird's mouth notch, as employed in Figure 5.3.

floor area of the lower structure. I believe these two floor plans represent both of the methods of patterned interior support mentioned above.

Depending on the state of the wood before a structure is burned, the patterns produced by roof thatch will also indicate structure style. The thatch (and entire roof element) of a rigid pole structure is expected to collapse on the feature floor as it burns, often to be buried by the walls if they themselves fall inward (notes on file SIUC). In the case of badly decayed wood the wall timbers and thatch of a flexed pole structure (intentionally burned) collapsed inward as well, retaining their curved form (McConaughy et al. 1985). However, Powell (1980:20) notes that in flexed pole structures burned when the wood is still green, the wall poles spring outward and straighten as the lashings catch fire, resulting in an absence of thatch on the structure floor. The burning of a five-month-old experimental flexed pole structure (Lacquement 2004:107) supports this expected pattern, as its thatch covering slid down the exterior walls as the house incinerated. Therefore, the presence of curved timbers and thatch on a structure floor can be one factor used to determine construction style in the instances where the wall poles are clearly not decayed.

The thickness and ubiquity of daub provides a final indicator of construc-

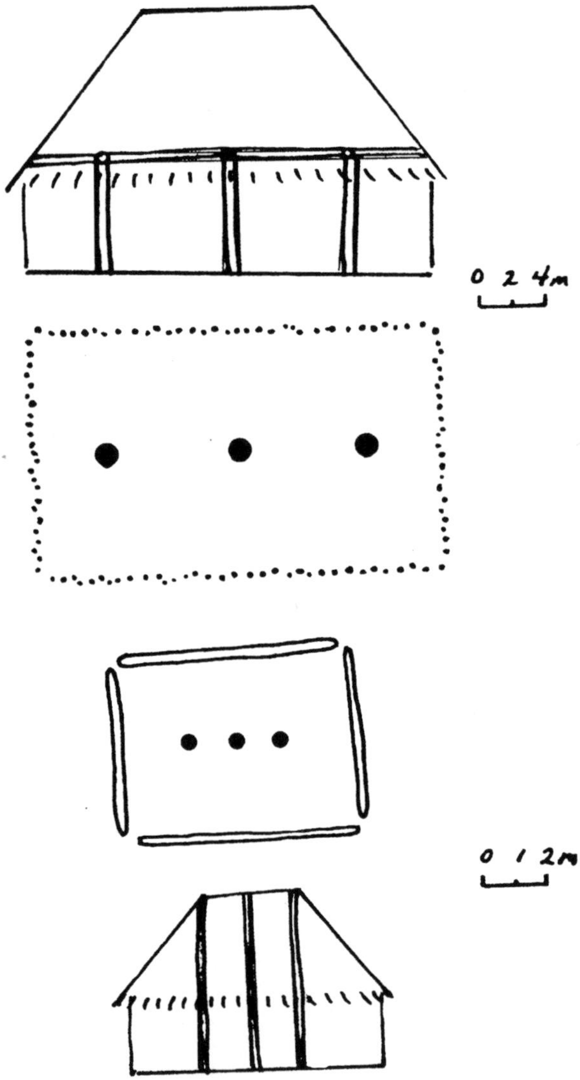


5.5. Possible above-ground correlates of two similar interior post layouts at Kincaid. Above, the arrangement of interior posts as well as structure size (≈ 13 x 8 m) indicates that tie beams may have been employed in the superstructure (after Mx°7 subzone 3D). Below, a similar but narrower post pattern from a much smaller structure (≈ 4 x 3 m) makes interior supports spanning to the ridgepole a more feasible arrangement (after House II, ZG, Mx°4).

tion technique. Le Page du Pratz (in Swanton 1911:60) notes that a layer of daub approximately 10 cm (4 in) thick or less was applied to the outer surface of flexed poled structures in the Lower Mississippi Valley. A much thicker application (approximately 30.5 cm [1 ft] thick) has been reported for rigid pole structures, plastered both inside and out (notes on file SIUC). It is likely that such a heavy application of daub may not be feasible for the roof of a flexed pole structure despite the remarkable strength of its arched shape. Therefore, substantial amounts of thick daub should only be recovered from a rigid pole house or from the peripheral areas of a burned flexed pole house.

### *Roof Styles*

If one can determine that a structure is rigid pole in design, the next step in analysis involves assessing roof style. Gabled roofs have often been cited both ethnographically and by archaeologists in association with rigid walls (Adair 2005:417–419; Cole et al. 1951; Hargrave 1991). A similar but more structurally sound hipped roof was more likely the form employed. Establishing this, however, is a more daunting task than determining whether a wall was flexed or rigid.

In large part, the difficulty in distinguishing between these styles archaeologically is due to the fact that roof elements leave little in ground indication of their presence. Elements of insubstantial size such as thatch and small stringers are less likely to survive, in contrast to wall elements, for example. With the exception of interior support posts, no soil stains are associated with roof construction. For these reasons, burned structures may present the best evidence for both wall and roof construction. Fortunately for the archaeologist, many Mississippian structures appear to have been intentionally burned and often covered in earth while still smoldering, resulting in excellent preservation of structural elements.

Gabled and hipped roofs are somewhat similar in appearance but architecturally very different. A hipped roof consists of four sides that meet either at a ridge pole in the case of rectangular houses, or at a central peak as is often the case in square structures. A hipped roof with a ridge pole results in two longer and two shorter sides, whereas the roof of a square structure would produce roughly equal sides, taking on a pyramidal appearance. These two styles would presumably have differing interior post patterns (compare those in Figure 5.5 above with Figure 178 of Black 1967:197). Gabled roofs result in a two-sided roof with two peaks perpendicular to the ground. Ideally, a thatched roof of either type would minimally have a 45-degree pitch in order to provide sufficient water-shed (Damato 2002).

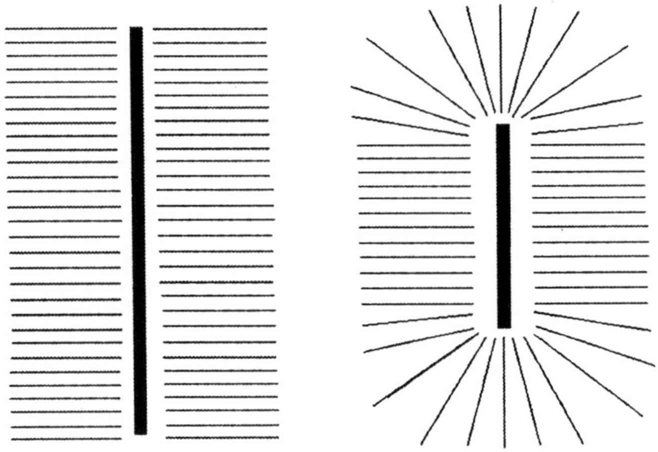

5.6. Expected distribution of collapsed roof thatch from gabled (right) and hipped (left) roofs.

For the determination of roof type, examining burned thatch is of greatest importance. Gabled and hipped roofs can fairly easily be distinguished from one another when directionality of this thatch is discernable. A gabled roof is two-sided, therefore its thatch would be expected to exhibit a bidirectional pattern as it collapses with the burning roof. A hipped roof is thatched on every side and should produce a four-directional or radial pattern in the ground (Figure 5.6). A similar analysis may prove useful for determining whether a flexed pole structure was constructed more like a dome (four thatched sides) or resembling a wigwam (two thatched sides), although no studies have yet examined this issue in depth.

Beyond investigating physical evidence for roof style, practical considerations must also be accounted for that lead to the conclusion that a hipped roof is more likely than a gabled roof for several reasons. For one, a gabled roof exposes a very large surface area to the elements, reducing its heating efficiency. This large surface area also makes gabled roof structures more susceptible to damage in high winds than those with hipped roofs (Federal Alliance for Safe Homes 2004), a factor of major importance in regions where violent seasonal storms are common (Swenson personal communication 2005). A hipped roof not only diverts strong gusts upward, but it also creates an overhang for all four walls, effectually extending their use-life. A final consideration is that the timber required for the walls of a hipped roof structure are all roughly equal in length, whereas the two shorter ends of a gable roofed structure require timbers that must reach the peak of the roof.

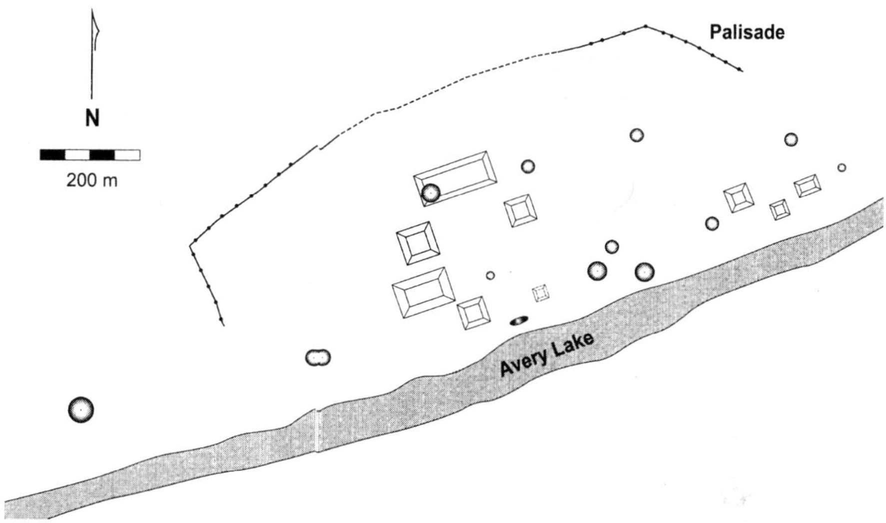


5.7. Kincaid Mounds site map.

## Kincaid

### *Site History*

In order to illustrate the utility of the above methods, the Kincaid Mounds site of southern Illinois will be used as an example. Kincaid Mounds, named after the landowners who erected their home atop Mound 8 (Mx°8) in 1876, lies near the Illinois/Kentucky border in both Pope and Massac counties (Figure 5.7). It stretches 1.6 km along the banks of Avery Lake and is situated on a high area within a floodplain north of the Ohio River at its confluence with the Tennessee and Cumberland Rivers, known as the Black Bottom. Not only is the Black Bottom rich in floral and faunal resources, but it is also ideal agricultural land due to annual alluvial deposits.

Indigenous peoples inhabited the Kincaid site periodically as early as Archaic times, although this project's focus is on the Mississippian occupation, spanning A.D. 1050 to 1400 and peaking at approximately A.D. 1250 (Butler 1991:271). The phases of early, middle, and late Kincaid originally designated by Orr (1951) fall within what is presently recognized as the Jonathan Creek (A.D. 1000–1100), Angelly (A.D. 1200–1300), and Tinsley Hill (A.D. 1300–1450) phases as set forth by Butler (1991) for this sequence (see also Clay 1997 and Muller 1986). Previously thought to incorporate 19 mounds (Payne 1994:86), a reexamination of the landscape at Kincaid has resulted in adjustments to this figure. To date there are 27 suspected mounds (Paul Welch personal communication 2006) and several additional low rises in the landscape, which have yet to be explored. The current site map reflects all confirmed mounds and many untested but obviously man-made earthworks as well as these mounds' presumed original shapes according to a recent study by Corin Pursell (personal communication 2006). Ongoing research at SIUC will certainly result in a more refined and accurate figure.

Kincaid witnessed an expansion in terms of social and political organization during the Mississippian time period as part of an elaborate ceremonial complex spanning the southeastern United States, evidenced by the massive earthworks that remain today. The end of the late Kincaid or Tinsley Hill phase (A.D. 1400) marked the abandonment of the region, which comprises a portion of what Williams (1990:173) terms the "Vacant Quarter." While the true extent of abandonment of this region and its cause remains a topic of debate (see Cobb and Butler 2002), the dispersion of Kincaid's Mississippian inhabitants marked the end of the indigenous use of the site.

Over a period of ten years (1934–1944), the Kincaid site underwent large-scale investigation conducted by the University of Chicago (UC) employing both field school and WPA labor forces. The list of crew members and students reads like a *Who's Who* of archaeology, including John Bennett, Robert Bell, Joseph Caldwell, Jesse Jennings, Richard S. MacNeish, Stuart Neitzel, Georg Neumann, Kenneth Orr, Frank Setzler, Edward Spicer, and John Murra, among others. Results of these excavations were published in Cole et al.'s (1951) edited volume, *Kincaid: A Native Illinois Metropolis.* While this volume is the most comprehensive account of the site to date, it was put together in a selective fashion long after excavations ceased. The Illinois Historic Preservation Agency (IHPA) acquired the majority of the Massac County portion of the Kincaid site, including the main mound group and plaza, in 1975. The Pope County portion, which contains one or two smaller plaza and mound groupings, remains under private ownership.

## Analysis

### *Materials*

This analysis considers the data available on architecture of the Mississippian component at the Kincaid Mounds site (Jonathan Creek through Tinsley Hill phases). Extensive excavations at the site as well as the preservation of charred logs and saplings of cedar, red oak, cypress, hickory, persimmon, and poplar; thatch, grasses, cane (often split or quartered), twine, and other unidentified fibers, twigs, and reeds; and massive amounts of daub recovered from burned structures make Kincaid an ideal site for in-depth analysis of construction techniques in the Lower Ohio River Valley. While field techniques employed during Kincaid's initial excavations were innovative in their own time, they are fraught with inconsistency and often lacking in the details routinely recorded in today's excavations. Reexamination of the original field notes in light of methodological advances and newly available comparative data clarifies and enhances interpretations of the Kincaid site and provides a more adequate resource for further analyses of southeastern sites.

Unless otherwise noted, the sources used in this analysis are two file cabinet drawers of handwritten notes, unpublished manuscripts, and weekly reports resulting from the original UC research and any of the original plan and profile maps that could be located from the 1934–1944 field seasons (on file at SIUC). While the most useful tools for an initial assessment of architectural variability are large plane table maps incorporating the many 1.5 by 1.5 m (5 by 5 ft) excavation blocks into larger continuous units, most of these are missing from the Kincaid files. Table 1 of John Bennett's (1940:47–51) master's thesis, *A Preliminary Study of the Kincaid Component and Its Affiliations,* has been very helpful in filling some of the gaps. Although not always substantiated by field notes and existing maps, Bennett's findings have provided information otherwise unavailable, as it seems to have been in large part compiled from the missing maps.

### *Methods*

Although there is at least partial information available for 127 structures at Kincaid, this study makes use of only the 27 for which floor areas can be calculated (Table 5.2). These include 15 of the 23 structures tabulated by Bennett (1940:47–52), supplemented in many instances with further data from field notes. In cases where there is contradictory data among sources, precedence is given in the following order: measurements taken from field maps, figures, and notes from Cole et al. (1951), dimensions given in Bennett's (1940) thesis, and finally the UC field notes. In many cases the only dimensions available are the estimates recorded in these notes. A cross check between recorded estimates with known dimensions reveals that these estimates are precise enough for the purposes of this analysis. Nondomestic architecture such as sweat lodges, granaries, and palisades has been noted at the site (Brennan 2005; Cole et al. 1951; Weigand and Muller 1967) but are excluded from this study. Aside from one recently excavated structure (West Mound F.2), all dates on Kincaid buildings are noted in relative terms as they were recorded in the field notes as determined using Orr's ceramic analysis.

5.2. Comparative Structural Data for 27 Kincaid Structures.

| Structure Designation | shape | fl. area ($m^2$) | walls | hearth | date | rebuilt | interior PM(s) |
|---|---|---|---|---|---|---|---|
| $Mx^o$4, F.13 (House 1) | Rectangle | 9.62 | WT | | Early Kincaid | X | X |
| $Pp^v$13, F.7 | Rectangle | 9.79 | WT | | | | |
| $Mx^o$7, structure 101 | Square | 10.22 | WT/SP | | Early Kincaid | | |
| $Mx^o$4, F.12 (House 2) | Square | 11.46 | WT | central (2) | Middle Kincaid | X | |
| $Mx^o$4, F.22 | Square | 12.26 | WT | central | Early Kincaid | | |
| $Mx^o$4, WT3/4/5 (House 2) | Rectangle | 12.9 | WT | | Early Kincaid | X | X |
| $Mx^o$4, F.23 | Rectangle | 13.94 | WT | | | X | |
| West Mound, F.2 | Square | 14.16 | WT | central | 1240 ± 60 | | X |
| $Mx^v$1D, F.1, E. Section | Rectangle | 15.68 | WT | central (2) | Early Kincaid | X | X |
| $Mx^o$4, F.31/8 | Square | 18.57 | SP | | Middle Kincaid | | |
| $Mx^v$1A, F.29 inner (1935) | Square | 20.89 | WT | | | | |
| $Mx^v$1A, F.29 outer (1935) | Rectangle | 27.88 | WT | | | | |
| $Mx^v$1C, F.19b | Square | 30 | SP | near edge of house | | | X |
| $Mx^o$4, F.7 (House 1) | Rectangle | 33.15 | WT | just east of center | Middle Kincaid | | X |
| $Mx^o$10, F.8 | Square | 33.49 | WT | one on each 1/2 | | | X |
| $Mx^v$1A, Structure 1, 1941 | Square | 33.5 | WT | central | | | |
| $Mx^v$1C, F.20 | Square | 35.14 | WT | central | Late Kincaid | | X |
| $Mx^o$4, WT51/59/60 | Square | 39.04 | WT | central | Middle Kincaid | | |
| $Mx^o$4, WT53-58 (House 2) | Rectangle | 41.83 | WT | | Middle Kincaid | | |
| $Mx^o$7, structure 102 | Square | 64.65 | WT | | Early Kincaid | | |
| $Mx^o$9, F.19 | Rectangle | 72.01 | WT | X | | X | |
| $Mx^v$1A, F.1/12 (1935) | Rectangle | 113.43 | WT | central | | X | |

| | | | | | | | |
|---|---|---|---|---|---|---|---|
| Mx°7, Subzone 3D | Rectangle | 117.53 | SP | | | Early Kincaid | X |
| Mx°7, L7, Z2A (House 1) | Square | 126.25 | WT | | | Late Kincaid | X |
| Mx$^{v}$1D, WT1/3/16 | Square | 183.77 | WT | X | | | |
| Mx°4, WT68/93 | Rectangle | 195.05 | WT | | | Middle Kincaid | |
| Mx°4, WT71/72/79 | Rectangle | 299.75 | WT | | | | |

WT = Wall Trench, SP = Single Post

A considerable lack of consistency in the field notes both from within and among different excavation areas and field seasons presented a notable problem during this analysis. Where such problems cannot be sorted out, these data have been excluded from the study. The level of detail demanded by field methodology today was not standard throughout UC notes, rendering the currently available data on Kincaid's buildings insufficient for more than a general understanding of the site's architectural history. The following will hopefully provide a solid foundation from which to build a more in-depth analysis as subsequent excavations provide new data.

*Findings*

Calculations of the 27 available floor areas at Kincaid reveal several distinct size classes (Figure 5.8). These fall into four categories: small (9.6 to 41.8 m$^2$, $n$ = 19), medium (64.7 to 72.0 m$^2$, $n$ = 2), large (113.43 to 126.25 m$^2$, $n$ = 3), and public (> 183 m$^2$, $n$ = 3). As expected, the largest class of structures is found within mound contexts and the smallest in village and premound village areas. Few architectural differences can be noted among the 27 structures in this analysis, excepting these spatial and size distinctions. Examples of wall trenches and individual posts, hearths, basins, central support posts, and daub are present across the board. The homogenous distribution of structural attributes between classes is broken only by evidence for possible functional specialization within the small class structures. Hearths are present in 50 percent of the small houses, accompanied by two examples of semi-subterranean basins. This may indicate the use of separate summer and winter dwellings as discussed by Sullivan (1995).

The buildings in the small class exhibit two clear peaks in floor areas at the 10 to 20 m$^2$ and 30 to 40 m$^2$ ranges. Based on the 11 small structures with available relative dates, these peaks appear to represent a temporal separation. Those buildings under 21 m$^2$ (small 1) span the early to middle Kincaid phases, whereas those falling within the 27 to 42 m$^2$ range (small 2) represent middle and late Kincaid structures. These data provide empirical evidence for the initial hypothesis (notes on file SIUC) that smaller houses with narrower wall trenches give way to larger ones with wider trenches over time. This sample does not support the hypothesis that floor plans change from rectangular to square in shape over time, although working out a chronology on those undated structures within this sample will lead to a more definite answer to this question.

A closer examination of small 1 structures exposes evidence of rebuilding and instances of superimposed (rebuilt) central hearths within the same struc-

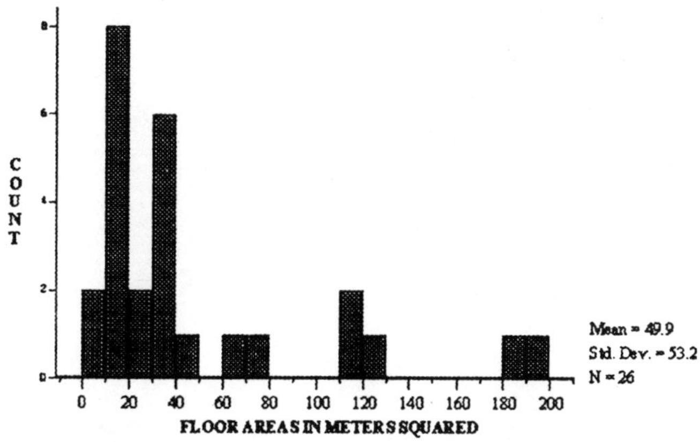


5.8. Histogram of floor areas from sixteen domestic and special purpose structures at the Kincaid Mounds site.

ture, allowing for the possibility that this class may represent a greater time depth than the small 2 class. Whether rebuilt structures during the earlier Kincaid phases actually indicate a longer phase duration, a greater attachment to place (i.e., the tendency to reoccupy specific locations), or simply a shorter structural use-life cannot be pinned down at this time without more precise chronological data. All other structural attributes recorded are evenly distributed between the small 1 and small 2 subclasses.

The medium and large size classes are tentative categories at the moment, as there are respectively only two and three buildings in each sample. Twenty-three meters squared separates the floor area of the small size class from the medium and 41 m separates the medium class from the large. While these data support a significant distinction among all three classes, a much larger sample is needed to confirm this conclusion. One possibility may be that the medium class is in fact on a continuum with the small 2 class. However, the specialized nature of the medium-sized features (structure 102 within a stockade in submound 7 and F.19 on the natural rise that forms the base of Mound 9) makes it more likely that they are properly placed within their own class. The only notable difference between the medium and large size classes is the presence of multiple patterned interior posts within two of the three larger structures—a factor that could be the result of both sampling bias and architectural necessity alike.

While using floor area as a parameter for studying architectural attributes is useful, it necessarily excludes at least one building at Kincaid that falls within

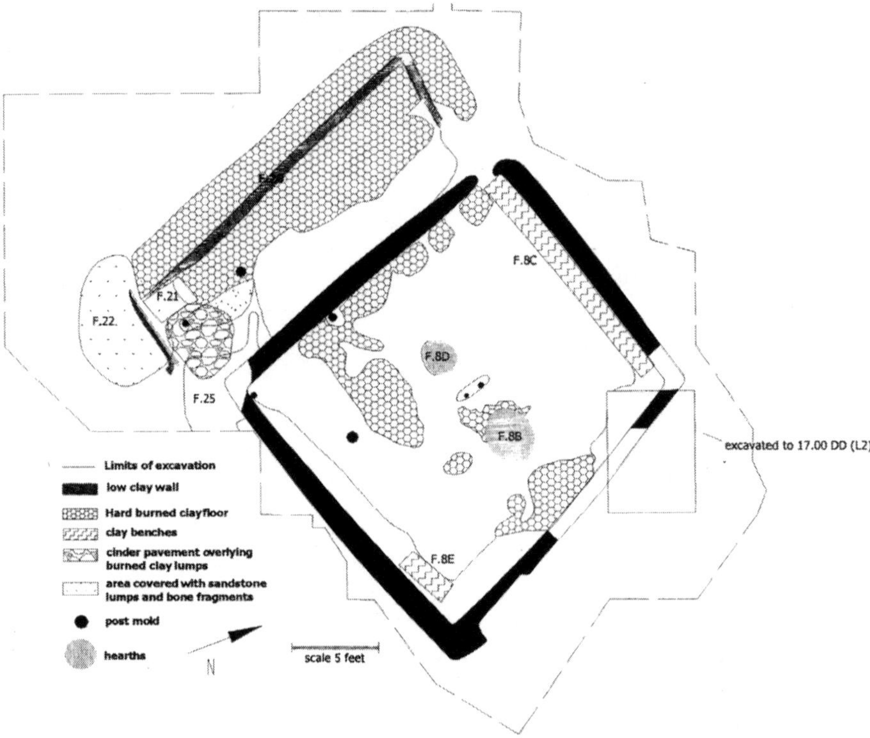


5.9. Feature 8, an elite structure excavated by the University of Chicago, positioned atop the conical portion of Mound 10 (Mx°10).

a similar functional category as the largest, public buildings. Feature 8 sits at the foot of the conical portion of the largest mound at Kincaid, Massac County Mound 10 (Mx°10) heading the main plaza (Figure 5.9). While classed as a small 2 structure based on size alone, this feature includes multiple clay benches, a partially hardened clay floor, and a central hearth on both the east and west sides of a plastered double pillar in the center of the structure. It is this feature's function that accounts for its elaborate interior and unique construction style, attributes indicative of southeastern ceremonial architecture (Payne 1994; Polhemus 1985) despite its small size.

Many of the attributes recorded from this architectural sample offer more ambiguous indicators of architectural form than floor areas. For example, hickory and oak are two of the more prevalent woods identified at Kincaid. Both of these are ideal building materials for flexed pole structures (Lacquement 2004), yet quite suitable for a rigid design as well. Posthole diameters were most often recorded as "small" or "large" during the Chicago excavations with no clarification as to actual measurements and no distinction made between postholes and post molds. Seemingly contradictory accounts have also been encountered. Namely, several instances in which small, closely spaced posts were noted, central supports were also recorded. The coincidence of these two attributes may be further cause to reconsider the assumption that small, closely spaced poles are always indicative of a singular style of construction—flexed pole.

Ambiguities aside, sufficient defining attributes remain to make a strong case for typical architecture at Kincaid (Table 5.3). Among these are the presence of woods associated with rigid poles such as cedar and cypress, interior posts of substantial width and depth aligned with a ridge pole or tie beams, and posts of a diameter greater than the upper limit established for hand bending (7.6 cm). The presence of massive amounts of daub still bearing the impressions of the walls they were once a part of have also been recovered from multiple contexts on site. In many instances this daub is nearly 30 centimeters thick and evidences the wattle that it once adhered to.

Additionally, three factors that point to roof style in particular have been recorded in detail. One amazing instance of charred wall and roof elements still lashed together perpendicular to each other as well as logs notched to either to receive a wall plate or perhaps to function as a bird's mouth notch both indicate a separate roof element. Also noted are several instances in which large quantities of burned thatch collapsed in the radial pattern that a hipped, but not a gabled, roof produces. Of the 17 instances where roofing material is recorded, six include a cane or split cane component.

## Discussion

Earlier reports of Kincaid architecture have posited structures as both flexed pole (Bennett 1944) and rigid pole with a gabled style roof (notes on file SIUC). Based on the evidence in the field notes and drawings, I conclude that the typical structure type at Kincaid fits neither of these previous interpretations. Rather, I believe that a rigid walled construction with a separate, hipped roof was the architectural style most commonly employed at Kincaid for both public and domestic buildings (Brennan 2005). These conclusions are supported by evidence reported above, including (1) structure size; (2) presence of heavy daub within structure context; (3) charred roof materials recovered in situ; and (4) post placement, depth, and function. Basic architectural principles have been used to further support my argument.

On a large scale, it is apparent that Kincaid exhibits most of the architectural traits typical of a Mississippian period mound center. Striking parallels

5.3. Architectural Attributes Evidenced in Excavation at the Kincaid Mounds Site.

| Architectural Attributes Present at Kincaid* | | Indicative of flexed | Indicative of hipped |
|---|---|---|---|
| wall posts | | | |
| | > 7.6 cm diameter | | X |
| | notched to receive wall plate | | X |
| | wide spacing of large posts | | X |
| | narrow spacing of small posts** | N/A | N/A |
| | curved | X (1 ex only) | |
| interior posts | | | |
| | patterned | | |
| | substantial width | | X |
| | substantial depth | | X |
| daub | | | |
| | heavy (> 4 in thick) | | X |
| roof | | | |
| | perpendicular elements bound together | | X |
| | thatch | | |
| | radial pattern | | X |
| wood types | | | |
| | cedar, cypress | | X |

* Factors that are indicative of both flexed and rigid structures have been omitted.
** The minimum diameter allowable for rigid pole construction has not been determined.

may be found in comparison with Cahokia, Angel, and Wickliffe mounds (126 km northeast, 215 km northwest, and 41 km southwest respectively). Nearly all of the square to rectangular houses of both the village and mound areas at Kincaid are oriented parallel to Avery Lake (northeast-southwest) and built from a rigid pole frame with a separate, thatched, hipped roof. Specialized features among elite and ceremonial buildings such as porchlike additions and clay benches and seats, a hallmark feature of many southeastern mound centers (Lewis and Kneberg 1946; Lewis et al. 1995; Payne 1994; Polhemus 1985) are also found at Kincaid. Less detail is known about the architecture from the village areas of Kincaid, as the UC excavations were heavily biased toward mound vicinities. Instances of stratigraphic superposition show a later tendency toward wider trenches as well as a shift from rectangular buildings to larger, roughly square ones—an observation first noted in the UC notes. An examination of the material contents of these features in conjunction with a more refined ceramic chronology will be needed to pull apart a finer grained temporal relationship in the absence of radiocarbon dates.

As all of the authors in this volume illustrate, there is no "Mississippian mold" shaping architecture of the Southeast. To characterize the architecture at Mississippian mound centers as "typical" does not do justice to the complexity of such sites and leaves archaeology without the information that Knight (this volume) has identified as being so critical. It is lamentable, then, that more specific assertions cannot be made about the architecture at Kincaid mounds, despite years of excavations. Current research, including renewed excavations at the site, make the exciting promise of providing details necessary to characterize Kincaid more fully.

## Conclusions

Marking shifts and trends in the organization and construction of prehistoric buildings can make a significant contribution toward archaeological interpretations of social dynamics. However, we must know what to look for and why in order to accurately discern variation and style within an architectural assemblage, in turn allowing us to make the inferences that will advance more theoretical research questions about the built environment. Too often, these interpretations are founded on loose empirical ground and have been formed with little to no cross-disciplinary consultation. Archaeologists must (literally) think above plan maps and post molds to determine how and why architectural changes came about. While data sets will vary from ideal to inadequate based on factors such as preservation and sampling biases, the above outlined methods may equip the archaeologist to make better-informed interpretations.

Above-ground architecture is only one of the many components of the built environment, a concept that Polhemus (1985:1) regards as "a patterned response to (the builders') perceived needs, desires, and world view." Investigations into the built environment (Rapoport 1969, 1982), "architectural grammar" (Lewis and Stout 1998), and landscape perspectives (Dalan et al. 2003) all deal in some way with the articulation of architecture and the societies that produce it. The utility of such approaches comes only with the realization that the built form is not determined by, but merely limited as a result of environmental constraints. Tracking architectural trends throughout history at both specific and broader levels will aid anthropologists in uncovering otherwise hidden relationships between man, society, and the built form.

## Acknowledgments

I am greatly indebted to Robert Swenson for enthusiastically giving of his time and expertise during our discussions about architecture and primitive technology. Any errors, however, are my own. Thanks are owed to Paul Welch and to Corin Pursell as well, for their helpful comments on earlier drafts of this chapter and to Daniel Smith for assistance with Figure 5.1.

# 6
# A Comparison of Burned Mississippian Houses from Illinois

*Mark A. McConaughy*

Many burned Mississippian structures have been excavated in Illinois over the last 50 years. These buildings have provided a wealth of information on construction techniques, materials, and architecture. It is becoming apparent that the stereotypic hipped or gabled roofed wall trench house, although relatively common, is by no means the only structural type built and/or used by the various Mississippian groups. This chapter will examine, compare, and contrast the different Mississippian structural forms that have been discovered in Illinois. Emphasis will be placed on both the archaeological floor plans and preserved structural remains.

## Previous Studies and Archaeological Evidence of Burned Structural Remains

Powell (1980) has made an extensive analysis of the mechanism involved in the burning and subsequent preservation of charred remains from the houses at the Orendorf site in the Central Illinois Valley. McMillan (1963), a registered architecture and fire insurance investigator, analyzed the destruction of the "Charcoal House" (Figure 6.1) and "Cross-Shaped House" (Figure 6.2) from the Eveland site in the Central Illinois Valley. Although not specifically cited elsewhere in the report, the interpretations of the burned structures presented in this chapter are based on the technical details of fires presented in these two papers.

Most burned remains of Illinois structures have been recovered from rectangular open corner wall trench houses that apparently had gabled or hipped roofs, the stereotypic Mississippian dwelling. Examination of the burned structures indicated that one variation of this hipped or gabled building form pos-

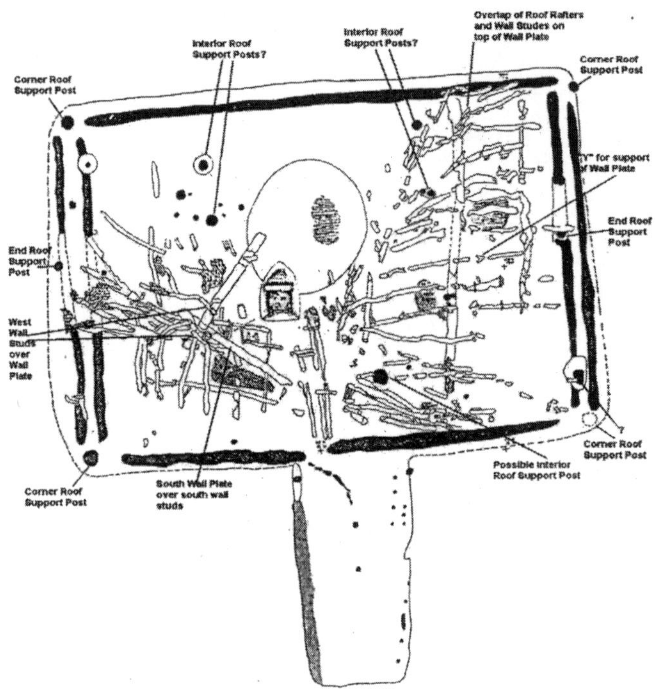


6.1. Plan of burned remains of a large structure, Eveland site, Fulton County, Illinois (adapted from Caldwell 1967b:140, Figure 1) (courtesy of the Illinois State Museum).

6.2. Excavated remains of a cross-shaped structure, Eveland site, Fulton County, Illinois (courtesy of the Illinois State Museum).

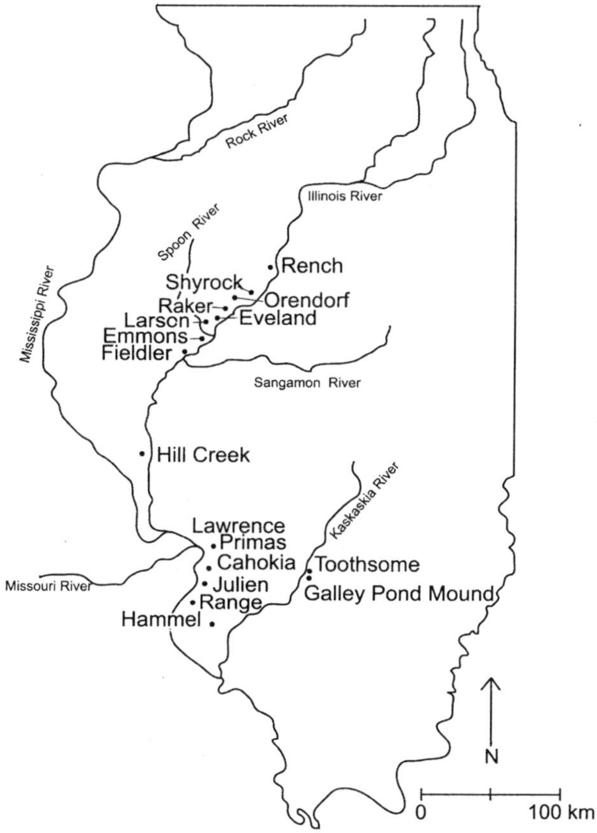


6.3. Map of sites with house structures used in this study.

sessed a cruciform floor plan, and may have been used for political and/or religious purposes. There also is at least one other structure style represented, a flexed or wigwam form. Burned Mississippian stage structures with intact charred logs have been found from at least 16 different sites in Illinois. In this chapter, the charred remains of 39 house structures are analyzed, including 23 from the Central Illinois Valley, two from the Lower Illinois Valley, 11 from the American Bottom, and three from southern Illinois (Figure 6.3).

The quality of structural evidence from charred elements in the Illinois area varies considerably from that of only a few logs, through those with preserved wall sections, to ones with portions of the roof superstructure still intact, such as House 2 from the Rench site (Figure 6.4). This uneven preservation of charred remains makes it difficult to directly compare individual dwellings. Therefore, buildings have been divided into different types based

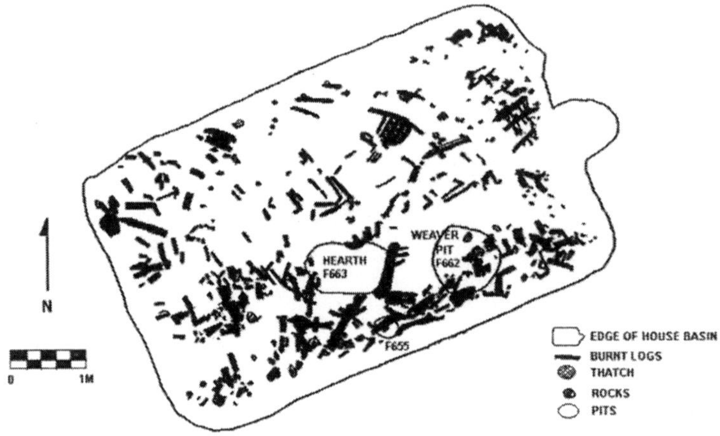


6.4. Plan view of House 2 from the Rench site (from McConaughy et al. 1985:185, Figure 2) (courtesy of the Illinois State Museum and Midcontinental Journal of Archaeology).

largely on wall form since charred wall posts are the most preserved of the burned members. Houses with similar wall construction are assumed to have the same roof form, particularly if from the same site. In cases where there are few preserved elements, house form is based upon wall trench and post mold data. However, for some dwellings, these data were not available and the classifications are more subjective.

## Hipped or Gabled Roof Structures

Thirty-five[1] of the 39 burned buildings examined for this study have tentatively been classified as possessing hipped or gabled roofs. Gabled roofs have two sloping sides and two vertical end panels, while hipped roofs have four sloping roof sections. The majority of structures classified as hipped or gabled roof houses in this study typically possess a square or rectangular open cornered wall trench foundation, and are normally constructed in an excavated house basin. Post molds or postholes are easily lost within wall trenches, therefore, most cases do not have data recorded for post characteristics such as size and spacing. In the limited evidence that was recovered, it appears that the wall posts of these hipped or gabled houses ranged from 8 to 16 cm and were spaced 20 to 30 cm apart. Other variations of hipped or gabled roof houses in this sample include structures that utilize larger corner posts in addition to wall trenches, such as the Charcoal House at the Eveland site and House 54 and House 79 at the Larson site. There are also examples of continuous or closed corner wall trenches such as the dwelling found at the Emmons and Structure 181 at the Orendorf site. In addition, there are several structures that were created either with individually set wall posts, such as Structure 2 at the Hill Creek site, and/or the use of interior roof supports. Interior roof supports are typically arranged either longitudinally to the house axis, a square formation near corners, or one roof support in the center of the structure.

In terms of the charred remains, most of structures in this study have preserved wall posts that are relatively straight. Logs from the same wall usually fell so that they extended from the outer edge of the house toward its interior in a roughly parallel pattern. These remains have been found in House 7, House 181, House 184, and House 208 at the Orendorf site (Conrad, personal communication 1985), House 1 at Tract 15A Cahokia, and the "Charcoal House" at the Eveland site, to name a few. Differential burning of logs and bindings may cause some wall or roof sections to twist as they fall, resulting in a torqued wall segment, indicated by a mass of charred logs. These torqued walls can be seen in the evidence from the "Charcoal House" and House 210 at the Orendorf site.

The wall posts of these structures are typically placed in wall trenches with horizontal cross beams tied to wall posts for added support. Cross beams usually are not interwoven with the upright wall posts to form a wicker or wattled framework, but apparently are tied either to the inside or outside of the wall. The only possible exception is House 2 at the Shryock site, where a preserved wall section in the north-central portion of the dwelling is described as possessing cross beams "overlapping at right angles to form a kind of wicker" (Wray n.d.).

Apparently, a specific method was used to decide which side of the wall the cross beams are tied. At Cahokia and the Larson site, the horizontal beams are tied to the inside of the uprights. Conversely, at the Eveland and Emmons sites, and perhaps the lower portions of the walls at the Orendorf site, horizontal elements are tied to the exterior side of the house wall. These sites are from different times and locations (Conrad 1973, 1991; Conrad and Harn 1972; Emmons et al. 1960; Hall 1975; Harn 1994), so the variation may be based on cultural or temporal differences. Yet perhaps upright poles with beams tied to the interior represent roof framework and not wall sections, while cross beams tied to exterior surfaces may be indicative of wall segments.

At the Orendorf site, several different methods of cross beam attachment are present. One interpretation may be that the builders alternated sides when tying horizontal supports to the walls. Another possibility, stated above, is that walls have cross beams tied to the exterior, roofs to the interior. Large preserved sections of straight vertical charred wall segments have been located in Structures 7 and 48 at the Orendorf site. Along other edges of House 48, horizontal beams are tied to the interior surfaces of some logs, and these are then covered with thatch. This suggests that cross beams tied to interior sides of logs at Orendorf are roof and not wall sections.

The roofs of these structures are supported by a central ridge pole. The ends of the ridge pole are placed on an A-frame set on top of large support posts in the corners of the house (McMillan 1963). A gabled roof with vertical end panels would not need additional interior support poles to hold up the ridge pole; however, a hipped roof with inwardly slanting end rafters would require them. The end rafters from both roof forms, hipped or gabled, usually have fallen so that they run diagonally from each corner toward the central section of the dwelling. Examples of end rafters in this position can be observed on the east side of the "Charcoal House" from the Eveland site (Figure 6.1), where diagonally running corner poles appear to be overlaid by other beams. There are four large corner poles in the "Charcoal House" that would have supported the roof framework. Additional examples of end rafters positioned in this manner include Feature 1 from the Lawrence Primas site (Pauketat and Woods 1986; Simon 2002), in which the long poles extend from the southwest wall toward the center of the structure, House 2 at the Shryock site (McConaughy 1985:Figure 15), and the northwest corner of House 1 at the Emmons site (Emmons et al. 1960:516).

Examples of Mississippian dwellings that have large post molds along their central long axis, implying a hipped roof form, are found with House 59 at the Larson site (Harn 1978), Structural Features 3 to 6 at the Toothsome (Binford et al. 1964:47), Houses 56 at Tract 15B, Cahokia, and House 1 at the Rench site (McConaughy et al. 1985) (Figure 6.5). A large charred post buried to a depth of 64 cm was found in the center of House 1 at the Lawrence Primas site (Pauketat and Woods 1986). Other structures also may have central support posts that were not depicted in the available or published maps since they would underlie some of the depicted charred structural remains.

Additional support for the roof superstructure sometimes is provided by four posts set diagonally interior of the corners of the house. Long horizontal poles are set on top and between these posts to provide support approximately halfway up the roof for other rafters. The "Charcoal House" from the Eveland site displays rafters of this type of framework along its eastern side (Figure 6.1). Longer side roof sections have a rectangular to trapezoidal form with logs extending from a wall plate or pole placed on top of the walls to the ridge pole. Wall plate poles may be represented by the remains from House 208 from the Orendorf site, the "Charcoal House" of the Eveland site, House 59 at the Lar-

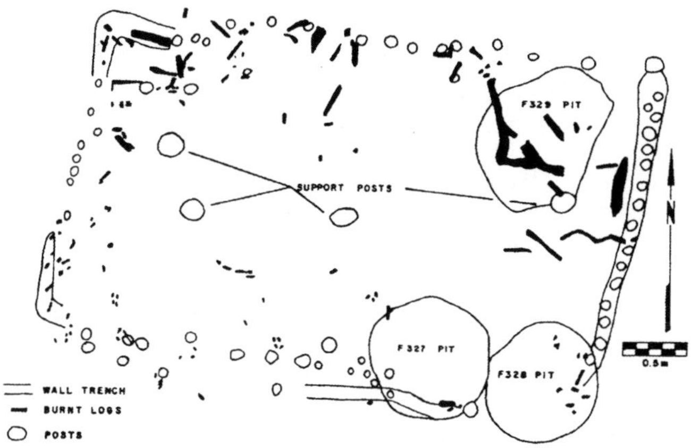


6.5. Plan view of House 1 at the Rench site (from McConaughy et al. 1985:184, Figure 1) (courtesy of the Illinois State Museum and Midcontinental Journal of Archaeology).

son site, House 56 from Tract 15B Cahokia, Feature 1 at the Lawrence Primas site, House 2 at the Shryock site, House 1 at the Emmons site, and Structure 1 at the Hill Creek site.

Smaller end panels tend to have a triangular shape with beams sloping toward the ridge pole from the end walls such as the "Charcoal House" and House 181 from the Orendorf site. Logs from House 181 have fallen in a radial pattern that suggests they were part of a roof superstructure. Conversely, Powell (1980:12) interprets these remains as wall posts. However, a radial pattern is the type predicted by the collapse of a hipped or gabled roof made of four separate roof panels. A similar arrangement is present in the much better preserved "Charcoal House" roof. The roof framework consisted of poles that extend from the wall plates across any support rafters to the ridge pole (for opposing view of this particular structure, see Reed this volume).

Portions of roof framework poles have been uncovered in the previously mentioned "Charcoal House" and House 181. Additional evidence of charred roof framework can also be observed at House 2 at the Shryock site and House 48 from the Orendorf site. Thin, lathlike pieces of wood were tied to the roof framework on the southeast side of the "Charcoal House" in the form of small, thin perpendicular pieces. These same pieces are found tied to the central section of roof framework of Feature 1 at the Lawrence Primas site. These pieces may have acted as a fastening point for thatching at the southeastern corners of House 7 and House 48 from the Orendorf site.

Charred thatching has been preserved at Cahokia (Collins 1990), the Orendorf site (Conrad 1991), the Lawrence Primas site (Pauketat and Wood 1986), and the Shryock site (Wray n.d.). Pieces of bark and thatch are found over roof sections of the Eveland "Charcoal House" (McMillan 1963:11).

The "Cross-Shaped" building at Eveland (Figure 6.2) probably is a ceremonial structure (Conrad 1973:3; Conrad and Harn 1972:8). This cruciform foundation has been found at the Eveland site (Conrad 1973; Eifert 1960), the Orendorf site (Conrad 1991), and Cahokia (Smith 1977:54–56). In spite of having a radically different floor plan, these cruciform shaped structures are believed to be built in a similar fashion to the hipped or gabled rectangular Mississippian dwellings.

McMillan's (1963) analysis of the construction and destruction of the "Cross-Shaped House" suggested that it was built with gabled roofs on ridge poles that were placed at right angles to one another. There is some suggestion that the walls of the "Cross-Shaped House" were daubed or plastered from the charred clay evidence of the southern side. However, it is not certain whether the plaster was applied to an outside wall or was the result of the collapse of an interior partition wall.

Although most burned structures have oxidized earth covering them, this is the result of the inhabitants extinguishing the fire and is not evidence of daub. If the fires had not been put out quickly and the embers covered, they would not have survived for future analysis. It is expected that any plaster covering would occasionally preserve structural impressions since it would have dried in place on the elements. Similarly, an earth embankment around the house would eventually become packed against the walls and produce structural impressions. A subsequent conflagration would fire the daub or dirt into ceramic molds of the superstructure. However, loose dirt tossed on the fire to extinguish it would not preserve such impressions. Besides the clay wall from the "Cross-Shaped House" at Eveland, the only other report of preserved impressions in daub associated with burned houses is from the Lawrence Primas site (Pauketat and Woods 1986). Therefore, based on the data examined for this chapter, it is believed that most Mississippian stage houses in Illinois (with the exception of sites in southernmost Illinois [Brennan this volume; Cole et al. 1951]) were neither covered with daub nor had extensive earth embankments.

## Wigwam Structures

Circular to oval Mississippian structures have been found at the Eveland site (Caldwell 1967a), the Julien site (Milner 1984:30–33, 180–181), the Range site (Mehrer 1982:24–27), the Bridges site (Hargrave 1983:139–140), the Orendorf site (Conrad 1991), and Cahokia (Smith 1977:58–63). These buildings were usually described as having a wigwam form (Caldwell 1967a) and are interpreted as ritual sweat lodges or possibly as storage facilities (Milner 1984:180–181). They rarely are described as single-family dwellings. Unfortunately, none of the "sweat lodges" were preserved by burning and their actual form cannot be confirmed from charred remains. (For additional information on structure and function of sweat lodges see Lafferty this volume.)

Of the 39 structures examined for this study, only two could be positively identified as wigwams, House 2 from the Rench site (McConaughy 1993:76–79; McConaughy et al. 1985) and Structural Feature 1 from the Toothsome site (Binford et al. 1964). Structural Feature 1 was a rectangular open corner wall trench dwelling with post molds averaging 7 cm in diameter spaced approximately 20 to 25 cm apart (Binford et al. 1964:23). House 2 at the Rench site was also rectangular, but there is no evidence of a wall trench. Post molds were roughly 5 cm in diameter. Although there is insufficient evidence for post spacing, it appears that the spacing of House 2 was similar to that of Structural Feature 1 at the Toothsome site, roughly 20 to 25 cm.

The charred remains of House 2 (Figure 6.4) from the Rench site indicate the sidewalls of this house are made from long, curved hickory (*Carya sp.*) and oak (*Quercus sp.*) studs. Three of these studs can be traced across preserved fragments in the north-central section of the structure, and smaller fragments of curved beams can be noted along the southern wall remains. Beams from opposing walls apparently were tied together at the apex of the curve to form a combined roof and wall framework (Figure 6.6).

Horizontal cross beams at the Rench site were tied to the exterior side of the wall/roof studs with a three-strand braided cordage made from what tentatively has been identified as basswood (*Tilia americana*) fibers. Examples of five closely spaced cross beams can be noted on the central section of the middle curved stud in the north-central section of the building. Thatching made from bulrush (*Scirpus validus*) is placed on top of these beams, apparently layered in alternating directions, to form a weatherproof roof. When the structure burned, the cross beams on the southeastern wall slid down the superstructure and piled up along the southern side of the house.

The narrower end walls of House 2 are composed of straight, vertical hickory and walnut (*Juglans sp.*) poles. Closely packed hickory cross beams are horizontally attached to the interior side of the end studs. A well-preserved portion of an end wall is present in the northeastern corner of the house. Apparently, the end walls were covered with thatch since a large quantity of bulrush was recovered along an end wall in the northwest corner of the dwelling. However, this thatch also could have fallen from roof members.

6.6. Reconstruction of wigwam architecture in Illinois (from McConaughy et al. 1985:189, Figure 6) (courtesy of the Illinois State Museum and Midcontinental Journal of Archaeology).

It is assumed that some of the wood fragments located in the central portion of House 2 along and paralleling its long axis are part of a ridge pole that would be supported on vertical posts of the end walls (Figure 6.4). However, they also may be preserved sections of horizontal pieces tied to the exterior of the wall/roof studs. There is no evidence of centrally located roof supports or of post molds indicative of central roof supports. The arched framework of the side walls would not necessarily need any further shoring to maintain the roof.

Late Woodland/Mississippian House 2 at the Rench site was cleaned out prior to its destruction. Examination of the charred wood used in the construction of this house indicated that it had aged and was badly decayed (McConaughy 1993:79; McConaughy et al. 1985). Presence of oxidized soil on top of the dwelling without any preserved impressions of thatch, wooden beams, and such indicated that the fire was intentionally put out. These data suggest that the house was purposefully burned and the fire extinguished, probably by the inhabitants of the dwelling.

One other burned Mississippian structure has been excavated that may be a wigwam dwelling. However, it originally was interpreted as a gabled roof house (Binford et al. 1964:21–27). Structural Feature 1 from the Toothsome site has curved side wall studs on the northwestern side (Figure 6.7). However, the horizontal cross beams are tied to the exterior side of the studs, instead of the interior as is found at the Rench site.

The Toothsome house also differs from the Rench House 2 structure in the

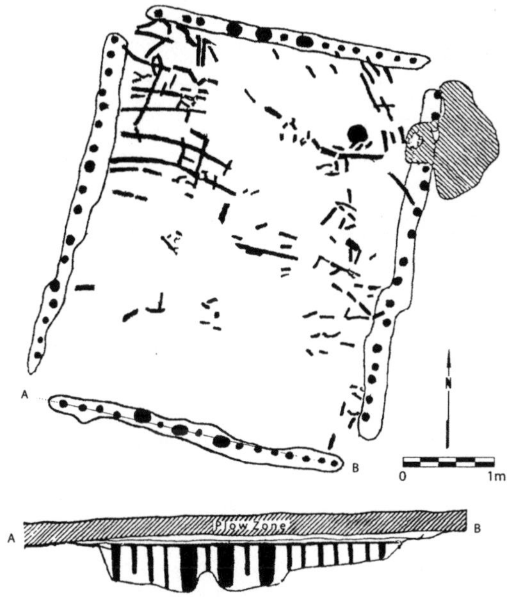


6.7. Plan view of Structural Feature 1 from the Toothsome site (adapted from Binford et al. 1964:21, Figure 5).

presence of a deep wall trench and three larger posts along the central portions of each end wall. Larger posts in the end walls may have held up ridge plates that were used to support the arched side studs. Apparently, the poles of the structures at Toothsome were tied together with two-ply cordage. Wall and roof coverings were not preserved but were assumed to have been thatch or matting since the framework has an open checkerboard pattern (Binford et al. 1964:24).

The curved side studs and lack of larger support posts or post molds in the central portion of the dwelling or in the corners suggested that Structural Feature 1 was not constructed along the same pattern as the burned gabled roof dwellings previously described. It is more likely that Structural Feature 1 from the Toothsome site possessed a wigwam style roof.

## Conclusions

Examination of 39 burned Mississippian structures from Illinois indicated that the interpretation of unburned Mississippian dwellings as gabled or hipped roof houses probably is justified. Burned examples of dwelling and rectangular ceremonial buildings indicate that they were constructed in largely the same fashion. However, larger "council" houses (Conrad 1973:3, 1991:124) may have minor modifications to the general plan, such as a ramp leading into the house.

In addition, it appears that the "ceremonial" cruciform structures found at Orendorf (Conrad 1991:133), Cahokia (Smith 1977:54–56), and Eveland (Conrad 1973:3, 1991:124; Eifert 1960) are variations of the hipped or gabled roofed theme.

In general, Mississippian stage construction techniques in Illinois were similar to those used in Missouri during the Powers phase (A.D. 1250–1400) (Price 1969). However, there are some differences. There is a lack of earthen embankments around the Illinois dwellings that are present around Powers phase houses (Price 1969:6–9). Also, wooden wall wedges are set to hold wall studs in place in the Powers phase buildings (Price 1969:6), while in Illinois, the wall studs usually are placed in deep wall trenches and do not require wall wedges for support. One possible exception to the absence of wall wedges in the Illinois sample is the wall sill found in Feature 1 at the Lawrence Primas site, which may have acted, in part, as a wall wedge (Pauketat and Woods 1986).

Wigwam dwellings have been discovered at the Rench site (McConaughy 1993:78–79; McConaughy et al. 1985) and the Toothsome site (Binford et al. 1964). However, the Toothsome house was not immediately recognized as a wigwam but was thought to be a gabled roof structure (Binford et al. 1964:24). This interpretation was based more on the presence of internal roof supports in Toothsome Structures 3 to 6 than on the preserved charred beams from Structure 1. It is possible that both the hipped or gabled roof and wigwam structures were built simultaneously by the same Mississippian inhabitants. These concurrent dual architectural forms may occur at the Rench site where House 1 is thought to represent a hipped roof domestic summer home, while House 2, the wigwam structure, is believed to be a domestic winter dwelling (McConaughy 1993:78–79; McConaughy et al. 1985). Rench House 2 and Toothsome Structure 1 demonstrate that it cannot automatically be assumed that all Mississippian houses had gabled or hipped roofs.

The presence of curved wood fragments in burned dwellings from Cahokia, Julien, and Orendorf demonstrates the tentative nature of the interpretation that they have gabled or hipped roofs. It is interesting that the Julien report used a wigwam as a house model for the farmstead reconstruction illustration (Milner 1984:198). Conversely, there are examples of curved wood pieces in what are clearly gabled or hipped roof structures from Orendorf and Lawrence Primas. The function of these pieces is unknown. Thus, the presence of curved logs does not necessarily mean that a structure is a wigwam.

Fortunately, one factor does seem to have utility in determining whether a dwelling is a wigwam or a gabled or hipped roof form. The location of roof support beams in the corners or along the longer axis of the house indicated to this researcher that these buildings had gabled or hipped roofs. Yet a lack of support beams in these particular areas lend support to the idea of wigwam architecture.

## 2006 Addendum

The preceding portion of this chapter was solicited for inclusion in this volume since the paper was widely circulated after its presentation at the Midwest Archaeological Conference meeting held in East Lansing in 1985. I have made some grammatical corrections and a few modifications to it that hopefully clarify some statements made in the original paper. However, it remains largely the paper presented back in 1985.

Looking back on the paper after 20 years provides a perspective that is not available to authors of the other papers in this volume. It presents me with a chance to clarify some assumptions and analyses behind interpretations made in the original paper, which Reed (see this volume) and others have addressed in the interim.

The original paper was not submitted for publication in 1985 because many of the floor plans from burned structures had not been published by the original researchers. Larry Conrad, Alan Harn, Duane Esarey, Andrew Fortier, Charles J. Bareis, George Milner, John Kelly, Timothy Pauketat, William Woods, and Michael Conner all permitted use of their data and plan maps of burned structures for the paper, but rightly wanted to be the first people to actually publish that information. Since that time, site reports with the plan maps have been published for some of the structures. In other cases, the researchers have now given permission to use those plans for this volume. I am grateful to all of them for unselfishly providing access to their information over the years.

When the paper was presented in 1985, I assumed that reconstructions of Mississippian houses as gabled and hipped roof structures by the earlier researchers cited in the 1985 paper were essentially correct and settled. Thus, I did have a predilection for interpreting most Mississippian structures as gabled or hipped roof buildings unless there was clear evidence to the contrary, as with House 2 at the Rench site and Structural Feature 1 at the Toothsome site. This was an unfortunate bias that may not be justified in hindsight.

Based on various structural analyses by Reed and others, I have since been convinced that there are more wigwam structures recorded than what I believed in 1985. For example, the interpretation of a long charred log in the southwestern portion of the Lawrence Primas structural as part of an A-frame brace for a gabled roof made in the 1985 paper is probably incorrect. Instead, this element is part of a curved wall section for a wigwam structure. In general, I am very supportive of interpretations of other structures that are included in my previous study as wigwams.

However, I am not yet ready to state that all of the structures that were previously identified as gabled or hipped roof houses really are wigwams. Nor am I going to say that they all are gabled or hipped roof buildings. Interpreting the types of structures built based on plan maps of charred remains is still more of an art than a science. Their interpretation is akin to analyzing Rorschach tests. Different people see contradictory things in the pictures. The physical charred remains are the actual data that archaeologists must rely upon, but the interpretations are subject to various degrees of reliability based on analyzers' biases. Nevertheless, I still believe that both rigid roof and flexible roof structures were built by Mississippians based on those plan maps and data.

I am not convinced that the larger posts and post molds found on the interior of some structures, like Rench House 1 (Figure 6.5) and Toothsome Structures 3 to 6 (Binford et al. 1964), represent either wall partitions, interior benches, or scaffolding for construction of the buildings. Wall partitions and benches do not need such large logs for support. Smaller logs and mats would suffice for partitions inside houses. Also, smaller posts would easily support interior benches. Scaffolding to build the structure might require larger logs to support multiple construction workers, but then why were these not present in all the wigwam structures? The presence of larger posts in the interior of House 1 at the Rench site and not inside House 2 of the same site suggests these two houses were built in a different fashion. House 2 clearly was a wigwam and did not require additional interior scaffolding during its construction. House 1 presumably was built by the same people who built House 2, based on associated artifacts (McConaughy 1993:78–79; McConaughy et al. 1985). Therefore, why would House 1 from Rench need scaffolding when it was built in the same soils and in close proximity to House 2 if it also was a wigwam?

Interpretation of the four larger interior posts of House 1 at the Rench site as roof plate support poles can also be criticized. They are not located exactly along the central axis of the house, but off slightly to one side or the other, which is also common of several houses discovered at the ICT-II track at the Cahokia mounds (Collins 1990). These slightly off-center interior postholes suggest they may not be support poles for a central ridge plate. This assumption presumes that the large poles were either intentionally notched with an ax or utilized a natural Y in a branching tree to support a ridge plate that was placed directly over or on them. In these cases, both arms of the cut notch or natural Y would go off at an angle from the top of the pole stem. Conversely, if the notch was on a side or the natural Y had one arm continuing straight up and a branch/arm going off the pole or trunk at an angle, then the pole would have to be offset from the central axis of the building to hold the ridge plate. I suggest the latter form is represented by the large interior posts of House 1 at the Rench site.

One continuing point concerns the interpretation of the Eveland "Charcoal House." There are larger posts set in the four corners of the structure as well as one each in the center of the narrower side walls that indicate support for a large wall plate. In addition there are larger posts set diagonally interior from the corners at least in the northwest corner. At least three other interior posts exist in the northwest, northeast, and southeast sections (the southwest section is covered by logs and there could be one there, too) according to the original map. I believe these represent support posts for rafter plates in a hipped roof.

A preserved corner of the wall plate(s) is preserved in the southwestern side of the "Charcoal House." It is an L-shaped form (i.e., building corner) made by the intersection of the two thickest surviving charred logs in this area. Two pieces of upright studs from the side wall go across the end wall plate, the rest are near it but do not cross it. However, the south wall brackets (upright studs and horizontal cross beams) go *under* the southern wall plate. If the "Charcoal House" was a wigwam then the southern wall studs curved over the top of the wall plate. It would be very difficult for the southern wall plate to fall on top of them if the studs actually were on top of the plate when the house burned. Thus, the presence of wall studs under the wall plate suggests this interpretation is incorrect and that the southern wall likely was a non-load-carrying section. It may have just hung from the wall plate and the studs did not go all the way to the roof.

One interpretation of the eastern burned section of the "Charcoal House" is that it represents continuous wall studs that curve over wall bracing and wall plate to the top of the roof of the structure. Conversely, I do not see the wall studs as continuous, based on examination of the original plan map of the "Charcoal house." Going from the eastern wall trench to the west, there is a low wall brace covered by vertical wall studs. Then the larger wall plate with roof rafters that overlap the wall plate are angled in to a point in the south-central portion of the structure. There also is a shorter rafter plate under the roof rafters close to the apex of the pointed end. I believe the vertical wall studs and the roof rafters were tied on the wall stud in pairs and they fell close to each other when the building collapsed in the fire. This accounts for the general appearance of them as continuous sections of one log instead of two separate pieces. The reason I view these as separate pieces is that one upright wall section (as I interpret them) in the middle of the eastern wall has a "Y" section that presumably is its top. The Y would support the wall plate. Also, on the original map, pieces of the roof rafters cross over the wall studs in the northeastern corner. Thus, they are not representative of single, curved beams. Therefore, my interpretation of the Eveland "Charcoal House" is the same as in 1985, that this structure possessed a hipped roof.

In conclusion, some Mississippian houses are rigid roof forms, either gabled or hipped. Other Mississippian houses are definitely wigwams, and there are more of this form than previously suspected. It is also probable that individual groups of Mississippians made both types of structures depending on need and use.

## Note

1. This number excludes the cross-shaped floor plan of the Eveland site, which is believed to be a form of hipped or gabled architecture and one identified structure from the Raker site, which did not provide enough evidence as to its roof form, but it is believed to exemplify evidence of a hipped or gabled form.

# 7
# A WPA Déjà Vu on Mississippian Architecture

*Lynne P. Sullivan*

Many students of late prehistoric architecture in the Southeast, including most of the authors in this volume, reference the work of Thomas M. N. Lewis and Madeline D. Kneberg (Lewis and Kneberg 1946; Lewis et al. 1995). As Lacquement notes in Chapter 1 (this volume), their 1940s ideas on flexed pole construction buildings with curved roofs are coming back into vogue, after a hiatus in which the alternate idea that wall trench houses had gabled or hipped roofs was more popular.

There are many good reasons that present-day researchers are rediscovering the flexed pole, rounded roof house. One of these is that the Works Progress Administration (WPA)–era researchers had evidence in the forms of careful excavations of well-preserved charred superstructures, and full-scale experimental models upon which to base their interpretations. In fact, their program of investigations looks very much like those of today.

Nonetheless, some seven decades have passed since this work was done. With a goal of gaining new insights into the formulation of their ideas, I revisit here the primary data upon which most of Lewis and Kneberg's interpretations of flexed-pole architecture were based. The data that figure prominently in the discussion of architecture in the Hiwassee Island report (Lewis and Kneberg 1946:50–53) and in Lewis's (1995:56–60) chapter on architecture in the Chickamauga Basin report derive from a particularly well-preserved, burned structure excavated in 1936 at the Hixon site in the Chickamauga Basin, and from little-known house reconstruction projects conducted by George A. Lidberg and Charles H. Nash, field supervisors for sites in the Kentucky Lake reservoir. The best documented of these projects was conducted by Lidberg at the Thompson Village site. Both the Chickamauga Basin and Kentucky Lake projects were done under the general direction of Thomas M. N. Lewis at the University of Tennessee as part of the archaeological investigations conducted before flooding of these Tennessee Valley Authority reservoirs.

## The Burned Building at the Hixon Site

The Hixon site (40HA3) was excavated in the summer and fall of 1936, under the field direction of Jesse D. Jennings and Robert S. Neitzel, both of whom trained at the University of Chicago. Hixon was the first site to be excavated as part of the Chickamauga Basin project (see Jennings's [1994:87–90] account of the field circumstances). Finding burned structures at Hixon was no surprise to Jennings and Neitzel or to Lewis. Jennings and Neitzel had excavated well-preserved, burned Mississippian structures in 1934 and 1935 at the Kincaid site in southern Illinois, and Lewis had seen burned, wall trench structure patterns with preserved superstructures in the Norris Basin (see Webb 1938). The structures at Hixon proved to be different from those encountered at Kincaid (see Brennan this volume).

The Hixon site mainly consisted of a platform mound, including submound deposits, surrounded by a palisade, but essentially devoid of village deposits (Lewis et al. 1995:372–418). House 68, the best-preserved burned structure, likely was a public building as opposed to an ordinary, residential house. The structure occurred at the very base of the mound, in construction stage C (or B2) on Floor R, and may have been contemporary with another burned structure, Feature 55. The overlying mound stage B (or B1) has been radiocarbon dated to A.D. 1235 (calibrated intercept) (Sullivan 2007).

The excavation of House 68 was supervised by Neitzel and was recorded on October 26, 1936. The building, which was approximately 43.5 m$^2$ (7.9 x 5.5 m), was of wall trench construction with open corners, although there are three posts in the gap in one of the corners (Figure 7.1). Wall posts averaged approximately 12.2 cm in diameter, and there were a few posts found inside the wall trench pattern, but there were no definite roof supports.

House 68 included a remarkably well-preserved section of interwoven, charred wooden poles (Figure 7.2). The saplings were 6 cm (2.4 in) to 9.1 cm (3.6 in) in diameter and crossed at right angles at intervals of about 30.5 cm (1 ft). More burned remains were found several feet beyond the building's northeast corner, including "a number of charred poles lying in juxtaposition and in the same direction as the long axis of the structure. Some of these were as long as 25 ft [7.6 m], and the diameters varied from 0.5 ft [15.2 cm] to 0.8 ft [24.4 cm]" (from original field report by Neitzel, Jennings, and Lewis on file at the McClung Museum and published in Lewis et al. 1995:383).

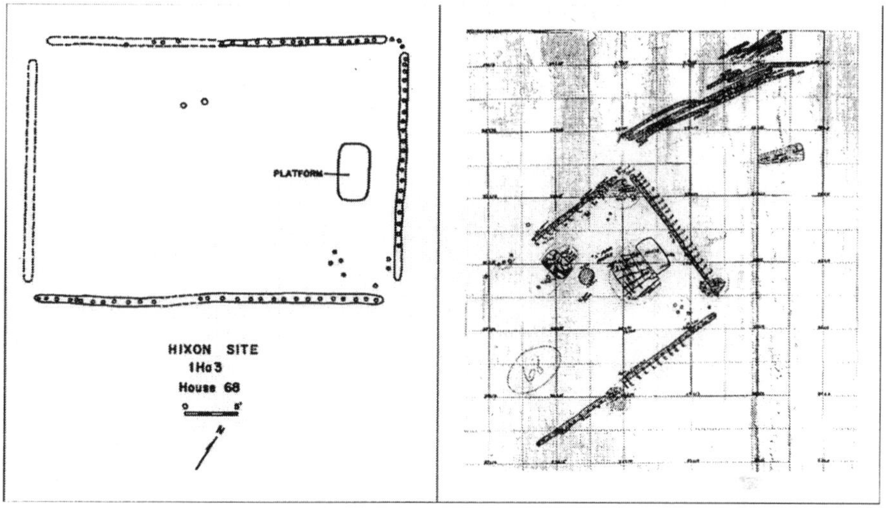


7.1. Floor plan (left) and field map (right) from the Hixon site excavations showing the plan of House 68 and the positioning of the charred poles associated with it (left) (from Lewis et al. 1995:383, Figure 24.11) (courtesy of the University of Tennessee) and (right) (courtesy of the Frank H. McClung Museum, the University of Tennessee).

7.2. Burned, interwoven superstructure from House 68 at the Hixon site (from Lewis et al. 1995:58, Figure 4.3) (courtesy of the University of Tennessee).

Lewis uses the Hixon site House 68 as prima facie evidence of flexed pole, curved roof construction techniques. In his chapter on architecture in the Chickamauga Basin report (Lewis 1995:57–58), he states,

> Charred poles present upon the floor of a building on the Hixon site were as long as 25 feet [7.6 m]. Their basal ends were close to the wall posts that apparently designated their former location. This instance further substantiates the conclusion that long poles were used; if such was the case it logically follows that such lengths could have been used only by bending them over to form the roof. . . . In several instances where charred superstructure remains lay upon the floor, an interweaving of the poles was noted. An interesting example of this occurred on the floor of House 68, a community building at the Hixon site. An interwoven section of framework was found near the center of the floor and therefore probably represented a section of the roof. This suggests that the process of bending the poles over to form the roof may have been carried out alternately with respect to the sides and ends of the structure. In other words, two opposing poles from the ends of opposite side walls were pulled inward and spliced together, and this was followed by splicing together the ends of the two poles from the two opposite walls.

Similar statements are made in the Hiwassee Island report (Lewis and Kneberg 1946:51):

> Charred poles present upon the floor of a building at another Chickamauga Basin site (Hixon site) were 25 ft [7.6 m] in length. Their basal ends lay *in situ* at the wall molds which designated their individual locations prior to the collapse of the burning structure. This example further substantiates the conclusion that long, limber poles were used, and it logically follows that such lengths could have been utilized only by bending them over to form the roof. . . . Where an abundance of charred superstructure remains lay upon the floors of community buildings in several other sites in the Chickamauga Basin, an interweaving of the roof framework was noted. In one instance, a well preserved section of carbonized framework lay upon the center of a floor. The diameters of the charred saplings were smaller than the wall postmolds and appear to be part of the roof framework composed of the tapering ends of the wall uprights. These crossed one another at right angles and were interwoven. This suggests that the practice of bending the poles to form the roof

> framework was probably carried out alternately from the sides and ends of the structure. By commencing this procedure at the ends of each of the four walls, it is apparent that a dome-shaped roof of woven framework would result.

A piece of evidence from the Hixon site structure that Lewis appears to ignore and that is at odds with his interpretation of a flexed pole, curved roof construction is the diameter of the long poles found lying along the long axis of House 68. Although Lewis discusses the length of these poles, he does not address the issue that their reported diameter (6 to 9.6 in) not only was larger than the average diameter of 12.2 cm (4.8 inches) of the postholes in the wall trenches, but these large diameters mean it is highly improbable that these poles could be bent.[1]

The positioning of these long poles, as reported in the original field report and shown in a field map, also appears at odds with Lewis's statement that the basal ends lay in situ at the wall molds. As the report states, the field map shows the poles lying side by side "and in the same direction as the long axis of the structure." Given their length (ca. 25 ft) and the length of the structure (26 ft), a reasonable conclusion is that these poles in some way were part of the building's framework that ran the full length of the structure, and due to their diameters, these poles were not woven, flexed, or bent, nor would they have fit into the postholes in the wall trenches. Yet the preserved section of lashed-together poles clearly was interwoven, and consisted of small-diameter saplings. What is unclear is whether this section was from a wall or the roof.

We are left with the dilemma that the archaeological evidence from a "type structure" for flexed pole structures appears to have some inconsistencies with the flexed pole model as presented by Lewis and Kneberg. Could a flexed pole structure have a woven roof and walls made of unwoven, not flexed, lashed-together poles? Alternatively, could Structure 68 have been a wigwam-type building (see McConaughy this volume) with long (not flexed) poles lashed parallel to the building's long axis, and forming the long walls and roof, while the building's two short ends were made of woven, flexed poles? In either case, a combination of flexed and not flexed poles appears to have been used to construct this building, such as Nash's (1968) description of intermediate architectural forms in west-central Tennessee.

## The House Reconstruction Project at the Thompson Village Site

Lewis and Kneberg gained insights into Mississippian architecture from early experiments in house reconstruction by Charles H. Nash and George A. Lid-

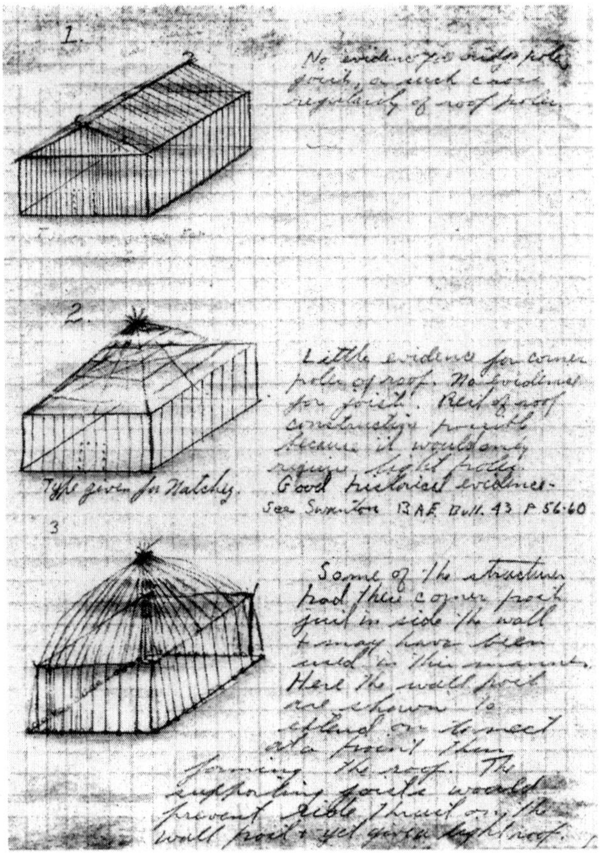


7.3. Sketches of house frameworks from Nash's field notes on the Link site (courtesy of the Frank H. McClung Museum, the University of Tennessee).

berg at sites on the Kentucky Lake reservoir. Nash was involved in reconstructing houses as early as 1936 at the Link site (71HS6), a Mississippian stage site where he was a supervisor. The framework for a reconstructed house model can be seen in the background of a photograph, dated May 6, 1936, of an excavated house pattern.[2] This framework appears to use small poles, but is rigid pole construction. Nash also sketched this type of framework and two others in his field notes (Figure 7.3). In the fall of 1939, Lidberg and his WPA crew were inspired to completely reconstruct one of the houses they were excavating at the Thompson Village site (40HY5). Lidberg's well-described project, discussed in detail below, is documented with photographs that show the reconstruction sequence. The framework is similar to that shown in Nash's sketch three. The information from these experiments obviously was known to Lewis and Kneberg when they wrote the Hiwassee Island report (Lewis and Kneberg 1946) and when Lewis drafted the architecture chapter for the Chickamauga Basin report in the early 1940s (Lewis et al. 1995).

Lewis hired Nash (a student at the University of Chicago) in 1936 and Lidberg in 1938 when the University of Tennessee geared up to run field projects in conjunction with the construction of Tennessee Valley Authority reservoirs (Lyon 1996:141). Nash already was supervising excavations in the Kentucky Lake area when Lidberg was hired. Lidberg had trained in Wisconsin with Will McKern at Milwaukee Public Museum, and had worked for nearly a year on several sites in the Chickamauga Basin, including Candy Creek, Varnell, and Ledford Island, before beginning work on the Kentucky Lake sites in 1939 (Lewis et al. 1995). He first worked at the Mississippian stage Williams site (40HY1) under Nash's direction and thus was well versed in excavation techniques and had seen some wall trench houses by the time of the Thompson Village project.

The Thompson Village site lay on the west bank of the Tennessee River, about seven miles (about 11 km) south of the Kentucky-Tennessee line in Henry County, Tennessee (see Figure 1.1). Two miles (about 3 km) north of the site the Big Sandy River meets the Tennessee. The palisaded site occupied an area perhaps 305 m (1,000 ft) along the river, extending 183 m (600 ft) inland. No mound was associated with the Mississippian occupation. A report has never been published on the Thompson Village site excavations.

Of the at least 15 structures excavated at Thompson Village, 14 were of wall trench and at least one was of single post construction (Table 7.1). Feature 11 was a complex of at least five superimposed structures, and the excavators had difficulty distinguishing one from another, but thought that the uppermost structures were of single post construction. Of the better-defined structure patterns, those with wall trenches typically were square with rounded, open corners and usually had a small, square or circular hearth not quite in the center of the floor. Only two of these structures had closed corners. The single post structure (Feature 2) was similarly shaped, but had larger corner posts that were not set in trenches. Both types of structures appeared to have been built in basins, probably less than 92 cm (3 ft) deep. Clear evidence of a basin was found for two structures (Features 8 and 21). Several of the houses had burned and carbonized superstructure material was present.

7.1. Excavated Structures at the Thompson Village Site (40HY5).

| Str. No. | Floor Area ($m^2$)/ Dimensions (m) | Post Diameter (cm) | Post Spacing (cm) | Wall Trench Width (cm) | Corners | Roof Supports | Daub |
|---|---|---|---|---|---|---|---|
| 1 | 18.7<br>4.39 x 4.27 | aver. 18.3<br>min. 4.6<br>max. 15.2 | ? | aver. 12.2<br>min. 9.1<br>max. 15.2 | open | none identified | yes |
| 2 | 33.4<br>5.48 x 6.1 | aver. 15.2<br>min. 15.2<br>max. 24.4 | aver. 48.7<br>min. 33.5<br>max. 67 | None | n/a | none identified | yes |
| 4 | ? | ? | ? | ? | ? | ? | yes |
| 5 | 19.3<br>4.45 x 4.33 | aver. 6<br>min. 6<br>max. 9.1 | aver. 15.2 | aver. 12.2<br>min. 9.1<br>max. 15.2 | open | none identified | none mentioned |
| 6 | 26.5<br>5.0 x 5.3 | aver. 7.6<br>min. 6<br>max. 12.2 | Aver. 12.2 | aver. 18.3<br>min. 12.2<br>max. 24.4 | posts? in 3 corners | none identified | none mentioned |
| 7 | 24.6<br>4.96 x 4.96 | aver. 6<br>min. 6<br>max. 9.1 | aver. 15.2 | aver. 15.2<br>min. 9.1<br>max. 18.3 | open | none identified | none mentioned |
| 8 | 14.5<br>3.81 x 3.81 | aver. 7.62<br>min. 6<br>max. 12.2 | aver. 12.2 | aver. 15.2<br>min. 12.2<br>max. 21.3 | open | none identified | none mentioned |

| | | | | | | | |
|---|---|---|---|---|---|---|---|
| 9 | 24.2<br>4.96 x 4.87 | aver. 7.62<br>min. 6<br>max. 9.1 | 13.7 | aver. 21.3<br>min. 18.3<br>max. 24.4 | open | perhaps<br>3 near<br>center | traces |
| 10 | 57.2<br>8.53 x 6.7 | aver. 6<br>min. 6<br>max. 15.2 | aver. 18.3 | aver. 18.3<br>min. 15.2<br>max. 24.4 | open | none identified | none |
| 11 | at least 5<br>superimposed<br>structures | aver. 6 | ? | aver. 12.2<br>min. 15.2<br>max. 18.3 | open | ? | yes |
| 12 | ? | ? | ? | aver. 12.2<br>min. 9.1<br>max. 18.3 | open | ? | yes |
| 21* | 15.6<br>4.27 x 3.66 | aver. 6<br>min. 6<br>max. 15.2 | aver. 24.4<br>min. 3<br>max. 222 | aver. 6<br>min. 18.3<br>max. 36.6 | closed | possibly | no |
| 22* | ? | aver. 27.4?<br>min. 15.2?<br>max. 39.6? | aver. 82.3<br>min. 36.6<br>max. 201.2 | aver. 6<br>min. 6<br>max. 15.2 | open | none identified | no |
| 23* | 4.6<br>2.74 x 1.68 | aver. 9.1<br>min. 6<br>max. 45.7 | aver. 18.3<br>min. 12.2<br>max. 48.8 | aver. 24.4<br>min. 21.3<br>max. 24.4 | closed | none identified | no |

All data taken from field notes, on file at the Frank H. McClung Museum, the University of Tennessee and converted into metric units.

* Features 21 to 23 were recorded by Douglas Osborne. All others were recorded by Lidberg.

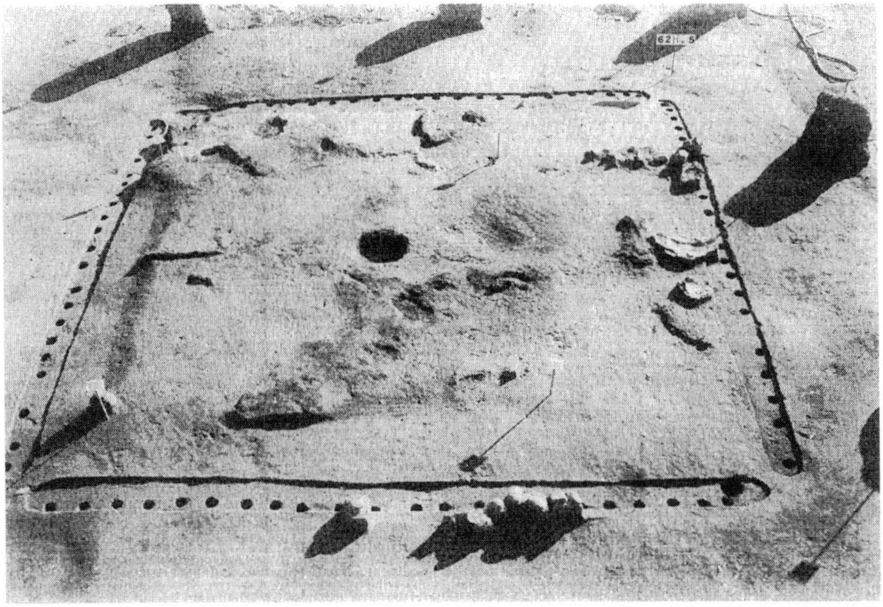

7.4. Excavated pattern of Feature 9 at the Thompson Village site (courtesy of the Frank H. McClung Museum, the University of Tennessee).

Feature 9 was the structure chosen for reconstruction (Figure 7.4). As can be seen in Table 7.1, it is typical of the wall trench structures at the site, but possibly had three interior posts. The feature form also indicated that "burned wattlework" was present and there was a "large patch of burnt floor" between the hearth and a refuse pit to the west, but "very little trace of burnt daub." The square hearth had a modeled clay rim and a flat bottom. A chipped stone hoe or spade was found near one wall (Lidberg n.d.).

Although Lidberg does not specifically state so in his field notes, it appears that one inspiration for the house reconstruction project was the need to find sufficient work to keep a large, mostly untrained field crew busy, with few supervisors and without compromising the quality of the archaeological fieldwork. On October 30, 1939, Lidberg wrote, "Work continues to present unarchaeological problems. Having a labor crew of approximately 70 men with but a small number of those capable and trained in working in structures, we find ourselves occasionally with more dirt being saved than we can accommodate. This is further complicated by cold wet weather. The only possible present solution to this is to train a second 'structure crew,' perhaps to do the less exacting work on the features" (Lidberg n.d.). His field notes abruptly end after an unusually long entry for that day, but the dates recorded on several standardized field forms postdate October 30. The date on the form for the reconstructed house, Feature 9, is December 4, 1939. Lidberg's notes do not indicate how many men were assigned to this project, or how many days it took to complete the house. Below is Lidberg's (n.d.) full account of the reconstruction of this structure. His original notes, diagram, and photographs are curated by the Frank H. McClung Museum at the University of Tennessee.

## Notes on the Reconstruction of a Middle-Mississippian Domestic Structure

> Feature 9 on site 7HY5 was a structure measuring about 16 ft square having wall trenches about .7 ft wide, including posts about .25 ft in diameter set therein [Figure 7.4]. A square fire basin had been built into the floor slightly off the center.
>
> After clearing the floor and locating the trenches and postmolds, a lateral profile was cut through all four trenches, bisecting the postmolds. These postmolds were hollowed out and a search was made for poles of a like diameter. We discovered that posts 30 ft [9.2 m] in length, which retained this small size at the base, could be found along the river bottoms. Posts of this length, if set in these postmolds and arched to a peak in the center of the structure, would make the roof about 22 ft [6.7 m] high. From this beginning, having learned that it was no difficult task to obtain such poles, we experimented to find the length needed to make the most easily constructed and most stable structure.
>
> There are two bases upon which our architectural theories were formulated, one: concrete evidence which was found associated with this structure or with others similar to it, and two: apparent necessary factors leading to the ease of construction and the stability and practicality of the finished building. Our final choice for the walls were ash poles measuring about 18 ft [5.5 m] in length, and producing a structure 12 ft [3.7 m] in height at the peak of the roof. These poles, when green, were pliable and bent easily, and the arch in the walls occurred high enough to make it possible for a person to stand upright near the wall.
>
> Along the bottom of the trenches, logs were laid horizontally to act as braces for the wall poles. This method of bracing was not used in the original structure, but there is evidence that such a brace was used in similar structures elsewhere. Poles were set in the bisected molds braced on the outside at the bottom by this log, and at the top, inside, by the earth floor (Figure 7.5). These poles were arched to the top and all were

7.5. WPA workers raising pole framework in postholes of Feature 9 (courtesy of the Frank H. McClung Museum, the University of Tennessee).

tied at the center with bark. Linden bark was used as the only binding material in the reconstruction. About 5 ft [1.5 m] from the ground a horizontal bracing pole was lashed to the wall frame, and still another about 3 ft [91 cm] above this (Figure 7.6). These poles increased the stability of the walls considerably, and burnt remains indicate that horizontal poles were used on the walls. It is my opinion that these wall frames, that is, all the poles with the braces, were "pre-fabricated." There seems little reason for, or advantage in, the use of wall trenches unless the wall skeleton was built and placed into the trench as a unit. The narrow trenches make the setting of individual poles less than .5 ft [15.2 cm] apart virtually impossible.

The suggested "pre-fabrication" technique would involve cutting the poles to proper length, laying them out on the ground parallel to each other, lashing them firmly together, and placing the entire unit in the prepared trench. There is also the possibility that the poles, rather than be tied in a peak, could have been interwoven at the top, forming a dome-shaped roof. When the opportunity again presents itself to enable us to again attempt to reconstruct a house, we shall try this method of roof construction.

7.6. WPA worker completing framework and cross bracing on reconstructed structure (courtesy of the Frank H. McClung Museum, the University of Tennessee).

Two types of split cane matting were used in the wattle work (Figure 7.7). The one was a series of individual mats laid upon the walls with the weft in a horizontal position, in the manner of modern plaster lathes. This wattle work proved unsatisfactory; the weight of the daub on the weft tended to tear the mats apart unless each element of the weft was tied to the warp. The other cane work that was applied to the walls consisted of the warp lashed to the wall poles in a horizontal position and the weft woven onto the wall vertically. This type of wattle work proved completely satisfactory and held the daub successfully. This wattle work extended from the ground level up to a height of about 6 ft [1.8 m]. Should the wattle work and daub have extended higher than this, too great a strain would have been exerted on the walls. Further, this much solid wall efficiently performs the function of wind break.

Over the wattle work we plastered a daub made of the sandy clay found on the river bank (Figure 7.8). In preparing the plaster, the clay was crushed and a small amount of grass was added. This mud plaster was spread over the wattle work about 0.1 ft [3 cm] to 0.2 ft [6.1 cm] in thickness and was pressed into the wattle work, so that even when quite

7.7. WPA workers installing wattle work on reconstructed house. "To the right the wall is covered with six separate cane mats, woven before placement on the wall. To the left the warp has been 'anchored' to the poles and the cane woven onto the wall" (original photograph caption, on file at Frank H. McClung Museum) (courtesy of the Frank H. McClung Museum, the University of Tennessee).

moist it adhered firmly to the wall. There seems little doubt that this daub was wholly covered with thatch extending from the roof. We found that it took very little rain to remove all of the unprotected daub, while that which was under the thatch withstood all rain for several months.

The thatch with which we covered the house was made from field grasses found along the river. Long canes were split, and between the two halves the root ends of the grass were tied. These became "shingles" 3 ft [91 cm] to 8 ft [2.4 m] in length which were tied to the poles and made a roof completely impervious to rain. We found that the roof allowed sufficient passage of air to dispel smoke from the interior without the use of a smoke hole. One theory explaining the repeated occurrence of "off-center" fire basins was this: with the wall poles tied at the center of the roof, it was necessary to place the smoke hole away from the center of the roof and that the fire basin's position corresponded to that of the smoke hole.

7.8. House reconstruction showing application of daub over wattle work (courtesy of the Frank H. McClung Museum, the University of Tennessee).

Lidberg's narrative ends here, but there is a photograph of the completed structure (Figure 7.9). He also provides a detailed diagram of the house construction (Figure 7.10). The notes for one photograph additionally state that the picture was made after "about 1.5 in of rain in 48 hours" and shows "the effect upon protected and unprotected daub." (The unprotected daub had slumped.)

Lidberg and his crew's reconstruction may be the only such project to use the actual postholes from a Mississippian period structure. The Thompson Village house and that at the Link site likely were the prototype studies for the reconstructed Mississippian houses at the Chucalissa site near Memphis, which became an archaeological park (see Figure 1.3 this volume). In 1940, after the Kentucky Reservoir work, Lidberg and Nash supervised excavations at Chucalissa, also under the direction of the University of Tennessee and Tom Lewis. Lewis was working with Shelby County and the National Park Service to develop Chucalissa as a tourist attraction. The excavations would provide the necessary information for interpretations and displays (Lewis 1940; Nash 1972). The fact that the Chucalissa wall trench house was reconstructed using a different framing technique for the roof from what was used at Thompson Village also suggests that Lidberg was involved in the effort. He states in his

7.9. Completed reconstruction of the Feature 9 house at the Thompson Village site (courtesy of the Frank H. McClung Museum, the University of Tennessee).

description of the Thompson Village reconstruction, "There is also the possibility that the poles, rather than be tied in a peak [as was done at Thompson Village], could have been interwoven at the top, forming a dome-shaped roof. When the opportunity again presents itself to enable us to again attempt to reconstruct a house, we shall try this method of roof construction." The house at Chucalissa has an interwoven, dome shaped roof.

Although Lidberg's experiment is not specifically mentioned, Lewis and Kneberg (1946:50; Lewis 1995:56) likely were referring to information from the reconstruction project when they noted the possibility of lashing the wall poles together on the ground (prefabrication) before setting them in the wall trench. They (Lewis et al. 1995:9) surely were referring to Lidberg's experiment when they stated that the buildings' outsides were plastered with clay and "the roofs were protected with grass thatching which probably extended beyond the walls as eaves to protect the clay plaster from rain."

What is curious is that Lewis and Kneberg do not mention the possibility of constructing the house roof in a way different from the "woven dome." Although Lidberg likely used Nash's sketched idea, the Thompson Village project demonstrated that an acceptable house could be built by simply tying the wall poles together at the top, making a peaked roof, rather than weaving them

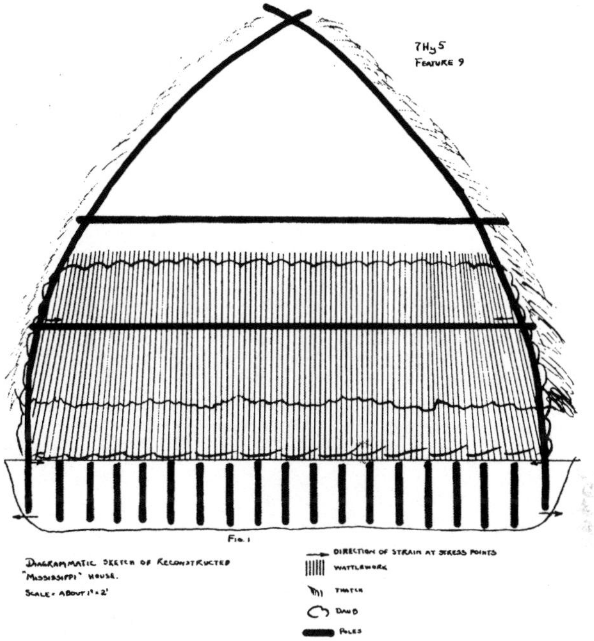


7.10. Lidberg's diagram of the reconstructed house at Thompson Village (courtesy of the Frank H. McClung Museum, the University of Tennessee).

together into a dome.[3] The walls, however, could have had interwoven sections. From the experiments discussed in this volume, it appears that Nash and Lidberg's approach has not been attempted again. Instead, the replicated structures have "woven domes."

## Past Ideas in Perspective

The evidence, in the form of large sections of charred superstructure, for flexed pole structures leaves little doubt as to why the archaeologists working in the Tennessee Valley (including Webb (1938:21–23, as well as Lewis and Kneberg) proposed this type of structure. The fact that they were using many of the same techniques we use today to learn about architecture, including experimental reconstruction, also is impressive, and it is somewhat humbling to know that such ideas are far from new.

Lidberg and Nash obviously deserve more credit than they have received for adding to our body of knowledge about Mississippian architecture. Lidberg and his crew made interesting observations and originated ideas about the construction of wall trench–style structures, including "prefabricated wall frames" and "thatched shingles." Also to Lidberg's WPA crew's credit, they used only materials they could find in the vicinity of the Thompson Village site. The fact that they happened to be doing fieldwork at the site in late fall likely was advantageous as they were able to find naturally dried grasses—a consideration for the seasonality of house construction.

Today's archaeologists owe a great debt to these earlier researchers. They gave us the basis upon which to move forward. But, it also is obvious that the early researchers were painting with broad brushes and did not study the details of the material evidence in the way that archaeologists now take great pains to do. An analogous situation is the fact that the WPA workers threw away debitage and unworked animal bones. Studies of these materials have now become specialty analyses that add considerable depth and new information to interpretations. In the same way, we now realize that the study of architectural remains must be done in more detail. The inconsistencies in Lewis's interpretations of the burned building at the Hixon site can now be recognized because we know more. Perhaps it is time to do some more rethinking of the exact nature of flexed pole structures and to imagine framework designs that are congruent with the archaeological evidence, but different from those drawn by Madeline Kneberg. The "wigwam" design is a beginning, but surely there are multiple ways to build such structures, and it is likely that prehistoric peoples of differing cultural affiliations had their own "bent" for building flexed pole structures as well.

## Acknowledgments

Thanks to David Dye for alerting me to the photograph and notes on house reconstructions from Nash's work at the Link site, and to Paul Welch for making me aware that Jennings and Neitzel had excavated the burned structures at Kincaid. Bobby R. Braly provided capable assistance with scanning the Thompson Village reconstruction description and diagram. This house reconstruction project has been known to and enjoyed by those people who have had the opportunity to peruse the McClung Museum's collections, but now this project can be enjoyed by a wider audience. Thanks also to the unknown WPA workers who helped with this interesting endeavor, and thanks to Cameron Lacquement for inviting me to participate in this book.

## Notes

1. There is no record of the wood species of any of the poles. The only identified archaeologically recovered wood specimen from the Hixon site was pine, but there is no record of its provenience.

2. This photo from the Link site (Digital ID# fhm00980), as well as the full set of photographs from the Thompson Village house reconstruction, and photographs of the excavations there and at the Hixon site, can be seen at http://diglib.lib.utk.edu/wpa/index.htm, thanks to a grant from the Institute of Museum and Library Services.

3. Which archaeologist first originated the idea of the "peaked roof" in the Southeast is not clear. Models of wall trench houses also appeared in a museum diorama at Moundville in 1936 (see Jones and DeJarnette 1936) and in 1938 in a movie titled *Temples and Peace* made by the National Park Service for the Moundville Museum (see Fundaburk and Foreman 1957:22). Both models had peaked roofs like Nash's 1936 sketch (Figure 7.3) and Lidberg's reconstruction. However, what is clear is that this peaked flexed roof form is not as prominent after Lewis and Kneberg (1946) published their concept of flexed architecture as having a basketlike roof and not a peaked roof.

# 8
# An Architectural Grammar of Late Mississippian Houses in Northwest Georgia

*Ramie A. Gougeon*

Domestic structures are mirrors that reflect in numerous ways the households that create them. The house as a physical structure is a shelter comprised of a variety of materials, encompassing a prescribed amount of space, and divided according to societal norms and probably to some degree by individual choice. The house also provides a rich source of information about culture, potentially revealing a variety of patterns of human behavior. In many ways, the *domus* contains elements of all of the dimensions of the household: the material, the behavioral, and the social (Wilk and Rathje 1982:618). As a material object, the house has to meet particular needs, the most important being to provide suitable shelter for a particular environment. In terms of behavioral needs, the structure must enclose enough space to perform a set of activities, while the social components of a household may reveal the status of individuals within a household, the status of the household as a whole, and ideas about gender roles.

According to Alexander (1979; Alexander et al. 1977), physical structures meet certain norms suggesting the presence of a "pattern language" accepted by a culture. More recently, this concept of shared perceptions exhibited through construction techniques has been referred to as "architectural grammar" (Lewis et al. 1998:2). In this chapter, I examine a sample of domestic structures from Late Mississippian sites as a means of surveying the common house form utilized in northwest Georgia in search of a particular architectural grammar.

## Establishing Architectural Grammar

Architectural grammar is present in all built environments, from the seemingly simple hut of a gatherer-hunter to the grandest estate of George Vanderbilt. Architectural grammar, as defined by Lewis et al. (1998:2–3), is the rules used to combine particular architectural elements in the creation of the built environment. Each piece of the grammar, consisting of archetypes created by the builder, must relate to other architectural patterns (e.g., the layout of towns, the placement of gardens, etc.) in particular ways (Alexander 1979), as well as to sociocultural patterns. In architectural grammars, the patterns are the elements from which a builder may choose from when designing a structure, town plan, or landscape. Due to the similarities in methodology, architectural grammar is commonly explained by comparisons to spoken or written languages. For example, English grammar consists of rules for combining words into an infinite variety of coherent arrangements. Syntax provides the meanings behind the combinations of phrases and sentences. As with any spoken language, an architectural grammar also allows for the creation of an infinite combination of patterns, but in meaningful ways. This prevents, as Alexander (1979:186) explains, finding kitchens on freeway interchanges.

Just as spoken or written languages are ordered, all architectural grammars are ordered by certain qualities that are held in common, regardless of particular cultural context. These include but are not limited to design intent, function, and context (Lewis et al. 1998:3–4). However, these traits are hardly independent, and can overlap greatly with one another as well as with other cultural elements such as religion, subsistence strategies, social structure, and such.

Design intent is associated with the anticipated duration of use of a structure, with the argument being that the longer the structure is planned to be used, the more architecturally complex the structure will be, and the greater the investment of labor (Lewis et al. 1998:3). Functionality comes into play in the design and construction of the built environment. As Rapoport (1990:11) notes, activity shapes form: if the form is not conducive to the performance of a particular activity, that activity may be more difficult or impossible to accomplish. The context or setting of the built environment also must be considered when defining an architectural grammar. Exploring context involves questioning aspects of locations such as where a house is located in the town, or where a town is situated along the river. Finding the boundary of the context may involve identifying where the grammar no longer applies. For example, we may question whether the specific architectural grammar for situating villages in relation to the principal town in a chiefdom in northwest Georgia applies to temporally and culturally similar chiefdoms across southwest Virginia (see Hally 1996; Meyers 2002).

## Recent Architectural Grammar Studies in the Mississippian Southeast

Some effort has been expended in recent years to define an architectural grammar for the Mississippian Southeast, though to date these studies have typically focused on the construction, orientation, and layout of mound sites and towns (Hally and Kelly 1998; Kidder 2004; Lewis and Stout 1998). The following examples are presented in the order of the largest to the smallest patterns in order to bring us to the main subject of this chapter. Examples from Georgia and nearby regions (an area approximately 400 kilometers in diameter, centered on Carters Lake) (Figure 8.1), were deliberately chosen with the idea that while there may be broad, pan-Mississippian architectural patterns (particularly at the largest scales of settlement patterns), the smaller patterns will likely reflect localized cultural expressions.

Hally's (1993, 2006) exploration of the geographical limits of chiefdoms provides a context for the placement of the towns comprising them. Although initially examined using data from northern Georgia and the adjacent portions of neighboring states, the 18-km extent of town spacing within a single chiefdom has been reexamined using data from other regions in the Southeast, including southwestern Virginia (Meyers 2002). Valley-specific evaluations are needed to further test Hally's model, and can provide refinements of Late Mississippian settlement patterns. For example, an analysis of Burke phase (A.D. 1400–1600) sites along an 8.5-km stretch of Upper Creek–Warrior Fork drainages in the upper Catawba River Valley of North Carolina revealed a three-tiered settlement pattern of households, communities, and multicommunity levels, including the elements of individual households/farmsteads, villages, and a mound center (Beck and Moore 2002).

Moving to a smaller geographical scale, a number of examinations of the patterning of space within towns and villages have been conducted at southeastern Mississippian period sites. Lewis and Stout (1998) explicitly examine architectural grammar at the town level across the Mississippian Southeast, focusing on specific examples from around the southern, south-central, and western areas of the region. Working with a sample of 33 Late Mississippian Dallas phase (A.D. 1300–1600) village sites in east Tennessee, Schroedl (1998) summarizes the development of both the settlement pattern and the layout of larger villages through the phase, using Toqua as a prime example (see Polhemus 1987). Early in the Dallas phase, villages were laid out with distinct public, ritual, and domestic areas, including a large community building and cemeteries. This pattern, once established, was maintained throughout the use and later reuses of the site. The largest villages were social, political, and religious centers, and had mounds, plazas, and palisades (Schroedl 1998:90). Schroedl contrasts Dallas phase village plans with east Tennessee Mouse Creek phase (A.D. 1300–1600) sites, noting the lack of villages as large as Toqua. Additionally, Mouse Creek sites do not have mounds, and community buildings are

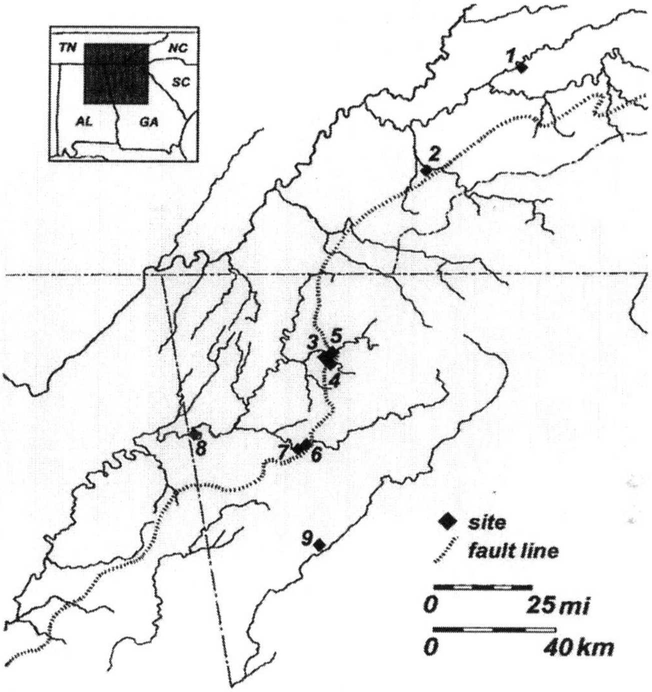


8.1. Locations of sites mentioned in this study. 1. Loy (40JE10) 2. Toqua (40MR6) 3. Little Egypt (9MU102) 4. Potts' Tract (9MU103) 5. Sixtoe (9MU100) 6. Etowah (9BR1) 7. Leake (9BR2) 8. King (9FL5) 9. Dog River (9DO34, 9DO39, 9DO45).

larger, suggestive of greater public access to ritual space and a less hierarchical social structure (see also Sullivan 1995).

In northwest Georgia, the most thoroughly examined Late Mississippian town is unquestionably the King site (Hally 1988, 2002; Hally and Kelly 1998). Here, the village layout pattern consists of a ditch and palisade surrounding a domestic structure zone with a central plaza. No mound is present at King, but a large structure located in the plaza is presumed to have been a community building.

Previous analyses of Mississippian households have produced a picture of the architectural signature of what has alternately been called a household aggregate, cluster, or unit (Hally and Kelly 1998; Polhemus 1987, 1998; Schroedl 1998; Sullivan 1995). For ease of description, I will refer to these as household units. A household unit is defined as the domestic structures and outdoor activity areas used by a household. These units are found at every level of the settlement pattern across the Mississippian Southeast. The Dallas phase household unit consists of a primary structure, a secondary structure, and outdoor activity areas (Polhemus 1987:1242–1244; 1990; 1998). Hally and Kelly (1998:57) suggest that structures facing a common outdoor activity area were part of extended family households, and tentatively identify four such units at the King site. The household unit pattern has also been discerned from excavations at Mouse Creek sites and prehistoric and historic Cherokee sites, though the forms of the structures comprising the household units are somewhat different between the three phases (Sullivan 1987).

The primary house of the household unit during the Late Mississippian subperiod in the southern Appalachian region was a roughly square structure with rounded corners (cf. prehistoric Cherokee houses, which are round [Sullivan 1995:105, Figure 5-2]). The primary house is commonly interpreted to be a "winter" structure due to its more substantial construction. Analysis of charred plant materials and other artifact classes to determine seasonality of destruction of a sample of these primary structures supports this interpretation (Hally 1981). This structure form is described in greater detail below. The secondary structure was an open sided, rectangular building with a roof. These are commonly held to be "summer" shelters, providing a shady area in which to work or rest. Artifacts and historic evidence support the idea that these shedlike structures were actually elevated granaries or corncribs (Polhemus 1987:1221). The third component of the household unit is the outdoor activity area associated with the primary and secondary structures. At Toqua, these areas were defined not only by the placement of structures around it but also by fired surfaces representing informal outdoor hearths (Polhemus 1990).

## Elements of Domestic Winter Structures in Northwest Georgia

This analysis focuses primarily on the winter structures for several reasons. First, because these structures were constructed in shallow basins, portions of the floor and/or post mold patterns are typically preserved even when the site has been subsequently plowed and evidence of the open areas under secondary structures has been destroyed. Second, during the winter months many household activities were conducted indoors where the more substantial structure provided insulation from the elements. In a way, winter structures may resemble a microcosm of household activities, with the dispersed activities of warmer months brought indoors under one roof. We might expect then that the winter structure was built for a broader spectrum of people and uses and reflects more social norms than we might find in a structure built for a limited subset of society or specialized activities. Third, some or all of the secondary structures may have been designed as storage facilities first. The absence of boundaries in the form of solid walls around the activity areas makes it difficult to discern discrete patterns of use, particularly if people were shifting their activities to follow the available shade during the course of the day. Likewise, during warmer months we can assume that some members of the household may have performed activities away from household structures altogether, removing elements of the broader social cues and activity patterns likely present in the winter structures. Last, the domestic winter structure was designed with a long anticipated use-life. The structures were built with a certain degree of architectural complexity lacking in a simple open-sided shed or hut, and likely had higher investments of human labor. Even if a raised storage shed had a long anticipated use-life, the actual amount of time anyone would spend in it would be minimal. Consequently, we might expect a low amount of architectural complexity, and limited spatial functionality.

Late Mississippian winter houses across northwest Georgia share many architectural features (Figure 8.2). The first is the house basin. This was a shallow excavated depression approximately 30 to 60 cm deep in which the superstructure was erected. It was only slightly larger than the structure itself, and soil from the basin was piled against the outside of the structure walls. House basins were found at Potts' Tract, Little Egypt, King, Leake, and Dog River sites (Hally 1970, 1980, 1988; Patton 1990; Poplin 1990).

The basin surface also served as the house floor. While it is possible that woven cane mats were used in portions of houses as floor coverings, the distribution of artifacts across entire basin surfaces at Little Egypt, for example, suggests that the inhabitants lived, worked, and ate on a compacted dirt floor (Gougeon 2002). A clean house floor was evidently important, as considerable evidence demonstrates that house basins were reused only after a clean layer of sand or soil was placed over the previous floor (Hally 1970).

Postholes are the most common and easily recognizable architectural elements representing domestic winter structures. They mark the location of exterior walls, central roof supports, interior partition walls, and furniture-like benches or beds that were located against exterior walls. Postholes can vary in size and are usually distinguished from the surrounding soil matrix by their darker fill and, in locations where subsoil is clayey, by their coarser grain size and looser compaction. Post molds, or the stain of the post placed in a posthole, are more difficult to discern unless the post burned. Post molds can provide additional information about construction techniques by revealing, for example, whether whole or split posts were used, and the average diameter of posts preferred for different structural elements.

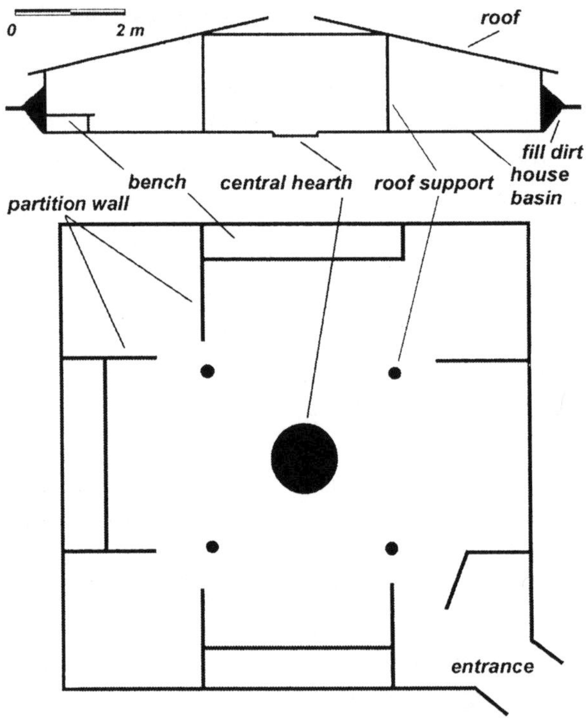


8.2. Profile and plan view of a typical Barnett phase winter domestic structure.

Exterior walls were constructed using single-set posts spaced 60 to 100 cm apart. The number of exterior wall posts in Barnett phase (A.D. 1475–1575) houses at King and Leake seems to be somewhat standardized, as it is common to find seven or eight posts in each wall regardless of the size of the structure (Hally 2002). This pattern was observed in three structures at Little Egypt as well (Gougeon 2002). Four posts were used to support rafters (beams giving form, slope, and shape to a roof) near the center of the structure. These four posts established a square area around the central hearth. While the interior roof supports were commonly whole posts, exterior walls and partition walls were typically constructed using split posts. Half and quarter posts have been recovered from postholes along structure walls at Little Egypt, and also near locations of central support posts (Gougeon 2002). In the latter location split and smaller whole posts may have been used to support sagging roof timbers as the main support posts rotted. It is also likely that exterior posts were replaced as they decayed. This would account for postholes that seem out of alignment with structure walls, as well as those that break up the almost standardized distances between posts.

The central feature of all Late Mississippian domestic winter structures is the hearth. The hearth is a prepared basin or surface in the floor of the structure that contained the fire used for cooking, heat, and light. The repeated firings left the basin and surrounding area rock hard and red in color. This surrounding area is sometimes referred to as a hearth apron. Polhemus (1987:1220) notes a wide variety of hearth forms, sizes, and elaboration from the large sample of structures at Toqua, but these appear to be the product of changes through time rather than being an indication of bipartite social or political organization. By the later stages of Toqua, hearths resemble those seen in Barnett phase sites in northwest Georgia: circular, shallow, and wider than in earlier structures.

Polhemus (1987:1221) notes that the area encompassed by the central posts was greatest in public buildings (31 to 40 percent of total floor area), followed by the homes of high status households (25 to 33 percent) and commoner houses (14 to 32 percent) during the Dallas phase at the Toqua site. A Brewster phase (A.D. 1450–1550) structure in a village area at the Leake site has a central hearth area that encompassed 16 percent of the total floor area (Patton 1990). The area within the central posts was much smaller in the elite and two commoner houses sampled at Little Egypt, ranging from 9 to 12 percent of the total floor space (Gougeon 2002).

The walls of winter structures were wattle, and possibly covered with cane mats in places. Wattle, a light frame of interwoven smaller diameter sticks or cane, was fixed to the structural frame (Curl 1992). Evidence of interwoven cane walls has been recovered from the Leake site (Patton 1990:20). Other walls in domestic structures include partition walls. Partition walls were non-load-bearing barriers separating one area from another (Curl 1992). A clay plaster (daub) was applied to some or all partition walls. Remnants of daubed partition walls were recovered at the Dog River, King, Leake, Loy, and Toqua sites (Hally 1988; Patton 1990; Polhemus 1987:207–208, 257, 283; 1998:52; Poplin 1990). Partition walls at Little Egypt are represented by posthole alignments extending from the exterior walls toward the center, sometimes with adjacent concentrations of fired daub (Hally 1980).

Partition walls for which there is no direct evidence can be inferred through analysis of artifact distribution. Partitions interrupted the even distribution of artifacts across the floor of the structure, and were also areas where tools, vessels, and refuse would have likely been deliberately placed or eventually come to rest. Examining contour maps of artifact density is one way of finding archaeologically invisible partition walls. Linear clusters of artifacts in areas that lack direct evidence of structural elements (like postholes) are probable indicators of partition walls. Most of the partition walls proposed for the structures at Little Egypt were inferred in this manner (Gougeon 2002).

Entrance trenches have been found at Toqua, Loy (Polhemus 1987; 1998), and King sites (Hally and Kelly 1998). These are presumed to have been low tunnel-like passageways located either at the corners of structures, as seen in structures at the King site, or in mid-wall as observed in structures at the Loy and Toqua sites, as well as some at King. No entrance trenches were found at Little Egypt, Potts' Tract, or Leake, though the place of entry may be inferred from the location of interior partition walls in the corners that might have been used to block drafts of air from entering the structure. It is possible that a type of entrance construction other than an entrance trench was used at some sites.

Fragments of tightly woven cane matting have been found at Little Egypt, Sixtoe (an Early Mississippian site), and Leake. At Sixtoe and Leake, cane matting was found fastened to wattle-and-daub walls (Kelly et al. 1965:184; Patton 1990:20). Cane matting recovered from Structure 1 at Little Egypt measured approximately 1.2 $m^2$, but it could not be determined whether it was placed on the walls or floor (Hally 1980:104). Cane mats are described in historic accounts as wall coverings, floor coverings, roof coverings, and as bedding or bench coverings. In archaeological contexts mats appear in different areas of the structures, which is likely an indication of the flexibility of their function.

Roofs were presumably covered with thatch (Polhemus 1987:223–224) or bark (Kelly et al. 1965:183; Polhemus 1987:223–224) secured to a light wooden frame of purlins fixed to larger rafters running from the tops of the exterior walls to the wall plates placed around the four center support posts.

The height of the exterior posts would, along with the height of the interior posts, determine both the height of the interior ceiling and the slope of the roof pitch. A steeply pitched roof might be too difficult to cover given its resulting greater surface area, although this would depend on the availability of grass, reed, bark, or other roofing materials, in addition to the number of structures being built at one time in a village. A flat roof would fail to shed water effectively and present the hazard of collecting too much snow in the winter, possibly resulting in a disastrous roof-collapse. Modern thatch installers recommend the pitch be no less than 45 degrees to shed water effectively, with 50 degrees being the minimum in areas that get snow accumulation (The Thatch Company n.d.). However, Poplin (1990:141) estimates the roof of a structure at Dog River (Str. 1, 9Do39) had a pitch of only about 15 degrees, with an exterior wall height of 1 m and a central clearance of approximately 2 m. His estimates are based on approximate lengths of rafter fragments, the dimensions of the structure, and the depth of the basin. The center of the roof would need to be nearly 5 m above the floor to achieve a 45-degree pitch in this same structure. Poplin's estimate of a 15-degree pitch seems far too low. For one, the low ceiling would trap smoke from the central fire over work and living areas. There might also be some thatching problems as described above, and most areas within the structure would be too small to stand in. Clearly, better-preserved structural elements are needed to further evaluate typical roof pitches.

The undersides of roofs were plastered with mud within the area enclosed by the central roof supports to suppress sparks that might cause fires (Hally 1980; Polhemus 1987). The central area of Structure 1 at Little Egypt was overlaid with a large mass of fired daub covering charred roof timbers and floor deposits (Hally 1980). This large daub mass represents the remains of the ceiling plaster. A hole was presumably left at the peak of the roof to let out smoke from the hearth. At the Loy site, this smoke hole was plastered with clay (Polhemus 1998:57), while at the Etowah site (a Middle Mississippian site) a structure was excavated with the neck of a jar plastered into the smoke hole (David Hally personal communication 2002).

Burial pits are commonly found within winter domestic structures. Historic accounts describe deceased household members being buried beneath the beds that they used in life (Hally 1988:13). When burial pits occur inside single-stage domestic structures they are commonly oriented parallel to the wall to which they are adjacent. This can be used to determine to which building stage the burial belongs in multistage domestic structures, and also assist in the identification of structures when the surrounding postholes, hearths, and other indicators have been lost to erosion, plowing, or other destructive processes.

## A Model for Developing an Architectural Grammar

Alexander and his colleagues (1977) have organized their ideas about architectural grammar around 253 identifiable patterns, beginning at the largest scale, the region, and following it to its smallest scale, "Things from Your Life" (i.e., knickknacks, collections, etc.). Their pattern language is presented from the largest to the smallest to emphasize the interconnectedness between each pattern, whether moving up or down in scale (Alexander et al. 1977:xii). As they put it, "no pattern is an isolated entity" (Alexander et al. 1977:xiii). That is, larger patterns contain smaller patterns, but are also built against other large patterns. Alexander and his colleagues do not imply that all 253 patterns are found in every architectural grammar, or that these patterns are applicable to every culture that has been, is, and is to come, or that their patterns are even completely correct. Theirs is clearly a Western perspective, looking primarily from the historical perspective of Western architecture in an attempt to guide the construction of future Western architecture. However, the patterns they define are general enough to be used in many cultural settings, and a number of the examples they provide are from non-Western societies.

Their grammar becomes less useful to the prehistoric archaeologist when used at the largest scales of the settlement system. Alexander et al. (1977:4) outline a typical metropolitan region to which their grammar best applies. The maximum region contains some eight million people, with major cities of perhaps a half a million people. Smaller towns would hold between seven to ten thousand people, with neighborhoods of five hundred to a thousand. It has been estimated that the King site, a single village in the polity, had a population of 250 to 475 people (Smith 2001). Although Alexander's larger patterns may not have direct correlations to the prehistoric period in question here, enough of the general principles, along with many of the patterns they propose for smaller scales within communities, are applicable and provide a useful point of departure for this study. It should be noted that when I use Alexander's patterns directly, the pattern number is provided in parentheses. Patterns of prehistoric architectural grammar are italicized.

## Architectural Grammar for the Late Mississippian Northwest Georgia

In the Late Mississippian subperiod in northwest Georgia, chiefdoms were *located along river valleys,* and by default provided residents with *access to water* (#25) for drinking, cleaning, food, transportation, and rituals. The principal town of a chiefdom was frequently placed at the intersection of two or more ecological zones, and controlled a polity of less than 40 km in extent (Hally 1993). Waterways and footpaths formed *transportation routes* between the settlements. Each town contained *a plaza,* a deliberately planned space for public ritual and community use. Flanking the plaza in some towns were one or more flat-topped *mounds,* again deliberately planned space for ritual use, though access to this space was presumably limited for the commoners. In nonmound villages, a large, nondomestic, *community building* was erected in the plaza and served as shared ritual, social, and political space (a prehistoric *local town hall* [#44]). A *domestic habitation zone* was established around the plaza, and could be surrounded by *a palisade* and/or *protective ditch. Main gateways* (#53), in the form of simple slot entrances (where the palisade walls would overlap for a distance, creating a passage between the wall faces), would control access to the village and also influence the orientation and placement of paths to and from the village.

In the habitation zone, households erected structures and established activity areas within and around smaller plazalike patios. These miniplazas are examples of *positive outdoor space* (#106), adhering to the idea that "left over" areas between buildings will not be used (Alexander et al. 1977:518). Positive outdoor space has a definite shape and is partially enclosed, typically by the adjoining building(s). "Left over" space might include buffer areas between structures of different household units and a palisade wall, for instance. In a way, positive outdoor space is as distinct as the buildings or features that frame them; they are recognizable as purposeful, demarcated spaces. This pattern can be observed in the site plan for the King site (Hally 1994:156, Figure 14.8; Hally and Kelly 1998:57, Figure 3.7), where outdoor activity areas are defined by the placement and orientation of structures.

The patio was partially enclosed by the placement of primary and secondary (or winter and summer) structures, ancillary constructions like racks for hide processing, privacy fences, outdoor hearths, storage pits, and even burial pits. The placement of structures around a patio also created a *hierarchy of open space* (#114). A well-designed open space has these qualities: it has a view into a larger space, and it provides a "back" against which people may sit, work, and otherwise feel less exposed (Alexander 1977:557–560). The hierarchy of open space can be imagined from the point of view of a person working under a granary with their view directed into the open space of the patio. From the patio, the public plaza (itself a positive outdoor space) is visible.

Access to winter structures was gained via the patio. The orientation of the entrance of the winter structure was determined by several factors, including the orientation of other structures in that household unit and the availability of space around the patio. In the Late Mississippian Southeast rules of exogamy dictated that individuals married outside of their lineage (Hudson 1976). Matrilineal practices likely included a matrilocal postmarital residence pattern, requiring the husband to move into his wife's household. Females did not move away from their mother's household upon marriage. Rather, they formed new households attached to their mother's, resulting in a pattern of multiple primary (winter) *structures oriented around a common patio* (Hally and Kelly 1998; Kelly 1988; Polhemus 1987). If the only available space were located south of the patio, the entrance would be oriented to the north. Examples of this include Structure 24 relative to Structures 2, 4, and 9 at the King site (Hally and Kelly 1998:52, Figure 3.3), and the diagram of Settlement Pattern Level II showing two household clusters around adjoining patio space at Toqua (Polhemus 1987:1244, Figure 13.3). Over time, *house clusters* (#37) of related households (household units) would form around the town plaza. A long-established village or town would have through the natural process of household growth a *mix of households* (#35) in various stages of development.

After the orientation of the structure and location of the entrance was determined, *a house basin* was excavated. The size of the basin appears to be dependent upon the specific stage of the life cycle of the household. That is to say, a newly formed household consisting of a wife, husband, and one or more children would build a smaller structure than a well-established, multigenerational household, which might include the wife's parents, unmarried sisters and older children of the wife, and the husband. Two options were available to the household: excavate a new house basin or reuse an existing one. In the latter case, the basin would be expanded (if the new structure was larger than the basin) and prepared with a layer of clean fill.

The planning of the interior space of the winter structure began with the placement of the *four roof support posts* and *central hearth.* As the exterior of the structure was completed, *internal partitions* could be secured to the exterior walls and benches could be constructed in the appropriate niches created by the partitions. As Alexander and his colleagues (1977:941) note, *structure follows social spaces* (#205). This is the notion of spatial functionality discussed above; a structure has physical spaces that are congruent with the social arrangements of people and their activities. The spaces set apart, partitioned, or left open within the domestic winter structure reflect a variety of social norms (gendered use of spaces, age differentiation) and anticipated uses (activity areas, sleeping areas, storage, etc.).

The layout of a winter structure was *imbued with symbolism* and social meaning. First, as Hudson (1997:211) discusses, a house with a central hearth and rooms along the exterior walls fits the widespread Mississippian motif of the equal-armed cross, symbolizing the four cardinal directions with a central fire. It is possible that the different directions had different meanings or values attached to them, including the notion of opposition seen in southeastern native belief systems (Hudson 1990, 1997).

Second, upon entering a structure one would recognize all of the symbolic cues that denoted *public* and *private spaces.* Polhemus (1990, 1998) differentiates between "public" and "private" spaces in Dallas phase structures in east Tennessee, a pattern that applies to Barnett phase structures in northwest Georgia as well (Gougeon 2002). The central hearth area is the public area in Polhemus's model. Private areas are marked by the benches along exterior walls, and also by the areas partially enclosed by partition walls. Even the *varying ceiling height* (#190) would convey an idea about public and private areas, as the greatest ceiling heights would be at the centrally shared area of the structure, and lowest along the edges of the structure above the private benches.

The layout and use of interior spaces set up by the placement of architectural elements like partition walls, hearth basins, and roof posts also contain information about other aspects of the social norms of the Late Mississippian subperiod in northwest Georgia. For instance, while the benches are separated from one another by virtue of being against each exterior wall, all had open and unobstructed access to the central hearth area. In this way, the household practiced *communal sleeping* (#186). So, while household activities were separated by gender, and most of the spaces within the structure were used by one sex almost exclusively (Gougeon 2002), the beds were within sight and sound of the other beds.

*Finishing the interior* of the structure likely followed certain patterns as well, but lack of solid archaeological evidence prevents a detailed analysis. Undoubtedly, tools, baskets, hides, and other objects were hung from rafters around the central hearth. Mats were placed on walls and floors, and benches had woven covers. We know that pots were used to store food in the corners of the structures and near work areas (Gougeon 2002). Painted, punctated, and incised daub from partition wall fragments recovered at Toqua (Polhemus 1987:208–209) provides tantalizing clues about other architectural cues and symbolism that may have been used inside domestic structures.

The *exterior of the building* was finished by piling the soil from the basin against the walls. The roof was thatched or covered with bark, and the underside was covered with a layer of daub. The entrance trench was covered, presumably, with a waddle-and-daub frame. We can assume a hide or cane mat was also used to block drafts.

## The Sum of Its Parts

The architectural grammar for the Late Mississippian subperiod in northwest Georgia contains the following patterns. This is by no means a comprehensive list, particularly at the largest scales, which are presented here to provide a context for the smaller patterns. As more domestic structures are excavated and reported, this grammar should be tested and amended.

### Chiefdom

1. Component villages located along river valleys
2. Access to water
3. Transportation routes connecting villages

Village/Town
1. Plaza
2. Mound(s) in principal town
3. Community building in secondary villages
4. Domestic habitation zone surrounding plaza
5. Palisade
6. Main gateways
7. Ditch

House Clusters
1. Positive outdoor space
2. Hierarchy of open space
3. Household's structures oriented around patio
4. Mix of households

House
1. House basin
2. Four roof support posts
3. Central hearth and apron
4. Seven posts in each exterior wall
5. Varying ceiling height
6. Internal partitions
7. Structure follows social spaces
8. Spaces imbued with symbolism
9. Division of public and private space
10. Finished interior
11. Finished exterior

An architectural grammar is more than just a list of architectural traits, however. It should be evident from the descriptions above that this architectural grammar also has rules for combining elements into meaningful patterns. Each pattern is tied to those "above" and "below" it in the hierarchy of patterns of the architectural grammar (Alexander 1979:186–187). The architectural grammar specifies the connections between the patterns necessary for someone to construct "coherent" arrangements of space.

This is perhaps summarized by the hypothetical construction of a new house in a growing Mississippian village. First, the placement and orientation of a new house within a household unit is ruled by the location of existing structures and the availability of space around the patio. Further, the new house cannot interfere with the patio space of a neighboring household unit, nor extend into the public plaza. A basin is excavated that reflects the current spatial needs of the household. (The pattern of overlapping hearths and posthole patterns suggest a new structure was constructed in the same location once the household grew or shrank.) Placement of the four central posts dictates the amount of space available for public and private areas, as well as the height and pitch of the roof. The orientation of the entrance influences the layout of activity areas within the structure, for instance, as coarse processing of materials occurred to the right of the entrance and adult female activities related to the preparation of food occurred across the central hearth from this area (Gougeon 2002). Although simplified, this example demonstrates the linkages between patterns in the architectural grammar I have outlined above.

## Conclusions

The purpose of developing architectural grammars for particular times and places is to explore those areas where architecture informs anthropology. These patterns are more than plans for the design of space. Each pattern also alludes to or contains information about an underlying human behavioral pattern, a social norm, or other cultural element. Because architectural grammars are specific to time and place, the comparison of grammars in different contexts (e.g., Dallas phase and Barnett phase) may be a valuable exercise as archaeologists seek to understand the prehistoric Southeast.

Our grasp of the architectural grammar of northwest Georgia, for example, can also inform archaeological investigations. If the pattern for the layout, orientation, construction, and use of a domestic structure is known we can make a more robust interpretation of a house or household unit, even in those instances when the archaeological record is incomplete.

As this chapter demonstrates, we are well on our way to having a complete architectural grammar for the Late Mississippian period in northwest Georgia. The study of architectural grammars can also contribute to diachronic studies of cultural change across the Southeast. With advances in our understanding of architectural grammars in northwest Georgia from earlier and later subperiods (Late Woodland, Early and Middle Mississippian), as well as from neighboring areas in the broader southern Appalachian region during the late prehistoric and early protohistoric periods, we can further our understanding of the Mississippian Southeast at a variety of scales—from differences between elite and commoner households within a village, to changes in social systems through time, to the transformation of chiefdoms of the late prehistoric into the coalescent societies of the protohistoric and early historic American South.

## Acknowledgments

This chapter is dedicated to my father, Rick Gougeon. On the day I grow weary of making my livelihood throwing dirt through screens and pondering the past, I'll take up a hammer and join you on your next project, Dad. My thanks to Cameron Lacquement for the invitation to participate, David Hally for continued guidance, and Amanda Edge-Gougeon for encouragement. This chapter was improved by the input from two reviewers, though I must admit I did not heed their every warning. All errors are therefore my responsibility alone.

# 9
# A Mississippian Sweat Lodge

*Robert H. Lafferty, III*

A structure, approximately 3 m in diameter, was excavated at the East site (3Po610), near Tyronza in Poinsett County, Arkansas, that possessed artifactual and architectural characteristics similar to that of historic Native American sweat lodges. The distribution of sweat lodges or sweat houses has been documented as being utilized by cultures ranging from the Eskimo of Alaska to the Maya of Mesoamerica (Lopatin 1960; Wissler 1938). In addition, the sweat lodge was described as a vital part of Native American life by early explorers and missionaries of the New World. In 1643, Roger Williams, a resident of Rhode Island, described the sweat lodge of the Natives as "a kind of little Cell or Cave, six or eight foot over, round, made on the side of a hill . . . into this frequently the men enter after they have exceedingly heated it with store of wood, laid upon an heape of stones in the mid[d]le . . . which sweating they use for two ends: First, to cleanse their skin: Secondly, to purge their bodies, which doubtlesse is a great means of preserving them" (Williams 1963:211–212). This chapter will provide a detailed examination of one particular prehistoric structure that may have been used for the purposes of sweating. The whole complex of this building at the East site, located in a clay midden, including post molds, different strata, and other miscellaneous features, is referred to as the Feature 410 complex. In this chapter, analyses of the artifacts, the architectural remains, and ethnohistorical accounts are presented in addressing the function of this structure.

## Archaeological Evidence at the East Site

The East site (3Po610) was excavated in the summer of 2004 by Mid-Continental Research Associates, Inc. (MCRA) under subcontract to Spears

Professional Environmental & Archaeological Research Service, Inc (SPEARS), for the Arkansas Highway and Transportation Department. The work was conducted to mitigate the impact of the enlargement of Highway 63 and the construction of a limited access ramp at Tyronza, Arkansas. The site was originally tested in 2003 by SPEARS (Spears and Walker 2003). The testing consisted of a controlled surface collection with 4-m precision, excavating five control columns and one backhoe trench, and then stripping the plow zone. The stripping revealed 195 stains that limited investigations suggested were cultural. These cultural features mainly included post molds but also three possible middens. Spears, Inc. and the State Historic Preservation Office agreed that the East site and three other sites in the nearby area were archaeologically significant and should be avoided or mitigated by data recovery.

The East site is on Sharkey clay (Gray and Ferguson 1977); however the B horizon was slightly oxidized, which is not consistent with the soil description for this particular area in Arkansas. The geomorphologic analysis (Guccione et al. 2006) suggests that the sediments were laid down about 5000 B.C. by the Mississippi River. At that time, the river occupied a course through Dead Timber Lake, located 50 m east of the surface manifestation of the site. In the intervening time, the reduced clays of the original backwater swamp were oxidized. There are data that there was an uplift of the ridges north of the site that caused Dead Timber Lake to form, though the timing of this event has not been defined.

The structure was found in Midden 1 at the extreme eastern edge of the surface scatter (Figure 9.1). The elevations were higher toward the west edge of the scatter, where the oxidized site matrix readily contrasted with the dark feature stains. Toward the east of the scatter, there were no artifacts on the surface, which was almost flat. The surface rose gradually to the small modern levee laid down by the Tyronza River, which periodically occupied the bottom of the Mississippi River Channel/Dead Timber Swamp. When the plow zone was stripped, Midden 1 appeared as a 4-m-wide dark band with pottery, bone, and carbon. Midden 1 dipped toward the southeast and plunged to almost 2 m below the more recent deposits. Four meters east of the western edge of midden 1, the surface sank under a sand blow that became thicker farther to the southeast. It is likely that in prehistoric times Dead Timber Lake was only several meters east of Midden 1.

There were artifacts, sporadic carbon concentrations, desiccation cracks with artifacts in them, and scattered fired clay concentrations. The midden was excavated in 1 by 1 m units by 5-cm-thick levels. Often, during August and September, when close to a floor the units were divided into four quadrants. A

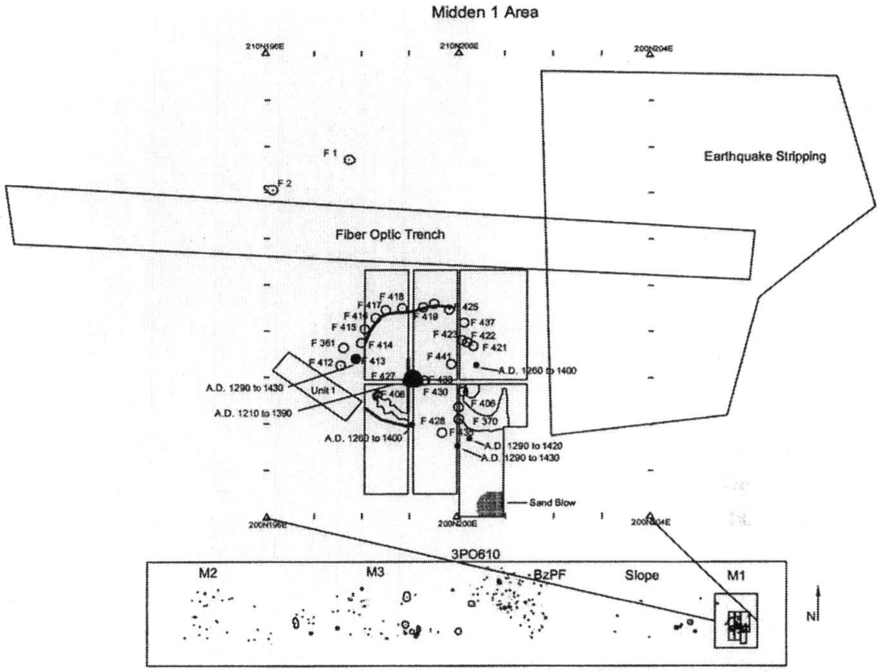


9.1. Map of the East site (3Po610).

large portion of the excavation levels near a floor were processed by flotation. Approximately 7 m³ from Midden 1 were processed by flotation. Samples of the light fraction from the flotation were analyzed by Drs. Gina Powell and Neal Lopinot. Several areas of fired clay that appeared to be in situ were found. The expected homogenous mass of clay was revealed as six large ceramic cones (Figure 9.2).

In all, seven cones were recovered. These were on the south edge of the Feature 410 complex. Several of the cones had not been fired past the three-quarters conversion point and were in poor shape. The cones are on average 16 cm high (14 to 17 cm range, Table 9.1) and are 13 to 14.5 cm in diameter at the base. The cones have flat bases and taper to a rounded end (Figure 9.2). Each cone weighed between 2.2 and 2.5 kg, averaging 2.33 kg. All seven cones had a projected total of 16.5 kg (≈ 36 lbs; Cone 5 was partial and Cone 1's weight includes some matrix). The three best-preserved cones have conical-shaped holes three-sevenths of the way from the bottom. These holes are about 4.4 cm deep and are 9.9 to 14 mm wide at the surface of the cone and taper to a point. This width is almost exactly the width of four white-tailed deer antler tips

9.1. Various Characteristics of Ceramic Cones from the East Site.

Tyronza Cone dimensions in millimeters

| | Height | Base Circum. | Min. width (base) | Max. width (base) | Top Circum. | Min. width (top) | Max. width (top) |
|---|---|---|---|---|---|---|---|
| Cone 1 | 140.2 | 450 | 103.3 | 145.1 | 245.7 | 52.2 | 76.3 |
| Cone 2 | 163.3 | 414 | 98.6 | 130.6 | 225 | 37 | 85.5 |
| Cone 3 | 156 | 415.4 | 114 | 139.5 | 240.4 | 63 | 85.4 |
| Cone 4 | 157.1 | 336.2 | 78.1 | 113.4 | 235.8 | 62.3 | 79.3 |
| Cone 5 | 153.7 | 349.2 | 96.7 | 113 | 194.3 | 54.9 | 64.4 |
| Cone 6 | 172.3 | 415.1 | 119.7 | 122.7 | 224.1 | 67.5 | 68.1 |
| Cone 7 | 170.2 | 434.9 | 115.2 | 129.1 | 184.5 | 66 | 69 |
| Average | 159.0 | 402.1 | 103.7 | 127.6 | 221.4 | 57.6 | 75.4 |

* not included in average

9.2. Photographs of ceramic cones from the Feature 410 complex.

| | | | Holes in Cones in millimeters | |
|---|---|---|---|---|
| Wt. | | | Depth | Width |
| 3400* | Cone 1 | poor shape | | |
| 2500 | Cone 2 | pretty poor shape | | |
| 2400 | Cone 3 | broken in two—poor shape | | |
| 2200 | Cone 4 | broken in two—pretty poor shape | | |
| 1500* | Cone 5 | surface removed over hole | 20.8 | 9.9 |
| 2250 | Cone 6 | | 45.1 | 14.1 |
| 2500 | Cone 7 | | 43.6 | 11.7 |
| 2370 | Average with Cone 5 | | 36.5 | 11.9 |
| | Average without Cone 5 | | 44.35 | 12.9 |

that are in MCRA's comparative faunal collection (Figure 9.2). The distal fork of these antlers would allow handling the cones when hot without them tipping over.

Cones 3 and 4 had not been completely fired and samples were taken for sediment size analysis. These cones are composed principally of very fine sand and coarse silt with 5 to 20 percent clay. There is no temper apparent with 10x magnification. Several samples from the cones are currently undergoing petrographic analysis.

These are not the first cones reported in the archaeological literature. They are the first ones that come from a context such as is described below. The earliest cones this author is aware of were described by A. V. Kidder from Pecos Pueblo and Forked Lightning Ruin (Kidder 1932). Several smaller cones have been reported from the Great Plains (Hoffman 1978). In the Lower Mississippi Valley, Price (1969) described five nearly identical cones from a house at the Turner site in southeast Missouri. A large number of other cones were found in domestic contexts at the Flurry and Snodgrass sites (Price personal communication 2005). Price noted that there were two different textures in the

Powers phase (A.D. 1250–1400) cones—one with a sandy texture and the other of almost pure clay. Interestingly Ford, Phillips, and Haag (1955:58) observed a similar distinction between the sandy tetrahedrons recovered from Mound A, at the edge of Wasp Lake, at the Jaketown site, and the Poverty Point objects found there, which did not possess a sandy texture.

It seems likely to me that the cones probably had at least two functions: as cooking pot supports and as heating elements in sweat lodges. In the following section, the context in which the seven cones were found is described in more detail. This author believes that the context is evidence that they were used as heating elements in a sweat lodge rather than pot supports, and therefore indicates that this structure was probably a sweat lodge.

## Context: Feature 410 Complex

The cones were recovered on the edge of a 3-m-diameter, bowl-shaped depression in Midden 1 at the eastern edge of the oxidized B horizon clay. There were several strata and almost a score of other features (Figure 9.1) that made up the Feature 410 Complex. These features and strata are hypothesized to represent different architectural, functional, and depositional units from the construction, use, and ceremonial destruction of the sweat lodge. The stratigraphy was quite complex and the origins of several deposition units are still not at all clear. The features, beginning at the bottom, are discussed below.

Feature 411 comprised the deposits on the floor of the structure. This 10-cm-thick mixture of burned clay, small bone fragments, and potsherds draped across the bottom of the structure. The bowl shape was clearly indicated on the north and west side of the structure, where it abutted the oxidized clay, but was less clear on the south and east sides. On the south and east sides, Feature 411 graded into the dark grayish brown clay A horizon soil. On the north and west sides it was obvious that the floor had been excavated into the oxidized clay and then leveled. The cones sat directly on this stratum. One shell-tempered sherd lay directly under Cones 3 and 4 (Figure 9.2). Another large shell-tempered sherd and a Mill Creek hoe flake were found just to the east of the cones.

Feature 356 was a layer of charcoal that was directly on Feature 411 and covered a slightly smaller area. It was composed of carbonized small hickory (*Carya sp.*), white oak (*Quercus sp.*), twigs, and cane (*Arundinaria gigantica*) that in some places had the appearance of a lattice when first uncovered. There were also substantial vine fragments. Parts of this carbon layer lay directly on the cones (Figure 9.2). A carbon date on a hickory twig from the top of Cone 7, dated to calibrated (cal) A.D. 1260 to 1400 (2 sigma is presented in all the ranges given below) with an intercept of A.D. 1300 (Beta #204247); all radiocarbon dates were calibrated using Ox-Cal, version 3.1 (Bronk Ramsey 2005). Another sample from this stratum dated to cal A.D. 1280 to 1410 with intercepts at A.D. 1320, 1350, and 1390 (Beta #198626). Also prominent in this feature were large amounts of charred grasses of at least two unidentified species.

Feature 370 was an unconsolidated mass of oxidized clay in the center of the bowl-shaped basin. It was directly on the carbon layer and was as much as 30 cm thick. In all, the volume of this feature contained about .4 $m^3$ of a mass of daub with leaf and grass impressions. Several fragments that were closely inspected had impressions showing cane and sapling at right angles. Most of the thousands of daub pieces were less than 4 cm in diameter, had small grass impressions, and their texture differed from the cones with little sand. The daub appears to have been used to seal up the structure. If this is so, then how did it become one mass and why are there parts of Feature 356 without any daub on it? Why did those parts of Feature 356 not turn to ash? Perhaps the burning of the supporting framework only got hot enough toward the center of the structure to carry the clay past the three-quarters conversion point.

There was a layer of sandy clay overlaying part of Feature 370 and most of the rest of Feature 356. This layer was up to 30 cm thick and fairly homogeneous. Sandy clay is a fluvial oxymoron—you simply do not get sand and clay deposited in the same environment by fluvial processes. The only nearby source for the sand is the sand blow, which lenses out 1.5 m southeast, and downhill of the structure. The sand particle sizes are not consistent with this sand blow being the source. First, it was hypothesized that the sand blow laid down a thin scatter of sand over an area larger than is currently preserved and that it was then redeposited by rainwater into the depression left by the collapsed structure. Problems with this interpretation are that there were no siltation bands, usually associated with waterborne deposition, and the sand blow is downhill. Another interpretation is that the sandy clay was used to intentionally bury the burned structure after it was burned. Interestingly, Cyrus Thomas, whose agents excavated about 20 burned structures at the nearby Tyronza Mounds, observed: "But there can be no doubt that it was a custom among the mound builders of this section to spread a layer of fresh earth upon the charred remains of one dwelling, often while yet smoldering, to the depth of 1, 2, or 3 feet" (Thomas 1985:206–207). The sediment size analysis of the sandy clay and two cones shows that they are 60 to 70 percent very fine sand and coarse silt and are 20 to 30 percent clay. This composition is different from the sand blow and other sampled natural soils.

Feature 427 was a 20-cm-deep pit in the center of the depression at the intersection of the balks. There was some evidence of firing in the bottom Feature 427 and that the Feature 411 floor fill did not cover it. Feature 427 produced a carbonized persimmon seed that was dated to cal A.D. 1210 to 1390 with an intercept at A.D. 1280 (Beta #204249). More than 600 calcified long bones from birds were recovered from this feature. The few that were identifiable were from teal and medium-sized ducks.

In the botanical samples from the floor deposits (Feature 411), the charcoal layer (Feature 356), and the central pit (Feature 427) there were nine morning glory (*Ipomoea sp.*) and six charred tobacco (*Nicotiana sp.*) seeds. These are considered medicinal/ceremonial species.

Thirteen small post molds were defined on the north, west, and east sides of the structure (Figure 9.3). Most had flat bottoms and were only about 5 cm in diameter, placed approximately 15 cm deep, and roughly spaced 30 cm apart. It is doubtful if any of these would have been preserved or recognized in matrix other than clay. Several of the post molds were angled toward the center of the structure. Feature 413, on the west side of the structure, produced a small amount of grass stem node carbon that was AMS dated to cal A.D. 1290 to 1430 with a calibrated intercept of A.D. 1400 (Beta #204248). Nearly identical results were obtained from twigs on the southeastern edge of Feature 356.

In summary, the structure was a 3 m in diameter, bowl-shaped depression surrounded by small post molds spaced about 30 cm apart and with a shallow pit in the center. The cones were on the floor of the depression, which, based on the thickness of Feature 411, had been used for a while. Mississippian artifacts found on the floor are consistent with the four early fourteenth-century radiocarbon dates. Feature 356, a layer of charred small hickory, white oak wood, vines, and cane, in addition to the angle of several of the post molds, suggests a structure with a domed roof created from a woven lattice of small wooden poles. There was also a fair amount of charred grasses. Feature 370 was a burned mass of daub on the charred layer near the center of the structure. Nearly identical results were obtained from twigs on the southeastern edge of Feature 356. The daub (Feature 370) and the charred layer (Feature 356) were capped with sandy clay. Several characteristics of this feature complex are consistent with its interpretation as a sweat lodge. There are a fair number of medicinal/ceremonial charred seeds, including tobacco and morning glory seeds. Sweat lodges were often used for healing. The prevalence of sweating in

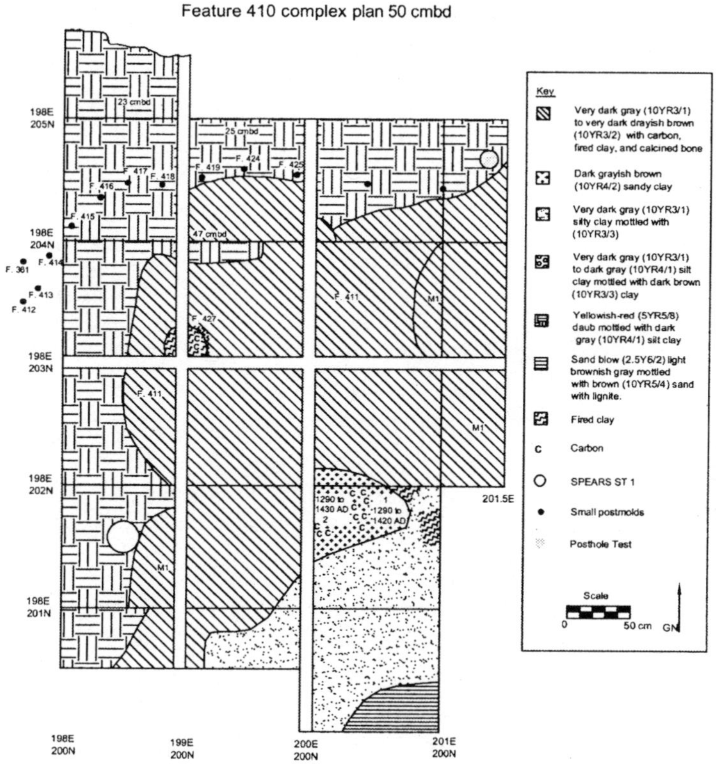


9.3. Feature 410 complex with the basin excavated to 50 cm below datum.

the ethnohistoric literature suggests that it is probably part of a common cultural tradition.

It is assumed the little posts went all of the way around the perimeter of the structure, resulting in about 30 posts. Either the post molds were not detected on the south and east side, where the soil was darker, or they were homogenized by the earthquake that caused the sand blow. If the posts met at the top each would have been at least 2.35 m long to span the 4.71-m dome, and longer if they overlapped. This framework would then have been reinforced with white oak and hickory saplings or branches, covered with grasses and leaves (probably attached to a sapling or branch), and plastered with clay. The .4 $m^3$ of clay would weigh 320 to 370 kg (700 to 800 lbs) and would have been 3 to 4 cm thick over this surface of the structure. The whole structure was either covered with an outer thatch to keep it from dissolving in the rain or the clay layer was intentionally fired.

## Ethnohistoric Analogies and Experimental Archaeology

Gravier, writing in the 1700s about the Tunica houses in the present-day state of Mississippi, describes a rather similar structure: "Their cabins are round and vaulted. They are lathed with canes and plastered with mud from bottom to top, within and without, with a good covering of straw. There is no light except by the door: it is as hot as a vapor bath" (Gravier, in Swanton 1911:315).

Driver and Massey (1957:314–315) note that water-vapor sweating was widespread in North America. They further note: "Although they were sometimes permanent structures, the majority were hastily assembled for a particular occasion and not used daily. They consisted of a light framework of poles and withes over which hides, pieces of bark, or mats were thrown to confine the water vapor. Often they were so low that the occupant had to stoop over to get inside. They were used most often for a purification rite by those seeking supernatural power or by the sick seeking relief from infirmities. . . . Among the Delaware each village apparently had an earth-covered sweathouse" (Driver and Massey 1957:314).

There are a number of illustrations of nineteenth-century sweat lodges from several cultures. The late nineteenth-century Sioux and modern Blackfoot (Figure 9.4) built structures very similar to the posited structure at the East site. The structures were and are about the same size and were constructed of similar materials. A late nineteenth-century sweat lodge pictured in Bucko (1998) holds at least five adults. The floors are covered with dried grass upon which everyone is sitting. Forked sticks, presumably for handling hot rocks, are in evidence. Other photographs from the early twentieth-century Cheyenne (Aadland 2000) show a pitchfork being used to handle the hot rocks and the fire for heating the rock 3 to 4 m away from the lodge.

Heckewelder (1971:225–226), describing the Indians of Pennsylvania and the Midwest during the eighteenth century, observed:

> The sweat oven is the first thing that an Indian has recourse to when he feels the least indisposed; it is the place to which a wearied traveler, hunter, or warrior looks for relief from fatigues he has endured, the cold he has caught, or the restoration of his lost appetite.
>
> This oven is made of different sizes, so as to accommodate from two to six persons at a time. . . . It is generally built on a bank or slope, one half of it within and the other above ground. It is well covered on the top with split plank and earth, and has a door in front, where the ground is level to go or rather creep in. Here, on the outside, stones, generally

9.4. Six Blackfoot sweat lodge frames on the margin of a small lake near Glacier National Park, Montana, in 2005.

about the size of a large turnip, are heated by one of the men appointed each day for that purpose. While the oven is heating, decoctions of roots or plants are prepared either by the person himself who intends to sweat, or by one of the men of the village, who boils a large kettle full for the general use, so that when the public cryer going his rounds calls out *Pimook!* "go to sweat!" everyone brings his small kettle, which is filled for him with the potion, which at the same time serves him as a medicine, promotes profuse perspiration, and quenches his thirst. As soon as a sufficient number have come to the oven, a number of hot stones are rolled into the middle of it, and the sweaters go in . . . Those sweat ovens are generally at some distance from an Indian Village, where wood and water are always at hand.

Catesby, writing in the 1730s concerning the Indians of the Southeast, notes:

There are three remedies that are much used by all the *Indians* of the northern continent of *America:* these are bagnio's or sweating houses, scarrification, and the use of *Casena* or *Yapon.* The first is used in intermitting feavers, colds and other disorders of the body: these bagnio's are

> usually placed on the banks of a river, and are of stone, and some of clay; they are of a form and size of a large oven, into which they roll large stones heated very hot; the patient then creeps in, and is closely shut up; in this warm situation he makes his lamentable groans, but after about an hour's confinement, out from his oven he comes, all reeking with torrents of sweat, and plunges into the river. However absurd this violent practice may seem to the learned, it may reasonably be supposed that in so long a series of years they have used this method, and still continue so to do, they find the benefit of it. (Catesby, in Swanton 1946:790–791)

Some experimental archaeology has been done. MCRA replicated a cone, using clay and sand that had been deflocculated with baking soda. It fired to nearly red hot. It produced a lot of steam and held together when put in a bucket of water. MCRA also constructed a modern sweat lodge in northwest Arkansas in 2004 that was about a meter larger than the East site's structure. It had eight small bamboo poles supporting the plastic roof covered with a plastic tarp and several hundred pounds of composting leaves. About 20 kg (44 lbs) of hot rocks in the pit were used to heat it, but it did not get quite hot enough. It was concluded that the structure should have been made smaller in diameter.

## Summary and Conclusions

In summary, the structure at the East site had the size, types of features, and contents that are similar to sweat lodges described in the ethnohistoric literature of North America. Its location on the edge of the site and on the margin of a lake is also consistent with sweat lodges' historic and modern placements. The medicinal seeds are consistent with the use of these structures for healing. The duck wing bones in Feature 427 could have been used as fans to bring the steam vapors down. The large number of the wing bones, careful alignment of the cones, and preservation of Feature 356 are consistent with a ceremonial burning and burial of the lodge.

In the many areas of the Southeast, only a few prehistoric sweat lodges are known archaeologically. They are best known at Cahokia (Milner 1984; Pauketat and Woods 1986; to name a few), and one, similar to the East site sweat lodge (and the others), was excavated at the Bellefonte site in northern Alabama (Futato 1977). These few examples stand in contrast to the thousands of domestic structures that have been described in the Southeast (see Knight this volume). This disparity is probably because the peripheries of habitation sites are often not intensively investigated. Locations are seldom investigated at some distance from habitation sites where sweat lodges were often placed. In the case of the Lower Mississippi Valley, sweat lodges are also probably buried under more recent alluvium. It is probable that a close look at their composition will show that those found in the different primary contexts will have different compositions. It also seems likely to me, given its ritual importance, that the sweat lodge was probably derived from the Late Archaic small winter earth lodges, which are about the same size.

# 10
# Interpreting Changes in Historic Creek Household Architecture at the Turn of the Nineteenth Century

*Robert J. Scott*

House construction is based on shared traditions and ideas about how dwellings should be built, where, of what materials, how they are to be used, and where different activities will take place. Change in domestic architecture can often be related to significant changes in cultural knowledge, attitudes, and technology within a given community or society. The historic Creeks selectively incorporated elements of European material culture and technology into their own throughout the eighteenth century but remained distinctively Creek (Waselkov 1989, 1997:185). With the exception of a specific subset of the population that was beginning to bring Euro-American architectural patterns into Creek country, most continued to erect homes of wattle-and-daub construction.

At the turn of the nineteenth century the historic Creeks were faced with an advancing frontier of white settlers and a U.S. government focused on civilizing the southeastern Indians. A decline in the overseas demand for deerskins had left a large number of Creek families without a means of acquiring European manufactured goods. The United States implemented a policy that encouraged southeastern groups to adopt stock raising, plow agriculture, spinning and weaving, and other elements of Western culture and society that Americans understood to represent civilization (Hahn 2004:275). The rhetoric surrounding this policy focused on the economic life of the Indians, requiring a reordering of the roles men and women played in household production, and accepting Western ideas of private property and the inheritance of wealth. Not required of this policy, but presumably implied in its mandate, were concomitant changes in other aspects of Creek material culture not related to the new economic enterprises recommended by the U.S. government.

Here I examine archaeological evidence from late Lawson Field phase (1783–1832) sites along the Lower Chattahoochee and Flint rivers for changes in Lower Creek domestic architecture at the turn of the nineteenth century. Written accounts and illustrations of Creek houses dating to the late eighteenth and early nineteenth centuries indicate a shift from vertical post, wattle-and-daub homes and storage facilities to horizontal log pole structures. The accounts of Benjamin Hawkins and others suggest that people living in the prominent core communities at the turn of the century were less receptive to the economic and social changes advocated by the civilization plan, an attitude that may have been expressed through the continued construction of wattle-and-daub dwellings and storage facilities. In contrast, those Creeks who decided to adapt to the new political and economic context that emerged in the Southeast at the turn of the century by raising livestock or growing crops for commercial exchange were beginning to build horizontal log and notch homes resembling those of frontier whites.

Limited test excavations at several late Lawson Field phase sites in Alabama and Georgia in the last 20 years (see Worth 2000 for a recent overview) and recent area-wide excavations at the Lawson Field site, the confirmed location of the Lower Creek town of Kasita, allow us to independently assess the extent to which changes in Lower Creek material culture really occurred during this period. The approximate locations of relevant Upper and Lower Creek communities discussed in this chapter are provided in Figure 10.1.

## Historical Context and Background

At the end of the eighteenth century the trade in deerskins was declining due to a drop in market demand in the United States and Europe and decimation of deer populations by years of over-hunting (Braund 1993; Crane 1956). In 1796 Hawkins arrived in Creek country as the first U.S. Indian agent to the southern Indians, charged with the task of promoting what would later be called Jeffersonian Indian policy. This plan focused on civilizing the southeastern Indians and transforming them into members of the newly founded United States. His obligation was "to lead the Indian from hunting to the pastoral life, to agriculture, household manufactures, a knowledge of weights and measures, money and figures . . . and lastly, letters" (in Mauelshagen and Davis 1969:7).

Central to the civilization plan was putting men in charge of the household and making them responsible for raising livestock and growing crops for commercial exchange. Women were to give up their influence over household production and focus on spinning cotton as their primary economic contribution

10.1. Map of Georgia, Alabama, and north Florida showing the locations of Lower and Upper Creek communities.

to the household. The response to this plan was varied. Some Creeks adopted this lifestyle while others objected to it, largely because of the incomprehensible changes in gender roles the plan called for (Saunt 1998; 1999). As the U.S. and European demand for deerskins declined, more Creeks were motivated to involve themselves in raising livestock because it provided a needed link to the commercial market and manufactured goods. Taking cattle, pigs, and horses to market was responsible for keeping the Indian trade alive, even if for just a short while longer, and it operated within the previously established workings of the trade system (Ethridge 2003). Also, Creek men generally approved of ranching as a reasonable alternative to the deerskin trade.

Ranching led to significant changes in settlement patterns and field location strategies. The establishment of settlements away from the large towns in the form of small dispersed villages and individual family farmsteads worked to weaken the influence of the matrilineages over household production and the ability of women to muster labor for the cultivation of communal fields (Saunt 1999:159; Waselkov 1997). The phenomenon of towns separating and establishing new villages was not new to the southeastern Indians and actually began earlier in the eighteenth century to accommodate the continued influx of people into Creek country. The settlement of Buzzard Roost was one such place, a satellite community established along the Flint River sometime in the 1760s. The scale and rate at which this occurred at the turn of the nineteenth century, though, was markedly different. In the 1770s William Bartram noted encountering very few farms or plantations outside of the towns. By 1798, however, towns were losing a small but steady stream of families to these outlying settlements (Saunt 1999:159). Eventually Creek settlement patterns came to resemble those of frontier whites but may not have necessarily resulted in a breakdown of the matrilineal kinship ties that were the basis of Creek social organization (Ethridge 2003:172–174).

The community of Upatoi, a daughter village of Kasita that was situated along a creek of the same name, provides one documented example of a group that separated from Kasita to accommodate livestock and agricultural production (Elliot et al. 1996; Ethridge 2003:170–174). Hawkins visited this community and described its members as "the best characters of any among the Lower Creeks" (Hawkins 1980:311). He was especially impressed by the requirements of the village headman, Tussekia Mico, that people living there fence all of their fields. Tussekia Mico was also an open supporter of the U.S. civilization plan and eagerly accepted Hawkins's offers to provide plows and spinning wheels for his community. Hawkins did not comment directly on the kinds of houses these individuals lived in, but does appear to have been generally impressed with the overall appearance of the community. Consequently, Upatoi is one of the few documented Lower Creek villages believed to have been identified archaeologically. Approximately 31 sites situated along Upatoi Creek and its smaller tributaries have been identified, each of which is assumed to represent separate single- or multiple-family households (Elliot et al. 1996).

Based on Hawkins's descriptions of Kasita and its surrounding villages, one gets the impression that while the branch settlements were more receptive to Euro-American influences, those still residing in the primary parent communities were not. Hawkins wrote in 1799 that none of the fields had fences surrounding them, only the potato gardens, which were presumably individual household garden plots. In another instance he stated that "the Cussetuhs have some cattle, horses, and hogs: but they prefer roving idly through the woods and down on the frontiers, to attending to farming or stock raising" (Swanton 1998:224). Adam Hodgson (1824), a missionary who visited Kasita in 1820, described a setting not much different from that seen by Hawkins: "The women were hard at work, digging the ground, pounding Indian corn, or carrying heavy loads of water from the river; the men were either out to the woods with their guns or lying idle before their doors" (Swanton 1998:224). These accounts are interesting, because they provide some evidence that the gender roles and economic responsibilities that defined social relations among the historic Creeks were still alive within the large core communities well into the early nineteenth century.

Hawkins also observed and documented this phenomenon at the Upper Creek town of Hoithlewaulee on the Tallapoosa River. Some members of this community had acquired a significant amount of property in the form of livestock and recognized the problems of maintaining their property. The majority of these animals were kept opposite the town on the other side of the river near the town's communal agricultural fields. Unable to keep their property from being taken, "the town eventually divided against itself; the idlers and ill-disposed remained in town, and the others moved over the river and fenced their fields" (Hawkins 1980:294). By the first decade of the nineteenth century the number of people in Creek country purchasing locks from traders and the U.S. Factory agent increased significantly, evidenced by the number of single and double bolt padlocks requested by Creek leaders between 1800 and 1810 (Saunt 1999:177). A certain subset of Muskogee-speaking Creeks, mainly mestizo traders and some town headmen, were requesting locks to secure their property as early as the late 1780s. At the time of his death in 1787 trader Charles McLatchy had on hand at his store in Apalache nine dozen padlocks and the paired hinges needed to install lockable doors (Saunt 1999: 176–177).

## Written Accounts and Illustrations of Creek Domestic Structures

Caleb Swan's (1855:692–693) description of dwellings he observed while traveling through Creek towns in 1791 is consistent with wattle-and-daub habitations. These structures had earthen floors and ranged from 12 to 20 ft on one side and 10 to 15 ft on the other, with walls 6 to 8 ft high made of vertical poles that were driven into the ground, had cane tied to them, and then were daubed with clay on the interior and exterior. The structures had pitched or gabled roofs supported by rafters and a central ridge pole with four to five layers of shingles and joints fastened with withes. He also mentions exterior chimneys made of poles and clay that rested on one of the gabled ends of the house. With the exception of the clay and pole chimney, Swan's description of Creek houses is very similar to the earlier accounts of Bartram and others who traveled through Creek country (Mereness 1916; Waselkov and Braund 1995).

One of the most often reproduced illustrations of a Creek Indian log cabin

10.2. "The Creek House in its best state of Improvement in 1790" (from the National Anthropological Archives, Smithsonian Institution [1169-A]. By permission).

was drawn by an artist named J. C. Tidball and published in a volume edited by Henry R. Schoolcraft (1855) titled "The Creek House in its best State of Improvement in 1790" (Figure 10.2). Cowie (2001:22) has most recently drawn attention to the fact that Swanton (1946:Plate 58) reprinted this lithograph and inappropriately attributed it to the reports of Caleb Swan. The lithograph was actually referred to by Schoolcraft in the same volume that reproduced Swan's reports of his journey through Creek country. I assume that the illustration was based on information collected by Schoolcraft from several different sources. This structure is obviously of horizontal log pole construction with a pitched roof and gabled ends, an exterior chimney, and a window, which does not appear to have glass in it. There is no indication that this structure sat on stone piers.

While traveling through Creek country in 1820, Adam Hodgson, a missionary, described the dwellings he saw while passing through the town of Kasita: "It appeared to consist of about 100 houses, many of them elevated on poles from two to six feet high, and built of unhewn logs, with roofs of bark, and little patches of Indian corn before the doors" (Hodgson 1824; Swanton 1998:224). The dwellings described by Hodgson appear to have been of horizontal log pole construction. Most likely the elevated structures were storage facilities. Unfortunately, Hodgson does not mention whether or not these houses had exterior chimneys or simple smoke holes in their roofs.

A sketch made in 1828 by Basil Hall shows a house of horizontal log pole

10.3. Basil Hall's 1829 sketch of a Creek Indian house on the Chattahoochee River (courtesy of the Lilly Library, Indiana University, Bloomington).

construction with an attached veranda or porch (Figure 10.3). This structure appears to rest directly on the ground and probably had a dirt floor. In the foreground is what appears to be a corn crib, also made of horizontal log pole construction, but elevated on six individually set vertical posts. On the left side of the picture there is what appears to be some form of ephemeral arborlike structure. There is no indication that the house had hinged windows or doors. Most likely though, windows and doors would have opened inward to allow operation from inside and may not have been visible when this sketch was made. The logs of both the dwelling and corn-crib appear to be unhewn, and it is assumed that the spaces between logs were packed with daub.

Polhemus (1975) noted the potential difficulty of identifying log cabins archaeologically in an earlier study of changes in Cherokee architecture during this time frame, based on various historical accounts and archaeological data. He cites one account of potential relevance to the present study left by a man named William Lewis who visited the Cherokee in 1776. This structure was built by first sinking four corner posts that were used as braces for unnotched horizontal wall poles. "Reeds" were used to make mats that were placed between the horizontal timbers and then covered with mud or clay on the interior (Polhemus 1975:150–151).

## Archaeological Data

One obstacle to studying variation in Creek domestic architecture during this time period archaeologically is that certain kinds of architecture do not leave sufficient material remains behind to identify what a building was made of, or how. For example, log homes do not require the excavation of postholes or foundations. The walls of these structures could have been built over simple wood sills or rested directly on the ground surface, which would leave no observable subsurface features that could be identified archaeologically. It might be possible, though, to detect drip lines through careful hand excavations as well as pathways or entryways into homes from differentially compacted soils. Probably the most conspicuous feature that might be encountered is an area of fire-hardened clay or earth left by a fireplace. Swan's description of a single set vertical post structure, mentioned above, would potentially leave an interesting archaeological signature of a rectangular pattern of post molds with a fire-hardened area at one end.

The presence of nails, "window glass," and burned clay or daub at a site must be interpreted critically for several reasons. Clear flat glass from Creek sites of this period is usually identified as window glass. The problem is that trade mirrors (also referred to as looking glasses) were still relatively common items among the Creeks in the late eighteenth and early nineteenth centuries. Mirrors can sometimes be identified from their rounded-off corners and beveled edges, but these may not be present on fragments of mirrors. The reflective agent used to make mirrors at this time is probably the best identifying characteristic but seems to have readily worn off once in the ground. A partial trade mirror, rectangular in shape, found in domestic contexts (a large trash-filled pit) at Kasita has only a small amount of the reflective agent remaining on its surface. Very few reports mention the presence or absence of any of these attributes on flat glass from historic Creek sites.

Burned clay or daub does not necessarily mean structures were of wattle-and-daub construction. Log cabins also require the use of clay "chinking" to fill in the spaces or gaps between logs, as seen in a photograph of a Cherokee log cabin in North Carolina dated 1888 (Figure 10.4). Differentiating between daub and chinking requires large pieces to be found with either split cane impressions or wide and deep concave impressions that would indicate the clay was pushed between two horizontally laid poles.

Finally, it is especially difficult to determine whether or not the nails recov-

10.4. Photograph of a Cherokee log cabin in North Carolina dated 1888 (from the National Anthropological Archives, Smithsonian Institution [1000-A]. By permission).

ered from Creek sites were used as fasteners in constructing log cabins. The single-pen log cabins shown in Figures 10.2 and 10.5 did not require the use of nails as fasteners. Documentary and historical research by Groover and Brooks (2003) on the material characteristics of Euro-American cow pen sites in western South Carolina has shown that dwellings were sometimes constructed without the use of nails. They provide one late eighteenth-century account describing a timber-framed house with wattle-and-daub walls where nails were used only to hold the boards of the structure's door together (Groover and Brooks 2003:96–97). It is possible that some Creeks were selectively using nails as fasteners in a similar manner. Most likely the ends of nails used to fasten metal hinges to shutters would have been bent to prevent injury and/or to increase their holding strength. In some cases it may be possible to identify facets on the head of a nail produced when it was driven into wood with a hammer. Wagner (1998:146) recognized that a small number of hand-wrought nails found during limited testing at Yuchi town (1RU63) (Hargrave 1998) were probably used as fasteners because of the presence of these facets on the heads of nails.

Architectural hardware in the form of hinges, locks, and door latches is more easily associated with standing structures. We do know from documentary evidence that by the end of the 1790s the number of large padlocks traded or purchased by the Creeks increased significantly (Saunt 1999:176–177). Several have been found at Creek sites dating to this time frame, but not in contexts that clearly associate them with a Creek structure. One problem is that the "ferrous lumps" found on Creek sites are usually only afforded attention if they resemble gun parts. Determining whether or not these objects could in fact be architectural hardware could prove crucial to understanding the transition from single post wattle-and-daub structures to log cabins or other architectural styles among the Creeks.

Domestic structures identified at Upper and Lower Creek sites dating to the eighteenth century include arbors and summer houses. In contrast to other Southeastern groups, Creek Indians in Georgia and Alabama stopped building winter houses by the beginning of the eighteenth century, a phenomenon that Waselkov (1994; Waselkov et al. 1990) has attributed to the impact of the deerskin trade (Hally 2002; Sheldon 1997). Summer houses are identifiable as rectangular patterns of post molds with interior burials and squared storage pits. At Fusihatchee the average area of space enclosed by these rectangular structures is 3.7 by 6.9 m (12.1 by 22.6 ft). At both Upper and Lower Creek sites, burials occur almost exclusively in the floors of dwellings as do the rectangular pits just mentioned. Sheldon (1997) noted the presence of these morphologically distinct features within 28 of 48 summer houses at Fusihatchee. This same pattern was encountered by Gordon Willey at Kasita in 1938 (Figure 10.5) and again in the course of investigations at the site by Panamerican Consultants, Inc., in 2001 (Lewis 2002; Scott 2004). These structures appear to have had wattle-and-daub walls with pitched roofs.

Rectangular features larger than the squared storage pits found in the floors of summer houses have been identified by a number of archaeologists as probable root cellars (Cowie 2001; Ledbetter 1997, 2002). In some cases these features have been found in association with clusters of posts, suggesting they were probably dug into the floor of a built storage facility. In those instances where these features were not associated with posts, the assumption is that the storage building was of horizontal log pole construction (Ledbetter 2002).

Sites that produce significant amounts of European manufactured ceramics, primarily pearlware, and traditional Creek pottery in association with small

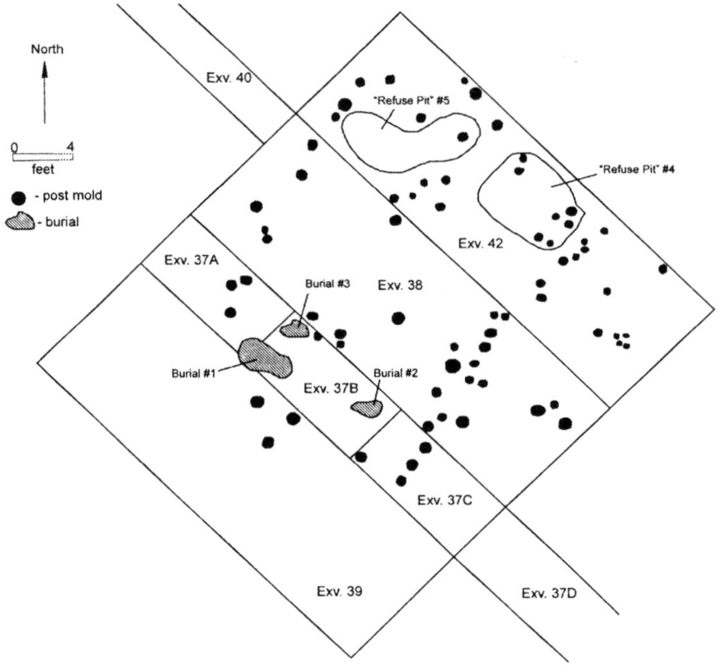


10.5. Plan view map of structure excavated by Gordon Willey at Kasita (9CE1) in 1938 (adapted from Lewis 2002, reproduced courtesy of C. T. Lewis, III).

numbers of architecture- and furniture-related objects are usually interpreted to have been settlements where a family lived in a log-cabin-like structure. Generally, very few subsurface features are found and post molds are almost nonexistent. In the case of one such early nineteenth-century site in central Alabama (1MC120), Waselkov (1984:15–18) was able to confirm the past existence of a Creek farmstead using federal land survey field notes from an 1832 census of Tukabatchee that identified one male head of household, a second adult male, and one adult Creek female. In this particular case investigators were able to mechanically strip the site to identify any subsurface features not detected by limited hand excavations, but none were found.

Excavations in 2001 at the Lawson Field site (9CE1), the confirmed location of Kasita, uncovered nearly 40,000 m$^2$ and identified several probable dwelling locations, in some cases associated with larger household feature clusters. The first of these was a single-post structure encountered in the central part of the project area. It was associated with a number of other feature types representing activity areas of the dwelling's occupants (Figure 10.6). Euro-

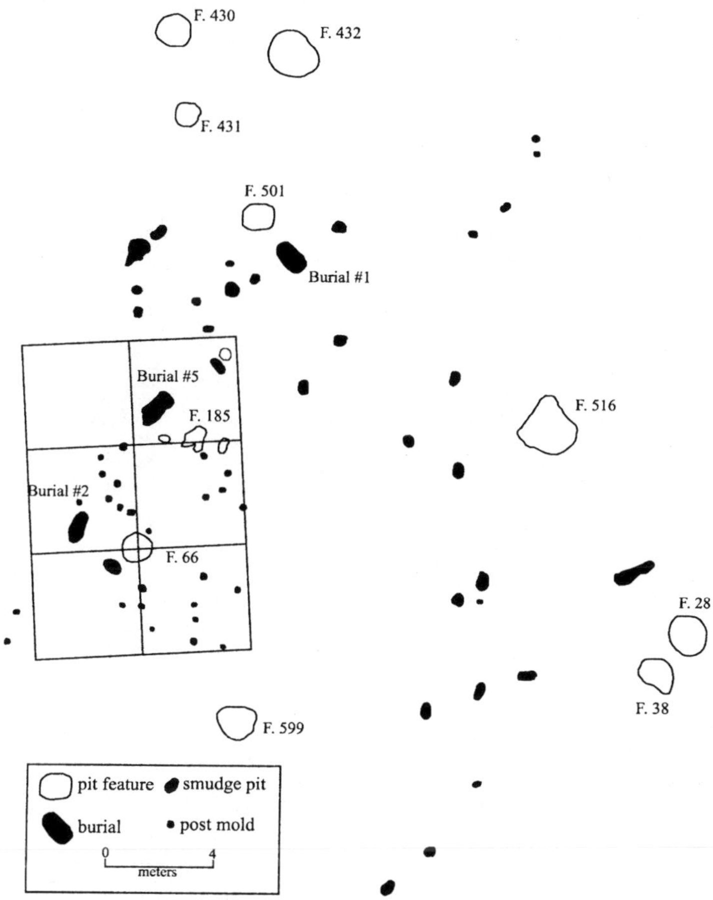


10.6. Plan view of single post structure and associated features at Kasita.

American manufactured ceramics, liquor bottles, and glass beads indicate an occupation date from the 1770s to mid-1780s. Test units excavated directly over this structure produced two clinched hand-wrought nails and a pintle-hinge (Scott 2004). There is no doubt that this was in fact a summer house similar to that described above, but it may potentially have had a window or door similar to those on a Houma Indian wattle-and-daub house photographed in 1900 (Figure 10.7). It is also interesting to note that the windows on this house are simple wooden shutters without glass.

A second feature cluster, located to the west of Household Cluster 1, was tentatively identified as the location of another residence at Kasita. This is

10.7. Photograph of a Houma Indian wattle-and-daub house dated 1900 (from Swanton 1911:Plate 13) (courtesy of the National Anthropological Archives, Smithsonian Institution).

based on the single rectangular pit and the clustering of feature types in this area (Figure 10.8). Two pearlware sherds were recovered from this feature, and a prismatic gunflint was found in a "borrow pit" within its immediate vicinity, indicating that these features date to the 1790s. The absence of posts around the squared storage feature suggests that a horizontal log pole structure may have once stood here. Post molds cluster to the south of the projected house, possibly representing a smaller ephemeral structure as shown in Basil Hall's 1828 sketch (Figure 10.3). Complete hand-wrought nails recovered from features in this area may or may not have been used as fasteners. Small sherds of clear flat glass were collected in very small quantities (Scott 2004). Although the available data fall short of conclusive, the presence of horizontal log pole structure within a Lower Creek town suggests this form of architecture was accepted or allowed within communities that were less receptive to U.S. Indian policy.

Investigations at two sites near the Flint River in southwest Georgia (9TR41 and 9TR54) considered to represent part of the community of Buzzard Roost by Southeastern Archaeological Services encountered important architectural

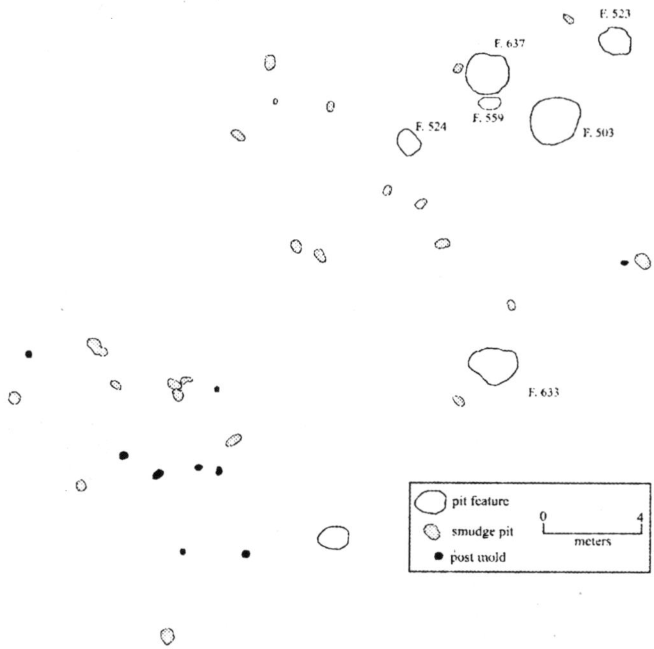


10.8. Plan view of features surrounding the hypothesized location of a horizontal log pole structure or structures at Kasita.

information on a daughter community of Kasita that was probably established to relieve the town's growing population. Mechanical stripping at one of these sites (9TR41) uncovered three discrete clusters of features, two of which were interpreted to be probable domestic structures that represented a mid to late eighteenth-century occupation (Ledbetter 2002:73). Structure 1 was identified by a rectangular arrangement of 41 post molds associated with five smaller pits (Figure 10.9). An attached outbuilding or veranda was also identified from another rectangular pattern of posts that extended from the western side of the primary structure. The second structure also consisted of a rectangular arrangement of irregularly spaced posts and additional posts on the interior. A large rectangular pit was excavated in the west half of the structure. Few nonaboriginal architecture-related artifacts were found, consisting only of a single piece of clear flat glass and one hand-wrought nail.

A second site (9TR54) located approximately 30 m west of 9TR41, encountered features in spatial arrangements different from those recorded at first (Figure 10.9). Large ovate and rectangular pits and a very small number of

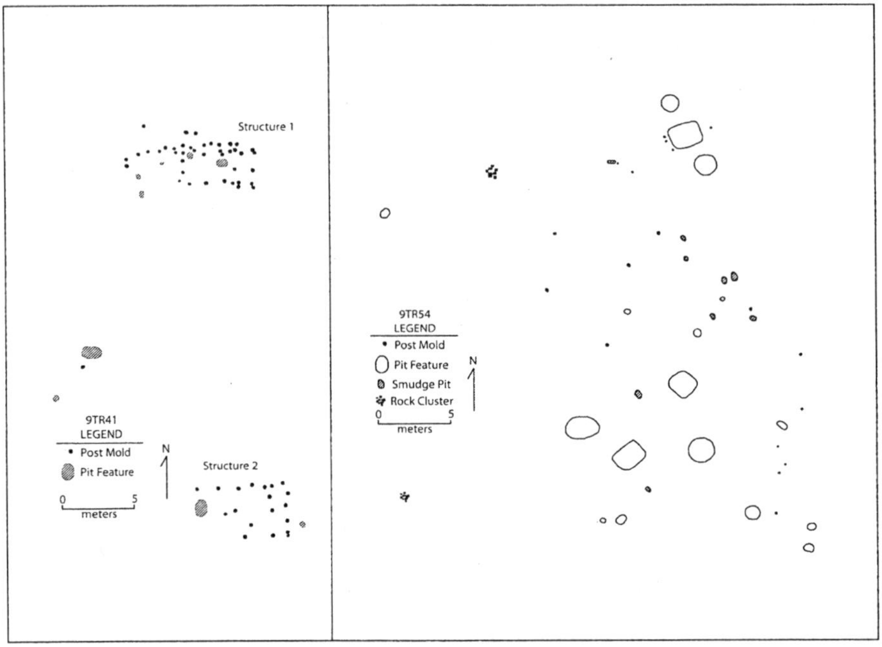


10.9. Maps of excavated features at 9TR41 (left) and 9TR54 (right) (adapted from Ledbetter 2002:74, 99, Figure 39, 62 respectively).

post molds occurred in distinct clusters. The three rectangular pits excavated at 3TR54 average 2 by 2 m. These features occurred in only two areas of the site. The first consisted of a single rectangular pit flanked on two sides by two basically round pits and three posts. Ledbetter (2002:127) noted the similarity of this feature and its associated posts to a root cellar excavated at the Victory Drive site near Columbus, Georgia, which dates to the early nineteenth century. He argued that this cluster of features represents some elements of domestic architecture, citing specifically the similarity of the rectangular pit to root cellars excavated at other early nineteenth-century Creek and Cherokee sites. The small number of posts suggests some other architectural form that did not require a large number of deeply sunken posts, one presumably of horizontal log and notch construction (Ledbetter 2002:110).

A second feature cluster at 9TR54 included two other rectangular features with dimensions similar to that excavated in the north portion of the site. Ledbetter also identified these features as probable structure locations based on the density of Creek pottery and diversity of nonaboriginal artifacts. No posts were identified in the vicinity of these rectangular features, suggesting any standing structure in this area probably would have been log-cabin-like.

A total of six hand-wrought nails and four pieces of clear flat glass were collected from features at 9TR54. One of these nails was bent at a 90-degree angle, indicating it could have been used as a fastener. The fragments of glass were too small to be identified as window glass, mirror fragments, or from a flat-sided container (Ledbetter 2002:200).

Limited test excavations carried out by Southern Research at three sites associated with the original location of Upatoi, the daughter village of Kasita established by Creeks receptive to the government's civilization plan, produced some data on the kinds of houses and other facilities built by these people. Sufficient evidence for a wattle-and-daub structure was found at only one of these sites, in the form of a series of post molds associated with a burial and interior storage pit. Although post molds were encountered at the other two sites, they were rare. The recovery of moderate amounts of Creek pottery, European manufactured ceramics, and architecture-related artifacts led the excavators to believe that horizontal log pole structures were present at both sites (Elliot et al. 1996:259). Considering the limited amount of excavation that was done at each of these three sites, it would appear that Euro-American style log cabins were not necessarily associated with social and economic changes sponsored by the U.S. civilization plan. This conclusion, though, requires taking Hawkins's comments about the people of Upatoi at face value.

Excavations at the Ochille Creek site (9CE379), a strictly early nineteenth-century Creek farmstead located on an unnamed tributary of Ochille Creek, identified what Cowie (2001:116–121) has argued represents the "Square Ground Plan" described by Bartram (Waselkov and Braund 1995:180–181). The square ground plan actually refers to the division of space use implied by Bartram's description of the function and positioning of different structures within a Creek household compound. In this particular instance, there is evidence that both log cabins and wattle-and-daub vertical post structures were used at the site contemporaneously.

Cowie (2001) identified two structure locations from posts uncovered in two separate but adjacent areas (the southern and western portions) of the site. The post mold cluster encountered in the western part of the site was argued to represent the remains of an open-air summer house based on the absence of architectural artifacts in a single 2 by 2 m test unit excavated in that area of the site. Associated with the southern post mold cluster was a large rectangular pit filled with a significant amount of charred maize that Cowie argued is a probable root cellar and represents what is left of a corn-crib or generalized food storage facility. The recovery of 137.1 g of burned clay and a relatively high percentage of kitchen-related artifacts from a test unit in the site's eastern portion were considered enough to indicate a wattle-and-daub winter house or kitchen. No posts or other subsurface features were identified in this vicinity. A log-cabin-like structure was hypothesized for the north edge of the site, based on the absence of posts and a relatively high percentage of architecture-related artifacts such as window glass and nails.

Given the limited area of the site investigated, the spatial distribution of Euro-American manufactured artifacts, Creek pottery, and food remains is consistent with the household use of space implied by Bartram's description of Creek houses. The identification of activity areas at the Ochille Creek site in this spatial configuration could be argued to reflect continuity in those cultural traditions enacted and maintained through the daily practice of various household activities. This would suggest then that changes in domestic architecture at the turn of the century do not necessarily reflect dramatic cultural and/or social transformations in all Lower Creek communities. The use of both "traditional" buildings and the architecture of Euro-Americans living on the frontier might be looked at as evidence of "creolization" in this aspect of Lower Creek material culture.

Limited investigations at a second site (1RU135) contemporaneous with Ochille Creek, situated on the west bank of the Chattahoochee River just north of the mouth of Uchee Creek, in Russell County, Alabama, failed to identify similar artifact patterning (Epenshade 1992). Four 2 by 2 m test units and earlier machine striping at 1RU135 failed to uncover any subsurface features other than a single post mold. Architecture-related artifacts consisted of two cut nails, two unidentified square nails, and a single fragment of clear flat glass identified by the investigators as window glass. Pearlware comprised a significant percentage of the artifact assemblage, making up one-third of the combined total of Euro-Americana and Creek pottery. The types of pearlware represented, and the occurrence of creamware as a minor constituent of the assemblage, led the investigators to assign an occupation span between 1810 and 1825 (Epenshade 1992:29). Again, given the limited area of the site investigated, interpretations of the kind of structure(s) that stood at this location are tentative and subject to revision. The near absence of posts is one indication that a dwelling was probably of horizontal log and pole construction.

## Summary

Historical accounts of Creek dwellings up to 1790 do not make specific references to any European or American architectural features or materials such as windows, nails, metal hinges on doors, locks, or chimneys that were selectively incorporated into the traditional wattle-and-daub domestic structures of the Lower Creeks. The accounts of Adam Hodgson and Benjamin Hawkins suggest that the people living in Kasita were not receptive to the U.S. government's attempts to make them more like frontier whites. It was hypothesized that resistance to the U.S. civilization plan may have been reflected in the retention of traditional architectural patterns in the larger towns. The possibility of a horizontal log pole structure at Kasita would seem to contradict the idea that those still residing in the core towns were more conservative, maintaining earlier cultural practices and traditional modes of domestic architecture. The occurrence of wattle-and-daub vertical post structures at Creek farmsteads dating after 1790 indicates that there was not necessarily an abandonment of this form of architecture by all Creeks who moved away from the large towns. There is also an indication that things like windows and doors were being selectively incorporated into "traditional" house forms by the 1770s and 1780s.

Variation in domestic architecture during this time frame might be looked at partially as the result of settlement dispersion. As Waselkov (1997:190–191) has discussed, such a dramatic shift in settlement patterns in conjunction with a growing reliance on the external market economy could have led to the increased economic autonomy of individual families. If the construction of dwellings had been a group activity (people of the same community who shared cultural models about how to build a house and what one should look like) but became a task for individual families performed on their own, we might expect to see more idiosyncratic variation in domestic architecture.

Wilk's (1990) study of changes in the domestic architecture of the Kekchi Maya of southern Belize provides a potentially interesting, though geographically and temporally removed, parallel or point of comparison to changes in historic Creek architecture at the turn of the nineteenth century. With the introduction of cash cropping and wage labor into Kekchi communities there was a significant weakening in group equality and cohesion. The source of income offered by cash cropping and wage labor, outside of the communal work put into agriculture for subsistence, meant that families no longer had to have the cooperation or approval of the community and neighbors and could walk away from community consumption standards. Without the help of the community in the construction of homes, families turned to nontraditional building materials that required less labor or effort in construction. Using boards or metal roofing became a symbol of rejection on the part of the village and symbolized the owner's independence (Wilk 1990:38).

Obviously, the materials from which frontier whites and Creeks made their homes were not significantly different, and one kind was probably not that much more difficult to make than the other. The similarity lies in the fact that an introduction of nontraditional materials and design appeared as a result of a family's separation from the consumption standards of their community. The outside market provided the income needed to make such a decision and a means outside of communal subsistence production to support a household, whatever its composition. To even consider this as a viable potential explanation for change in Creek domestic architecture, though, requires the assumption that there was a significant breakdown in communal labor, not only in food production but also in other group activities such as house construction. In the case of the historic Creek this would have meant a weakening in the authority or influence of matrilineages in household production and consumption, which is assumed in the notion that the dispersion in settlement patterns caused by the need to accommodate livestock led to the establishment of patriarchal households (Saunt 1999:159).

Ethridge (2003:173) has argued, though, that settlement dispersion alone could not have resulted in a loss of matrilineal ties. Late prehistoric societies that would later come together after multiple traumatic events to become the historic Creeks, Chickasaw, Cherokee, and Choctaw changed settlement strategies in a cycle that began with the emergence of the first chiefdoms in the Southeast. Increases in the size of communities would have required the fissioning and establishment of new daughter or satellite settlements. Even though in this case a shift in settlement patterns was required for Creek families to accommodate livestock, this was not a change in cultural practice among the Creeks and alone cannot be considered responsible or used as evidence for a breakdown in communal labor or matrilocal control of "household" production and consumption.

Ultimately, though, the adoption of the log cabin as the primary structure type for dwellings may not have required much negotiation in shared cultural models of what domestic architecture should look like. With the exception of timbers being laid horizontally instead of set vertically in the ground, there were probably very few differences in form and probably no real differences in the materials used to build a house. Trees and clay were available to everyone; the plants used to make rope were accessible to everyone. Creek houses most certainly had dirt floors, and the logs the houses were made of were unhewn. The elements of frontier Euro-American architecture that were new included the presence of windows and doors with hinges, the use of nails as fasteners, and external chimneys. Hinged windows and doors could have been installed without any metal hardware or nails used as fasteners. The adoption of horizontal log and notch construction may simply represent people manipulating cultural practices that were visible to frontier whites while maintaining their traditional use of space and material culture out of sight.

## Acknowledgments

I owe a special thanks to Marvin D. Jeter and Ian W. Brown for their suggestions regarding the content and style of this chapter and to Cameron H. Lacquement for inviting me to be part of the SEAC symposium that spawned publication of this work. My family kindly provided the money needed to pay for permission to use a number of the figures presented in this chapter and to them I am extremely grateful. I take full responsibility for any errors or misrepresentation of other research presented and/or cited herein.

# 11
# Conclusions

## Taking Architecture Seriously

*Vernon J. Knight, Jr.*

I would like to comment briefly on some of the prospects for the study of indigenous late prehistoric and early historic architecture in the Eastern Woodlands. The chapters in this volume point to several subject areas that beg for further investigation.

It is difficult to know how many late-period structure foundations have been excavated archaeologically and are on record for the Eastern Woodlands. A very rough estimate is that the number is above 4,000, perhaps somewhere between that and 5,000. Whatever the actual number, the point is that there is a large available sample, accumulated over more than seven decades.

With such a large documented sample and such a long history of investigations of such structures, one might reason:

that basic typology and traditions of domestic housing would be well worked out and their geography over time would be a matter of record.

that enough would be known of the above-ground correlates of below-ground features to understand the distinctive signatures of different types.

that this information would be understood at a basic level by those who would convey it to the public via illustrations, dioramas, and living history exhibits.

that sharedness of formal designs of domestic housing across geographic space would be a common index of the relatedness and interaction of peoples, in the same manner that pottery is often used.

that most excavators would be familiar enough with the applicable range of pole frame architecture to know what to look for and what to record in the field.

Unfortunately, one could easily argue that none of this is the case. Why is this so? While there are no doubt many reasons, the following come to mind.

First, it strikes me that we might be lulled by received terminology into thinking that the main problems already have been solved, or that any empirical differences we might find consist of minor variations on known themes. But as it turns out, some of our common terminology is misleading. For example, it is still routinely taught that Mississippian houses were of "wattle-and-daub" construction. This term arbitrarily emphasizes specific aspects of wall construction (as opposed to floor plan, roof form, roof covering, and so on) as the diagnostic feature. Many have learned to envision this "wattle" as small-diameter, horizontal lathwork woven among closely spaced vertical poles, and to envision the daub as tempered clay packed around this lathwork to form a smooth, bare wall. With this terminology so firmly entrenched, it might come as a big surprise that most of the excavated structures at large Mississippian centers like Cahokia and Moundville never had any daub applied to their walls. It might also be surprising to many to learn that wall daub bearing structural impressions conforming to the imagined stereotype—and here I have in mind Glenn Black's often reproduced cutaway drawing depicting a wattle-and daub-house (Figure 1.4 this volume)—is extraordinarily rare if it exists at all. The term "wattle" is by itself potentially misleading in its implication of interlacing where there might be none, a situation made worse by the peculiar substitution of that word for daub by some of our best authorities.

Another factor perhaps inhibiting our understanding of the subject is that complete excavation of structures has become much less common in recent years than it used to be. Preservation concerns, and the high cost of broad horizontal exposure in excavations, are no doubt responsible for this. As a result, comparative work has come to depend on examination of older, often sketchy excavation records, and fewer archaeologists have much first-hand experience in excavating and interpreting structural remains. Fewer still are called upon to place their finds in a macroregional perspective.

Finally, in general, our colleagues have gotten away from broad-scale comparative studies of material culture of the kind that might reveal the geography of housing traditions. This trend, I think, is to our detriment.

The negative assessment presented thus far has its silver lining, however, which is that the whole subject seems open for fresh ideas and new initiatives. We seem poised for significant steps forward in how we understand indigenous housing in eastern North America. The chapters in this volume can serve as guideposts in one important respect. They take architecture seriously. These authors want to understand what cultural models governed the design of structures, how they were built, how much effort went into building them, what they were made of, how durable they were, what the walls and roofs really looked like, and how well these buildings kept out the elements. They want to understand what the interior spaces were like, and how these spaces were used in the context of domestic units and larger communities.

How do we take architecture more seriously? From what I have already said, we might begin by agreeing on less prejudicial terminology, rather than "wattle-and-daub," "pole and thatch," or other terms with imbedded assumptions in the absence of proof. Beyond this, it seems to me that we can improve our mastery of at least three areas: field observation, experimental archaeology, and use of ethnographic analogy.

## Field Observation

Almost all late-period architecture in the Eastern Woodlands was framed using vertical poles set in the ground, leaving collections of postholes as a ubiquitous form of evidence. Given this circumstance, it is sometimes amazing what passes for "houses" in archaeological reporting. It seems obvious that given any random shotgun-blast pattern of sufficiently numerous postholes, it will always be possible (and tempting) to read-in structures, often long after the fieldwork is concluded, where structures may or may not exist. Also, using a subjective and often post hoc connect-the-dot method, the desire to conjure buildings out of posthole scatters too often results in crazily misshapen and asymmetrical wall lines and internal "roof support" posts that make no sense as planned, weight-bearing units. But historical records make it abundantly clear that indigenous peoples did not build their houses that way. Wall lines were regular, posts were evenly spaced, roof supports were symmetrical, and angles were roughly true. It follows that problems of interpretation, like that of obvious houses that are missing one or more wall lines (e.g., Figure 4.5 Type IV this volume), or houses that are lacking regular wall lines altogether (e.g., Figure 4.5 Type V this volume), are problems of field observation, not the sobriety of the original builders.

A fairly obvious antidote is for excavators to become more cognizant of the above-ground structural requirements of buildings within known indigenous architectural traditions. For example, in separate roof components without internal roof bracing there are span limitations. In flexed pole arrangements there are bending limitations for posts of a given diameter. The presence or absence of corner posts in rectilinear floor plans means something. And posts can be used for bracing during construction and can be removed later upon the structure's completion. In short, the excavation of any structure should hardly proceed without one or more working hypotheses about that structure's framing principles and probable above-ground appearance. Any resulting puzzles, such as oddly aligned components, missing wall posts, or missing roof supports, should be resolved while still in the field, when there is still a chance to reconcile the field observations with a plausible architectural model. Where structures were rebuilt in place or where extraneous posts complicate interpretation, careful and systematic attention to posthole depth, size, fill characteristics, and intrusion sequences often reveals which sets of posts go together. Where necessary structural components really are found to be missing, post-occupational site formation processes may be to blame, but evidence for any such disturbances must be recorded as well.

There will always be intractable palimpsests of dense postholes, but even for these sets there is interest in developing mathematical procedures that discern trends of spacing or alignment, and allow postholes meeting specified conditions to be factored out of the set.

## Experimental Archaeology

Despite outward appearances, there really has been a considerable amount of experimental archaeology directed toward late prehistoric architecture of the Eastern Woodlands. To date these studies, however, are scattered and largely unpublished. One contribution of this volume is to bring together much of that bibliography for the first time. Several such studies are reported or referenced within these pages.

The most useful experimental replication of architecture has to do not merely with creating a plausible above-ground structure for exhibit purposes or living history. Rather, as in the work reported by Reed, Lacquement, Blanton, and Gresham herein, such studies are designed to test alternative framing and covering solutions, alternative construction materials, quantification of effort, and archaeological signatures. Such experiments can and should be modified in their course, to yield to unexpected successes and failures in each component. Above all, to be of value such studies have to be published.

As Blanton, Gresham, and Brennan suggest in their chapters, one need not reconstruct an entire building to get answers to specific questions about alternative solutions. Experiments with lathwork, daubing, roof covering, rafter and wall stresses, insulation value, and so forth can be done much less expensively as stand-alone experiments. Lacquement's (2004) wood bending experiments controlling for species and different base diameters are of this type.

## Ethnographic Analogy

For the Eastern Woodlands we are fortunate to have descriptions of indigenous domestic architecture by such careful observers as Le Page du Pratz for the Natchez (Swanton 1911:59–60) and James Adair for the Chickasaw (Adair 2005:448–450). The account by Le Page du Pratz has been used repeatedly as an analogy for flexed pole construction, while that by Adair has been used similarly as an example of rigid pole architecture. It would be of much interest to attempt accurate above-ground reconstructions using either of these detailed eighteenth-century accounts. To my knowledge this has not been done.

As with all ethnographic analogies, however, such descriptions must be applied to archaeological remains with great caution. The specific Natchez house described by Le Page du Pratz may be fairly unusual, even for the Grand Village of the Natchez. The use of long corner poles bent over diagonally to define the roof dome, as described by Le Page du Pratz, does not match any of the excavated archaeological remains of contemporary houses at the Grand Village (Neitzel 1965, 1983), while an independent observer (Charlevoix, in Swanton 1911:59) mentioned that the majority of Natchez houses were not daubed. Similarly, the Chickasaw rigid pole summer house described by Adair may be unusual as well. It had a gable roof with poles at both ends and the center accepting a roof tree, whereas it is clear from late-period archaeological remains of that region that the more common roof form of rigid pole houses was hipped, with four roof supports symmetrically arranged.

Nonetheless, these and other accounts do give us guidance on certain problematic issues. For example, the French accounts of Natchez houses help us understand key aspects of thatched, flexed pole structures. First, it seems probable that in general, flexed pole structures are seldom associated with daub, as without a separate roof component there is no eave to protect the daub from the wash of rain. However, the French accounts confirm that at least some flexed pole houses were daubed, and they tell us how it was done. The daubed wall was covered inside and out with woven cane matting, and moreover, the manner in which the roof thatch is described as cropped suggests that there was at least some overhang protecting the wall below.

Second, the sandwiching of roof thatch between carefully joined cane matting on the exterior and interior of the house answers a second question, that of fireproofing. Without some form of fireproofing, roof thatch is an extraordinarily vulnerable and dangerous building material, as several experiments have shown.

Third, Le Page du Pratz describes a cross-braced horizontal frame that served as a ceiling of rafters below the arch of the roof. This cross-braced frame also would have kept the wall poles from bowing inward as they were bent to form the roof, a key consideration especially if the walls were to receive daub.

## The Question of Flexed vs. Rigid Pole Architecture

An unresolved question that emerges in this volume as a debate, with proponents on both sides of the issue, is that of the distinction between flexed and rigid pole architecture. More specifically, the issue has to do with the correct interpretation of square or rectangular structures in which the wall posts are numerous, closely spaced, and of small diameter, often without corner posts. These traits are interpreted by some as among the signatures of flexed pole structures without a separate roof component. Others argue that additional traits such as wall daub, internal roof supports, and presence of structural woods unsuitable for bending co-occur with small pole construction and instead indicate rigid pole construction with a separate roof component.

This is an old question, and my impression is that it is one of those issues where powerful biases are at play that will have to be overcome in order to reach a consensus. Still, the problem seems eminently solvable. To achieve closure on this point will require a combination of enhanced field documentation of newly excavated structures, focused experimental archaeology, and ethnographic analogy.

There is probably no simple answer to this question. From the available evidence it appears that wall daub was used with a flexed pole technique at least occasionally, probably in conjunction with rainproofing using tightly woven cane matting, as Le Page du Pratz describes. Blanton and Gresham's chapter in this volume explores some of the problems arising from the application of daub to a flexed pole wall. Also, it seems likely that at some times and places in the evolution of domestic architecture in the Eastern Woodlands, separate roof components were used with small pole wall construction. Brennan's chapter in this volume offers a helpful list of potential diagnostics to address the issue.

Such proposed diagnostics no doubt can be refined and added to. For example, a documented trait of some small pole structures from Illinois to Tennessee is a gradation of posthole size along wall lines, with larger and deeper posts near the center grading to smaller and shallower posts at the ends. Such a condition probably points directly to flexed pole construction, where longer-reaching and structurally more important poles are required in the center of a dome-shaped roof. In contrast, such a gradation of wall pole sizes makes little sense in a rigid pole framework, where strength at the corners of the structure is precisely at issue.

I will add a cautionary note about the diagnostic value of central roof support posts in deciding the question in favor of separate roof components. It is well known that some large, rectangular Mississippian buildings incorporated two or three large central posts delineating a ridge pole. A convenient example is William S. Webb's "Trench Wall House Type A′" [A-prime] defined at the Jonathan Creek site in Kentucky (Webb 1952:48–51), a type whose walls were composed of numerous poles of small diameter set in wall trenches. In such cases, the existence of a central ridge pole does not rule out the possibility of a flexed pole framework (see Blanton and Gresham this volume). The fact that ridge poles can be used to good effect in large flexed pole structures is amply attested in the literature on communal houses of the tropical forest tribes of South America, and indeed, much closer to home in summer houses of Eastern Woodlands tribes as illustrated by Reed in this volume.

As a final comment, to those interested in this fundamental debate between flexed pole vs. rigid pole construction, I recommend a close reading of Charles Nash's *Residence Mounds: An Intermediate Middle-Mississippian Settlement Pattern,* published as Occasional Paper No. 2 of the Memphis State University Anthropological Research Center (Nash 1968). Based on excavations at the Link and Slayden sites in Central Tennessee, Nash defined house forms that he felt were both architecturally and chronologically intermediate between classic small-log and large-log types. These "intermediate" houses, which Nash believed were of flexed pole construction, combined small, closely spaced wall posts with wall trenches somewhat wider than the classic "small-log" style, often with closed corners. Walls in these buildings, according to Nash, were associated with massive amounts of daub, which collapsed to form a mounded ring of clay along the wall lines with the destruction of the buildings. Nash was also an early experimenter with house reconstructions of both flexed and rigid pole designs, and photographs documenting the construction of both forms are included in the Memphis State publication.

# References Cited


Aadland, Dan

2000 *Women and Warriors of the Plains: The Pioneer Photography of Julia E. Tuell.* Mountain Press Publishing, Missoula, Montana.

Adair, James A.

2005 [1775] *The History of American Indians: Particularly Those Nations Adjoining to the Mississippi, East and West Florida, Georgia, South and North Carolina, and Virginia,* edited by Kathryn E. Holland Braund. University of Alabama Press, Tuscaloosa.

Alexander, Christopher

1979 *The Timeless Way of Building.* Oxford University Press, New York.

Alexander, Christopher, Sara Ishikawa, and Murray Silverstein

1977 *A Pattern Language.* Oxford University Press, New York.

Andersen, Kaj Blegvad

1977 *African Traditional Architecture: A Study of the Housing and Settlement Patterns of Rural Kenya.* Oxford University Press, Nairobi.

Anderson, David G., and Joseph Schuldenrein

1985 *Prehistoric Human Ecology along the Upper Savannah River: Excavations at the Rucker's Bottom, Abbeville, and Bullard Site Groups.* 2 vols. National Park Service, Atlanta.

Beck, Robin A., Jr., and David G. Moore

2002 Burke Phase: A Mississippian Frontier in the North Carolina Foothills. *Southeastern Archaeology* 21(2):192–205.

Bennett, John W.

1940 A Preliminary Study of the Kincaid Component and Its Affiliations. Unpublished master's thesis, Department of Anthropology, University of Chicago.

1944 A Note on Middle Mississippi Architecture. *American Antiquity* 9:333–334.

Biermann, Barrie

1971 Indlu: The Domed Dwelling of the Zulu. In *Shelter in Africa,* edited by P. Oliver, pp. 96–105. Praeger Publishers, New York.

Binford, Lewis R., James Schoenwetter, and Melvin L. Fowler

1964 Archaeological Investigations in the Carlyle Reservoir, Clinton County, Illinois. Archaeological Salvage Report No. 17. Southern Illinois University Museum, Carbondale.

Black, Glenn A.

1944 Angel Site Vanderburgh County Indiana: An Introduction. *Indiana Historical Society* 2(5). Indianapolis.

1967 *Angel Site: An Archaeological, Historical, and Ethnological Study.* 2 vols. Indiana Historical Society, Indianapolis.

Blanton, Dennis B.

n.d. The Experimental Construction of a Mississippian "Small Pole" Structure at Etowah. Unpublished manuscript in possession of the author.

Blitz, John

1980 Variation in Mississippian Structures at Lubbub Creek. Southeastern Archaeological Conference, Bulletin 23, pp. 11–14.

1993 Ancient Chiefdoms of the Tombigbee. University of Alabama Press, Tuscaloosa.

Bradley, Ray S., and P. D. Jones

1993 "Little Ice Age" Summer Temperature Variations: Their Nature and Relevance to Recent Global Warming Trends. *The Holocene* 3:367–376.

Bradley, R. S., and P. D. Jones (editors)

1992 *Climate since A.D. 1500,* pp. 606–622. Routledge, London and New York.

Braund, Kathryn E.

1993 *Deerskins and Duffles: Creek Indian Trade with Anglo-America, 1685–1815.* University of Nebraska Press, Lincoln.

Brennan, Tamira K.

2005 Architectural Variation at the Kincaid Mounds Site. Unpublished master's thesis, Department of Anthropology, Southern Illinois University, Carbondale.

Breyer, Donald E., Kenneth J. Fridley, David G. Pollack, and Kelly E. Cobeen

2003 *Design of Wood Structures ASD.* McGraw-Hill, New York.

Bronk Ramsey, Christopher

2005 OxCal Program version 3.10.

Brown, Ian W.

1983 Plaquemine Culture Houses in the Natchez Bluffs Region, Mississippi: Excavations at the Lookout Site. *Mississippi Archaeology* 18(1):14–26.

1985 Plaquemine Architectural Patterns in the Natchez Bluffs and Surrounding Regions of the Lower Mississippi Valley. *Midcontinental Journal of Archaeology* 10(2):251–305.

Bucko, Raymond A.

1998 *The Lakota Ritual of the Sweat Lodge: History and Contemporary Practice.* University of Nebraska Press, Lincoln.

Bushnell, David I., Jr.

1922 *Villages of the Algonquian, Siouan, and Caddoan Tribes West of the Mississippi.* Bulletin 77. Bureau of American Ethnology, Washington, D.C.

Butler, Brian M.

1991 Kincaid Revisited: The Mississippian Sequence in the Lower Ohio Valley. In *Cahokia and the Hinterlands: Middle Mississippian Cultures of the Midwest,* edited by Thomas J. Emerson and R. Barry Lewis, pp. 264–273. University of Illinois Press, Urbana.

Caldwell, Joseph R.

1967a The House that "X" Built. *The Living Museum* 28(12):92–93.

1967b New Discoveries at Dickson Mounds. *The Living Museum* 29(6): 139–142.

Callahan, Errett H.

1981 Pamunkey Housebuilding: An Experimental Study of Late Woodland Construction Technology in the Powhatan Confederacy. Unpublished Ph.D. dissertation, Catholic University of America, Washington, D.C.

1985 The St. Mary's Longhouse Experiment: The First Season. *Archaeological Society of Virginia Quarterly Bulletin* 40:12–40.

1992 North American House Projects. *Bulletin of Primitive Technology* 3:31–33.

Cheatham, Scooter

1992 Caddo House Reconstruction: Anatomy of a Project. *Bulletin of Primitive Technology* 3:22–24.

Clay, Berle

1997 The Mississippian Succession on the Lower Ohio. *Southeastern Archaeology* 16:16–32.

Cobb, Charles R., and Brian M. Butler

2002 The Vacant Quarter Revisited: Late Mississippian Abandonment of the Lower Ohio Valley. *American Antiquity* 67:625–642.

Cole, Fay-Cooper, Robert Bell, John Bennett, Joseph Caldwell, Norman Emerson, Richard MacNeish, Kenneth Orr, and Roger Willis
1951 *Kincaid: A Prehistoric Illinois Metropolis.* University of Chicago Press, Chicago.
Collins, J. M.
1990 *The Archaeology of the Cahokia Mounds ICT-II: Site Structure.* Illinois Cultural Resources Study No. 10. Illinois Historic Preservation Agency, Springfield.
Conrad, Lawrence A.
1973 The Nature of the Relationship between Cahokia and the Central Illinois River Valley. Paper presented at the 52nd Annual Meeting of the Central States Anthropological Society, St. Louis, March 29–31.
1991 The Middle Mississippian Cultures of the Central Illinois Valley. In *Cahokia and the Hinterland,* edited by Thomas E. Emerson and R. Barry Lewis, pp. 119–156. University of Illinois Press, Urbana.
Conrad, Lawrence A., and Alan D. Harn
1972 The Spoon River Culture in the Central Illinois River Valley. Manuscript on file at Dickson Mounds Museum, Lewistown, Illinois.
Cowie, Sarah
2001 Early Nineteenth-Century Evidence of the Creek Square Ground Plan: Phase II Archaeological Testing and Limited Phase III Data Recovery of the Ochillee Creek Site (9CE379). Report Submitted to Environmental Management Division, Directorate of Public Works, U.S. Army Infantry Center, Fort Benning, Georgia, by Southern Research, Ellerslie, Georgia.
Crane, Verner W.
1956 *The Southern Frontier, 1670–1732.* University of Michigan Press, Ann Arbor.
Crowley, Thomas J.
2000 Causes of Climate Change over the Past 1000 Years. *Science* 289:270–277.
Curl, James Stevens
1992 *Encyclopedia of Architectural Terms.* Donhead, Wimbledon, London.
Curren, Caleb
1984 *The Protohistoric Period in Central Alabama.* Alabama Tombigbee Regional Commission, Camden.
Dalan, Rinita A., George R. Holley, William I. Woods, Harold Watters, Jr., and John A. Koepke
2003 *Envisioning Cahokia: A Landscape Perspective.* Northern Illinois University Press, DeKalb.

Damato, Rick

2002 Antidote for the Ordinary: Thatch by Africa Roofing. *Roofing Contractor.* Electronic document, http://www.roofingcontractor.com/CDA/Archives/d258c64552c58010VgnVCM100000f932a8c0, accessed October 2004.

DeJarnette, David L., and Steve B. Wimberly

1941 The Bessemer Site: Excavation of Three Mounds and Surround Village Areas near Bessemer, Alabama. Museum Paper 17. Geological Survey of Alabama, University of Alabama.

Denyer, Susan

1978 *African Traditional Architecture: A Historical and Geographic Perspective.* Africana Publishing, New York.

Dickens, Roy S.

1976 *Cherokee Prehistory: The Pisgah Phase in the Appalachian Summit Region.* University of Tennessee Press, Knoxville.

Driver, Harold E., and William C. Massey

1957 *Comparative Studies of North American Indians.* Transactions of the American Philosophical Society, Vol. 47, Pt. 2. Lancaster Press, Lancaster, Pennsylvania.

Eifert, Virginia S.

1960 A Tenth-Century Indian Village Is Uncovered. *The Living Museum* 22(7):535.

Elliot, Daniel T., Karen G. Wood, Rita Folse Elliot, and W. Dean Wood

1996 Up on the Upatoi: Cultural Resources Survey and Testing of Compartments K-6 and K-7, Fort Benning Military Reservation, Georgia. Report Submitted to Environmental Management Division, Directorate of Public Works, U.S. Army Infantry Center, Fort Benning, Georgia, by Brockington and Associates, Inc., Norcross, Georgia.

Emmons, Merrill, Pat Munson, and Joseph R. Caldwell

1960 A Prehistoric House from Fulton County, Illinois. *The Living Museum* 22(5):516–517.

Ensor, Blaine

1993 Big Sandy Farms: A Prehistoric Agricultural Community near Moundville, Black Warrior River Floodplain, Tuscaloosa County, Alabama. Alabama Museum of Natural History Office of Archaeological Research, Tuscaloosa.

Epenshade, Christopher

1992 Archaeological Assessment of 1RU135, A Nineteenth-Century Creek Site, Uchee Creek Recreation Area, Fort Benning, Alabama. Report submitted to N.A.F. Procurement Office, Fort Benning, Georgia, by Brockington and Associates, Inc., Norcross, Georgia.

Ethridge, Robbie
2003 *Creek Country: The Creek Indians and Their World.* University of North Carolina Press, Chapel Hill.

Faherty, Keith F., and Thomas G. Williamson
1989 *Wood Engineering and Construction Handbook.* McGraw-Hill, New York.

Federal Alliance for Safe Homes
2004 Strengthening Your Home against High Winds. *Blueprint for Safety News* 1(2). Federal Alliance for Safe Homes, Tallahassee, Florida.

Fenton, William N.
1978 Northern Iroquoian Cultural Patterns. In *Northeast,* edited by Bruce G. Trigger, pp. 296–321. Handbook of North American Indians, Vol. 15, William C. Sturtevant, general editor, Smithsonian Institution, Washington, D.C.

Ford, James A., Philip Phillips, and William G. Haag
1955 *The Jaketown Site in West-Central Mississippi.* Anthropological Papers of the American Museum of Natural History, Vol. 45, Pt. 1. American Museum of Natural History, New York.

Frescura, Franco
1981 *Rural Shelter in Southern Africa.* Ravan Press, Johannesburg.

Fundaburk, Emma L., and Mary D. Foreman
1957 *Sun Circles and Human Hands: The Southeastern Indians Art and Industries.* Emma Lila Fundaburk, Luverne, Alabama.

Futato, Eugene M.
1977 The Bellefonte Site: 1JA300. Office of Archaeological Research, Research Series No. 2. University of Alabama, Tuscaloosa.

Gebremedhin, Naigzy
1971 Some Traditional Types of Housing in Ethiopia. In *Shelter in Africa,* edited by Paul Oliver, pp. 106–123. Praeger, New York.

Gorman, Rebecca A., and Geoffrey Duchenin
2004 Burning Down the House: Site Formation of Pole and Thatch Native Structures through Fire. Paper presented at the 61st Annual Southeastern Archaeological Conference, St. Louis, Missouri.

Gougeon, Ramie A.
2002 *Household Research at the Late Mississippian Little Egypt Site (9MU102).* Unpublished Ph.D. dissertation, Department of Anthropology, University of Georgia, Athens.

Gray, James L., and Dick V. Ferguson
1977 *Soil Survey of Poinsett County, Arkansas.* U.S. Department of Agriculture, Soil Conservation Service.
Gresham, Thomas, and Dan Simpkins
n.d. Excavation of an Experimental Mississippian House Site at Etowah. Unpublished manuscript in possession of the authors.
Groover, Mark D., and Richard D. Brooks
2003 The Catherine Brown Cowpen and Thomas Howell Site: Material Characteristics of Cattle Raisers in the South Carolina Backcountry. *Southeastern Archaeology* 22(1):92–111.
Grove, Jean M.
1988 *The Little Ice Age.* Routledge, London and New York.
Guccione, Margaret J., John D. Horn, Phillip Hays, and Jackson Cothren.
2006 Geomorphology, Stratigraphy, Vegetation, and Paleoseismology of the Tyronza, Arkansas Area and Archaeological Sites 3Po608, 3Po610, and 3CT340/341. In Data recover at the Gilmore site: 3CT40/341, edited by C. Spears. SPEARS report to the Arkansas Highway and Transportation Department.
Guidoni, Enrico
1975 *Primitive Architecture.* Translated by Robert Erich Wolf. Harry N. Adams, New York.
Hahn, Steven C.
2004 *The Invention of the Creek Nation, 1670–1763.* University of Nebraska Press, Lincoln.
Hall, Robert L.
1975 Chronology and Phases at Cahokia. In *Perspectives in Cahokia Archaeology,* pp. 15–31. Illinois Archaeology Survey Bulletin No. 10, Urbana.
Hally, David J.
1970 Archaeological Investigation of the Potts' Tract Site (9-Mu-103), Carter's Dam, Murray County, Georgia. University of Georgia, Laboratory of Archaeology Series, Report No. 6. Athens.
1980 Archaeological Investigation of the Little Egypt Site (9MU102), Murray County, Georgia, 1970–1972 Seasons. Report submitted to the National Park Service, United States Department of the Interior.
1981 Plant Preservation and the Content of Paleobotanical Samples: A Case Study. *American Antiquity* 46:723–742.
1988 Archaeology and Settlement Plan of the King Site. In *The King Site: Continuity and Contact in Sixteenth-Century Georgia,* edited by Robert L. Blakely, pp. 3–16. University of Georgia Press, Athens.
1993 The Territorial Size of Mississippian Chiefdoms. In *Archaeology of*

*Eastern North America: Papers in Honor of Stephen Williams,* edited by James B. Stoltman, pp. 143–168. Archaeological Report No. 25. Mississippi Department of Archives and History, Jackson.

1996 Platform Mound Construction and the Instability of Mississippian Chiefdoms. In *Political Structure and Change in the Prehistoric Southeastern United States,* edited by John F. Scarry, pp. 92–127. University Press of Florida, Gainesville.

2002 As Caves Below Ground: Making Sense of Aboriginal House Form in the Protohistoric and Historic Southeast. In *Between Contacts and Colonies: Archaeological Perspectives on the Protohistoric Southeast,* edited by C. B. Wesson and M. A. Rees, pp. 90–109. University of Alabama Press, Tuscaloosa.

2006 The Nature of Mississippian Regional Systems. In *Light on the Path,* edited by Thomas J. Pluckhahn and Robbie Ethridge, pp. 26–42. University of Alabama Press, Tuscaloosa.

Hally, David J. (editor)

1994 *Ocmulgee Archaeology, 1936–1986.* University of Georgia Press, Athens.

Hally, David J., and Hypatia Kelly

1998 The Nature of Mississippian Towns in Georgia. In *Mississippian Towns and Sacred Spaces: Searching for an Architectural Grammar,* edited by R. Barry Lewis and Charles Stout, pp. 49–63. University of Alabama Press, Tuscaloosa.

Hargrave, Michael L.

1983 Mississippian Wall Trench Structures and Settlement Organization. In *The Bridges Site (11-Mr-11): A Late Prehistoric Settlement in the Central Kaskaskia Valley,* edited by Michael Hargrave, Gerald A. Oetelaar, Neal H. Lopinot, Brian M. Bulture, and Deborah A. Billings, pp. 121–175. Southern Illinois University, Research Paper No. 38, Carbondale.

1991 A Selectionist Perspective on Change in Late Prehistoric (A.D. 600–1400) Domestic Architecture in the American Bottom Region of Southern Illinois. Unpublished Ph.D. dissertation, Department of Anthropology, Southern Illinois University, Carbondale.

1998 *The Yuchi Town Site (1RU63), Russell County, Alabama: An Assessment of the Impact of Looting.* Cultural Resources Research Center, U.S. Army Construction Research Laboratories. Prepared for Environmental Management Division, Department of the Army, Headquarters U.S. Army Infantry Center, Ft. Benning, Georgia. DoD. Project

Harn, Alan D.

1972 A Mississippian House A.D. 1972. *The Living Museum* 34(5):124–126.

1978 Mississippian Settlement Patterns in the Central Illinois River Valley.

In *Mississippian Settlement Patterns,* edited by Bruce D. Smith, pp. 233–268. Academic Press, New York.

1994 The Larson Settlement System in the Central Illinois River Valley. Reports of Investigations 50. Illinois State Museum, Springfield.

Harvey, Dennis E.

1977 Preliminary Analysis of Wood Utilization at Two Mississippian Sites. *Missouri Archaeologist* 38:272–280.

Hawkins, Benjamin

1980 A Sketch of Creek Country in the Years 1798 and 1799. In *The Letters, Journals, and Writings of Benjamin Hawkins, Vol. 1,* edited by C. L. Grant. Beehive Press, Savannah.

Heckewelder, John

1971 [1876] *History, Manners, and Customs of the Indian Nations Who Once Inhabited Pennsylvania and the Neighboring States.* Arno Press, New York.

Heilman, James M., Malinda C. Lileas, and Christopher A. Turnbrow

1988 History of 17 Years of Excavation and Reconstruction—A Chronicle of the 12th Century Human Values and the Built Environment. Vol. 2. Dayton Museum of Natural History, Ohio.

Hodgson, Adam

1824 Letters from North America, Written during a Tour in the United States and Canada. Hurt, Robinson, London.

Hoebel, E. Adamson

1949 *Man in the Primitive World.* McGraw-Hill, New York.

Hoffman, Jack L.

1978 Identification of Perforated Ceramic Cone-Shaped Artifacts from the Southern Plains and Adjacent Areas. *Plains Anthropologist* 23(79): 7–11.

Hudson, Charles

1976 *The Southeastern Indians.* University of Tennessee Press, Knoxville.

1990 Conversations with the High Priest of Coosa. In *Lamar Archaeology: Mississippian Chiefdoms in the Deep South,* edited by Mark Williams and Gary Shapiro, pp. 214–230. University of Alabama Press, Tuscaloosa.

1997 *Knights of Spain, Warriors of the Sun.* University of Georgia Press, Athens.

Hughes, M. K., and H. F. Diaz

1994 Was There a "Medieval Warm Period" and if so, Where and When? *Climatic Change* 26:109–142.

Iseminger, William R., and Joyce A. Williams

1998 Experimental House Burning at Cahokia Mounds. *Rediscovery* 4:31–48. Illinois Association for the Advancement of Archaeology.

Jackson, Douglas K.
1996 The Vaughn Branch Site: Late Woodland and Mississippian Occupations in the American Bottom (11-Ms-1437). Transportation Archaeological Research Program Research Reports No. 42. Illinois Archaeology Transportation Research Program, University of Illinois at Urbana-Champaign.

Jackson, Douglas K., Andrew C. Fortier, and Joyce A. Williams
1992 The Sponemann Site 2: The Mississippian and Oneota Occupation. American Bottom Archaeology, FAI-270 Reports, Vol. 24, edited by Charles Bareis and John A. Walthall, Illinois Department of Transportation and University of Illinois Press, Urbana.

Jenkins, Ned
1982 *Archaeology of the Gainesville Lake Area: Synthesis.* Report of Investigation 23. University of Alabama Office of Archaeological Research, Tuscaloosa.

Jennings, Jesse D.
1994 *Accidental Archaeologist: Memoirs of Jesse D. Jennings.* University of Utah Press, Salt Lake City.

Johnson, Hunter B.
1999 Archaeological Excavations at Pride Place (1Tu1) and Its Role in the Moundville Chiefdom. Paper presented at the 56th Annual Meeting of the Southeastern Archaeological Conference, Pensacola, Florida.
2001 Archaeology at Pride Place (1Tu1) and Its Position in the Moundville Chiefdom. Paper presented at the Annual Meeting of the Society for American Archaeology, New Orleans, Louisiana.

Jones, P. D., K. R. Briffa, T. P. Barnett, and S. F. B. Tett
1998 High-Resolution Palaeoclimatic Records for the Last Millennium: Interpretation, Integration and Comparison with General Circulation Model Control Run Temperatures. *The Holocene* 8:455–471.

Jones, Walter B., and David L. DeJarnette
1936 Moundville Culture and Burial Museum. Museum Paper 13. Alabama Museum of Natural History, Tuscaloosa.

Kelly, Arthur R., Frank T. Schnell, Donald F. Smith, and Ann L. Schlosser
1965 Explorations in Sixtoe Field, Carter's Dam, Murray County, Georgia, Seasons of 1962, 1963, 1964. Report submitted to U.S.D.I. National Park Service, Atlanta.

Kelly, Hypatia
1988 The Architecture of the King Site. Unpublished master's thesis, Department of Anthropology, University of Georgia, Athens.

Kelly, John E.

1989 The Range Site: The Emergent Mississippian Dohack and Range Phase Occupations 2 (11-S-47). Illinois Department of Transportation. University of Illinois Press, Urbana.

1995 The Fingers and Curtiss Steinberg Road Sites, Two Sterling Phase Mississippian Farmsteads in the Goose Lake Locality. Illinois Department of Transportation. Department of Anthropology, University of Illinois at Urbana-Champaign.

Kennedy, William, and Andrew Sawyer

2005 Making the Past Visible at Sunwatch Indian Village. *SAA Archaeological Record* 5(3):23–25.

Kidder, Alfred Vincent

1932 *The Artifacts of Pecos.* Phillips Academy, Andover, Massachusetts.

Kidder, Tristram R.

2004 Plazas as Architecture: An Example from the Raffman Site, Northeast Louisiana. *American Antiquity* 69(3):514–532.

Knight, Vernon J., Jr., and Vincas P. Steponaitis

1998 A New History of Moundville. In *Archaeology of the Moundville Chiefdom,* edited by V. J. Knight, Jr. and V. P. Steponaitis, pp. 1–25. Smithsonian Institution Press, Washington, D.C.

Lacquement, Cameron H.

2004 How to Build a Mississippian House: A Study of Domestic Architecture in West-Central Alabama. Unpublished master's thesis, University of Alabama, Tuscaloosa.

2005 The Experimental Building of a Flexed Pole Early Mississippian Structure. *Bulletin of Primitive Technology* 30:59–67.

Larson, Lewis H., Jr.

n.d. Unpublished descriptions and plans of certain Mound C, Etowah structures. On file at West Georgia College, Anthropology Department, Carrollton.

Lawson, John

1967 [1709] *A New Voyage to Carolina; Containing the Exact Description and Natural History of That Country: Together with the Present State Thereof. And a Journal of a Thousand Miles, Travel'd Thro' Several Nations of Indians. Giving a Particular Account of Their Customs, Manners, &c.,* edited with an Introduction and notes by Hugh Talmage Lefler. University of North Carolina Press, Chapel Hill.

Ledbetter, Jerald

1997 *The Victory Drive Site, 9ME50, Muscogee County, Georgia.* Southeastern

Archaeological Services, Inc., Athens. Report prepared for the City of Columbus Water Works, Columbus.

2002 *Archaeological Investigations at Buzzard Roost 9TR41, 9TR54, and 9TR106, Taylor County, Georgia.* Report to the Georgia Department of Transportation Office Environment/Location. Southeastern Archaeological Services, Inc., Athens, Georgia.

Lewis, C. Thomas

2002 Kasita Revisited: A New Look at the 1938 Kasita (9-Ce-1) Excavations. Paper presented at the 59th Annual Southeastern Archaeological Conference, Biloxi, Mississippi.

Lewis, R. Barry, and Charles Stout (editors)

1998 *Mississippian Towns and Sacred Spaces: Searching for an Architectural Grammar.* University of Alabama Press, Tuscaloosa.

Lewis, R. Barry, Charles Stout, and Cameron B. Wesson

1998 The Design of Mississippian Towns. In *Mississippian Towns and Sacred Spaces: Searching for an Architectural Grammar,* edited by R. Barry Lewis and Charles Stout, pp. 1–21. University of Alabama Press, Tuscaloosa.

Lewis, Thomas M. N.

1937 *Annotations Pertaining to Prehistoric Research in Tennessee.* University of Tennessee Record 40(6). University of Tennessee Press, Knoxville.

1940 Master Plan Pertaining to the Excavation and Preservation In Situ of Prehistoric Remains Contained in Fuller Park, Memphis, Tennessee. Mss. on file, Frank. H. McClung Museum, University of Tennessee, Knoxville.

1995 Architectural Industry. In *The Prehistory of the Chickamauga Basin in Tennessee,* 2 vols., edited by Lynne P. Sullivan, pp. 54–78. University of Tennessee Press, Knoxville.

Lewis, Thomas M. N., and Madeline Kneberg

1941 *The Prehistory of the Chickamauga Basin in Tennessee.* Tennessee Anthropology Papers No. 1. Division of Anthropology. University of Tennessee, Knoxville.

1946 *Hiwassee Island: An Archaeological Account of Four Tennessee Indian Peoples.* University of Tennessee Press, Knoxville.

Lewis, Thomas M. N., Madeline Kneberg Lewis, and Lynne P. Sullivan (editors)

1995 *The Prehistory of the Chickamauga Basin in Tennessee,* 2 vols. University of Tennessee Press, Knoxville.

Lidberg, George A.

n.d. Unpublished field notes, site 7HY5, on file, Frank H. McClung Museum, University of Tennessee, Knoxville.

Litchford, Michael

2002 This Old House: A Reconstruction of a Mississippian Temple. *Bulletin of Primitive Technology* 24:72–79.

Little, Keith J.

2000 Late Holocene Climate Fluctuations and Culture Change in the Southeastern United States: Evidence from the Tennessee Valley. Unpublished master's thesis, University of Alabama, Tuscaloosa.

Lopatin, Ivan A.

1960 Origin of the Native American Steam Bath. *American Anthropologist* 62(6):977–993.

Lorant, Stefan

1946 *The New World: The First Pictures of America.* Duell, Sloan, and Pearce, New York.

Lyon, Edwin A.

1996 *A New Deal for Southeastern Archaeology.* University of Alabama Press, Tuscaloosa.

Mann, M. E., R. S. Bradley, and M. K. Hughes

1998 Global-Scale Temperature Patterns and Climate Forcing over the Past Six Centuries. *Nature* 392:779–787.

Martin, Paul S., George I. Quimby, and Donald Collier

1947 *Indians before Columbus.* University of Chicago Press, Chicago.

Mauelshagen, Carl, and Gerald H. Davis (editors)

1969 Partners in the Lord's Work: The Diary of Two Moravian Missionaries in Creek Country. School of Arts and Sciences Research Papers No. 21. Georgia State College, Atlanta.

McConaughy, Mark A.

1985 A Comparison of Burned Mississippian Houses from Illinois. Paper presented at the Midwest Archaeological Conference, East Lansing, Michigan.

McConaughy, Mark A. (editor)

1993 *Rench: A Stratified Site in the Central Illinois River Valley.* Illinois State Museum Reports of Investigations No. 49, Springfield.

McConaughy, Mark A., Claude V. Jackson, and Frances B. King

1985 Two Early Mississippian Period Structures from the Rench Site (11PA), Peoria County, Illinois. *Midcontinental Journal of Archaeology* 10(2):171–193.

McElrath, Dale L.

1987 Emergent Mississippian and Mississippian Communities at the Radic Site (11-Ms-584). Illinois Department of Transportation by the University of Illinois Press, Urbana.

McKenzie, Douglas
1964 The Moundville Phase and Its Position in Southeastern Prehistory. Unpublished Ph.D. dissertation, Department of Anthropology, Harvard University.

McMillan, Carl W.
1963 A letter to Don Dickson, October 7, 1963, on file at the Dickson Mound Museum, Lewiston, Illinois.

Mehrer, Mark William
1982 A Mississippian Community at the Range Site (11-S-47), St. Clair County, Illinois. FAI-270 Archaeological Mitigation Projection Report No. 52, Urbana, Illinois.

Mereness, Newton D.
1916 A Ranger's Report of Travels with General Oglethorpe, 1739–1742. In *Travels in the American Colonies,* edited by N. D. Mereness, pp. 215–236. Macmillan, New York.

Meyers, Maureen S.
2002 The Mississippian Frontier in Southwestern Virginia. *Southeastern Archaeology* 21(2):178–191.

Milner, George R.
1984 The Julien Site. American Bottom Archaeology FAI-270 Site Reports. University of Illinois Press, Urbana.
1998 *The Cahokia Chiefdom: The Archaeology of a Mississippian Society.* Smithsonian Institution Press, Washington, D.C.

Mitchell, William J.
1990 *The Logic of Architecture: Design, Computation, and Cognition.* MIT Press, Cambridge.

Muller, Jon
1986 *Archaeology of the Lower Ohio River Valley.* Academic Press, New York.

Nash, Charles H.
1968 *Residence Mounds: An Intermediate Middle-Mississippian Settlement Pattern.* Master's thesis, University of Mississippi, Oxford. Memphis State University Archaeological Research Center Occasional Papers No. 2, Memphis.
1972 *Chucalissa: Excavations and Burials through 1963.* Memphis State University Anthropological Research Center, Occasional Papers No. 6, Memphis.

Neitzel, Robert S.
1965 *Archeology of the Fatherland Site: The Grand Village of the Natchez.* American Museum of Natural History, Anthropological Papers No. 51, Pt. 1, New York.

1983 The Grand Village of the Natchez Revisited: Excavations at the Fatherland Site, Adams County, Mississippi, 1972. Archaeological Report No. 12, Mississippi Department of Archives and History, Jackson.

Norrish, Dick
1989 Demonstration Houses Are Burned. *Cahokian:* Cahokia Mounds Museum Society, Collinsville, Illinois.

Orr, Kenneth
1951 Change at Kincaid: A Study of Cultural Dynamics. In *Kincaid: A Prehistoric Illinois Metropolis,* edited by Fay-Cooper Cole, pp. 293–359. University of Chicago Press, Chicago.

Patton, Robert
1990 *An Investigation of Domestic Architecture at the Leake Site (9BR2), Bartow County, Georgia.* Unpublished bachelor honor's thesis, Department of Anthropology, University of Georgia, Athens.

Pauketat, Timothy R.
1986 *Predicting Occupation Span from Ceramic Refuse: A Case Study from the American Bottom.* Unpublished master's thesis, Department of Anthropology, Southern Illinois University, Carbondale.
1998 The Archaeology of Downtown Cahokia: The Tract 15A and Dunham Tract Excavations. Illinois Transportation Archaeological Research Program Monograph, University of Illinois, Urbana.
2003 Resettled Farmers and the Making of a Mississippian Polity. *American Antiquity* 68(1):39–66.

Pauketat, Timothy R., and William I. Woods
1986 Middle Mississippian Structure Analysis: The Lawrence Primas Site (11-MS-895) in the American Bottom. *Wisconsin Archeologist* 76(2): 104–127.

Payne, Claudine
1994 Mississippian Capitals: An Archaeological Investigation of Precolumbian Political Structure. Unpublished Ph.D. dissertation, Department of Anthropology, University of Florida.

Peebles, Christopher
1983 Prehistoric Agriculture Communities in West Central Alabama. 2 vols. University of Michigan, Ann Arbor.

Polhemus, Richard R.
1975 Cherokee Structure Change. The Conference on Historic Site Archaeology Papers 8:139–154.
1985 Mississippian Architecture: Temporal, Technological, and Spatial Patterning of the Structures at the Toqua Site (40MR6). Unpublished master's thesis, University of Tennessee, Knoxville.

1987 *The Toqua Site: A Late Mississippian Dallas Phase Town.* Report of Investigations 41. Department of Anthropology, University of Tennessee, Knoxville.

1990 Dallas Phase Architecture and Sociopolitical Structure. In *Lamar Archaeology: Mississippian Chiefdoms in the Deep South,* edited by Mark Williams and Gary Shapiro, pp. 125–138. University of Alabama Press, Tuscaloosa.

1998 Activity Organization in Mississippian Households: A Case Study from the Loy Site in East Tennessee. Unpublished Ph.D. dissertation, Department of Anthropology, University of Tennessee, Knoxville.

Poplin, Eric

1990 *Prehistoric Settlement in the Dog River Valley.* Report prepared for Douglasville–Douglas County Water and Sewer Authority. Brockington and Associates, Inc., Atlanta.

Porter, James W.

1974 Cahokia Archaeology as Viewed from the Mitchell Site: A Satellite Community at A.D. 1150–1200. Unpublished Ph.D. dissertation, Department of Anthropology, University of Wisconsin, Madison.

1977 The Mitchell Site and Prehistoric Exchange Systems at Cahokia: A.D. 1000 ± 300. In *Explorations into Cahokia Archaeology,* 2nd ed., edited by Melvin L. Fowler. Illinois Archaeological Survey, Inc. University of Illinois, Urbana.

Powell, Terry J.

1980 An Archaeological Study of Burned Structures at the Orendorf Site, Fulton County, Illinois. Unpublished Ph.D. dissertation, Department of Anthropology, Southern Illinois University, Carbondale.

Price, James E.

1969 *A Middle Mississippian House.* Museum Brief No. 1. University of Missouri, Columbia.

Rapoport, Amos

1969 *House Form and Culture.* Prentice-Hall, Englewood Cliffs, New Jersey.

1982 *The Meaning of the Built Environment: A Nonverbal Communication Approach.* Sage, Beverly Hills, California.

1990 Systems and Activities of Systems of Settings. In *Domestic Architecture and the Use of Space,* edited by Susan Kent, pp. 9–20. Cambridge University Press, Cambridge.

Redwine, Charles P.

2002 Large Log Structures as Scara: Architecture and Ethnohistory at the

Powers Site. Paper presented at the 59th Annual Southeast Archaeological Conference, Biloxi, Mississippi.

Reed, Nelson A.

n.d. A Study of the Prehistoric Material Culture of the Cahokia Area. Report prepared for the Illinois Department of Conservation, May 1977.

Regnier, Amanda L.

2006 An Examination of the Social Composition of Late Mississippian Towns in the Alabama River Valley through Ceramic Styles. Unpublished Ph.D. dissertation, University of Alabama, Tuscaloosa.

Rogers, J. Daniel, and Bruce D. Smith (editors)

1995 Mississippian Communities and Households. University of Alabama Press, Tuscaloosa.

Saunt, Claudio

1998 "Domestick . . . Quiet being broke": Gender Conflict among the Creek Indians in the Eighteenth Century. In *Contact Points: American Frontiers from the Mohawk Valley to the Mississippi, 1750–1830,* edited by Andrew R. L. Clayton and Fredrika J. Teute, pp. 151–174. University of North Carolina Press, Chapel Hill.

1999 *A New Order of Things: Property, Power and the Transformation of the Creek Indians, 1733–1816.* Cambridge University Press, Cambridge.

Scarry, C. Margaret

1995 *Excavations on the Northwest Riverbank at Moundville: Investigations of a Moundville I Residential Area.* Report of Investigations 72. University of Alabama Museum, Office of Archaeological Services, Tuscaloosa.

1998 Domestic Life on the Northwest Riverbank at Moundville. In *Archaeology of the Moundville Chiefdom,* edited by V. J. Knight Jr. and V. P. Steponaitis, pp. 63–101. Smithsonian Institution Press, Washington, D.C.

Schoolcraft, Henry R.

1855 *Information Respecting the History, Condition, and Prospects of the Indian Tribes of the United States,* Vol. 5. Lippincott, Philadelphia.

Schroeld, Gerald F.

1998 Mississippian Towns in the Eastern Tennessee Valley. In *Mississippian Towns and Sacred Spaces: Searching for an Architectural Grammar,* edited by R. Barry Lewis and Charles Stout, pp. 64–92. University of Alabama Press, Tuscaloosa.

Scofield, W. Fleming, and W. H. O'Brian

1963 *Modern Timber Engineering.* Southern Pine Association, New Orleans.

Scott, Robert J.

2004 Artifact Distributions, Activities, and Material Culture at the Historic Lower Creek Town of Kasita. Unpublished master's thesis, Department of Anthropology, University of Alabama, Tuscaloosa.

Sheldon, Craig T., Jr.

1997 Historic Creek "Summer" Houses of Central Alabama. Paper presented at the 62nd Annual Meeting of the Society for American Archaeology, Nashville.

Sheldon, Elisabeth S.

1982 Continuity and Change in Plant Usage from the Mississippian to the Historic Period. Unpublished Ph.D. dissertation, Department of Biology, University of Alabama, Tuscaloosa.

Simon, Mary L.

2002 Red Cedar, White Oak, and Bluestem Grass: The Colors of Mississippian Construction. *Midcontinental Journal of Archaeology* 27(2):273–308.

Smith, Harriet M.

1977 The Murdock Mound: Cahokia Site. In *Explorations into Cahokia Archaeology,* pp. 49–88. Illinois Archaeological Survey Bulletin No. 7, Urbana.

Smith, Marvin T.

2001 The Rise and Fall of Coosa, A.D. 1350–1700. In *Societies in Eclipse: Archaeology of the Eastern Woodland Indians A.D. 1400–1700,* edited by David S. Brose, C. Wesley Cowan, and Robert C. Mainfort, Jr., pp. 143–155. Smithsonian Institution Press, Washington D.C.

Spears, Carol S., and Leslie Walker

2003 Significance Testing at Sites 3Po608 and 3Po610, 3CT340, and 3CT341 on the Proposed Marked Tree I-55 (Hwy. 63) Corridor, Poinsett and Crittenden Counties, Arkansas. SPEARS Project Report 156. AHTD Job Number 00184. Prepared by SPEARS Inc., West Fork, Arkansas. Submitted to the Arkansas State Highway & Transportation Department, Environmental Division, Little Rock.

Speck, Frank G.

1909 *Ethnology of the Yuchi Indians.* University of Pennsylvania Museum Paper 1(1). Philadelphia.

Steponaitis, Vincas P.

1998 Population Trends at Moundville. In *Archaeology of the Moundville Chiefdom,* edited by V. J. Knight, Jr. and V. P. Steponaitis, pp. 26–43. Smithsonian Institution Press, Washington, D.C.

Sullivan, Lynne P.

1987 The Mouse Creek Phase Household. *Southeastern Archaeology* 6(1):16–29.

1995 Mississippian Household and the Community Organization in Eastern Tennessee. In *Mississippian Communities and Households,* edited by Daniel Rogers and Bruce D. Smith, pp. 99–123. University of Alabama Press, Tuscaloosa.

2007 Shell Gorgets, Time, and the Southeastern Ceremonial Complex in Eastern Tennessee. In *Chronology, Iconography, and Style: Current Perspectives on the Social and Temporal Contexts of the Southeastern Ceremonial Complex,* edited by Adam King, pp. in progress. University of Alabama Press, Tuscaloosa.

Swan, Caleb

1855 State of Arts and Manufactures, with the Creek Indians, in 1791. In *Information Respecting the History, Condition, and Prospects of the Indian Tribes of the United States,* edited by H. R. Schoolcraft, Vol. 5:691–693. Lippincott, Philadelphia.

Swanton, John R.

1911 Indian Tribes of the Lower Mississippi Valley and the Adjacent Coast of the Gulf of Mexico. Bulletin 43. Smithsonian Institution, Washington, D.C.

1942 Source Material on the History and Ethnology of the Caddo Indians. Bulletin 132. Smithsonian Institution, Washington, D.C.

1946 *The Indians of the Southeastern United States.* Bureau of American Ethnology Bulletin No. 137. U.S. Government Printing Office, Washington, D.C.

1998 *Early History of the Creek Indians and Their Neighbors.* University Press of Florida, Gainesville.

The Thatch Company

n.d. *Thatch FAQs—The Thatcher's Art.* Electronic document, http://www.thatchco.com/thatchpg/faq.htm, accessed March 2006.

Thomas, Cyrus

1985 [1894] *Report on the Mound Explorations of the Bureau of Ethnology.* Smithsonian Institution Press, Washington, D.C.

Trigger, Bruce G.

1968 The Determinants of Settlement Patterns. In *Settlement Archaeology,* edited by K. C. Chang, pp. 53–78. National Press Books, Palo Alto, California.

United States Department of Agriculture

1987 Wood Handbook: Wood as an Engineering Material. Agriculture Handbook 72. Washington, D.C.

Wagner, Mark J.

1998 Euro-American Artifacts. In *The Yuchi Town Site (1RU63), Russell*

*County, Alabama: An Assessment of the Impact of Looting*, by Michael L. Hargrave, Charles R. McGimsey, Mark J. Wagner, Lee A. Newsom, Laura Ruggiero, Emanuel Breitburg, and Lynette Norr, pp. 133–175. Construction Engineering Research Lab (Army), Champaign, Illinois.

Walthall, John A.

1977 *Moundville: An Introduction to the Archaeology of a Mississippian Chiefdom.* Alabama Museum of Natural History, University of Alabama, Tuscaloosa.

Walthall, John A. and Steve B. Wimberly

1978 Mississippian Chronology in the Black Warrior Valley. *Journal of Alabama Archaeology* 24(2):118–124.

Warrick, Gary A.

1988 Estimating Ontario Iroquoian Village Duration. *Man in the Northeast* 26:21–60.

Waselkov, Gregory A.

1984 Intensive Subsurface Archaeological Investigations at the I-85 Shorter-Milstead Interchange, Alabama. Report submitted to the Environmental Technical Section of the State of Alabama Highway Department.

1989 Seventeenth-Century Trade in the Colonial Southeast. *Southeastern Archaeology* 8(2):117–133.

1994 The Macon Trading House and Early European-Indian Contact in the Colonial Southeast. In *Ocmulgee Archaeology, 1936–1986,* edited by David J. Hally, pp. 190–196. University of Georgia Press, Athens.

1997 Changing Strategies of Indian Field Location in the Early Historic Southeast. In *People, Plants, and Landscapes: Studies in Paleoethnobotany,* edited by Kristen J. Gremillion, pp. 179–194. University of Alabama Press, Tuscaloosa.

Waselkov, Gregory A., and Kathryn E. Braund (editors)

1995 *William Bartram and the Southeastern Indians.* University of Nebraska Press, Lincoln.

Waselkov, Gregory A., John W. Cottier, and Craig T. Sheldon, Jr.

1990 Archaeological Investigations at the Early Historic Creek Indian Town of Fusihatchee (Phase I, 1988–1989). Report to the National Science Foundation (Grant No. BNS-8718934). Manuscript on file, Department of Sociology and Anthropology, Auburn University, Montgomery, Alabama.

Wauchope, Robert

1938 *Modern Maya Houses: A Study of Their Archaeological Significance.* Carnegie Institution of Washington, Washington, D.C.

Webb, William S.
1938 An Archaeological Survey of the Norris Basin in Eastern Tennessee. Bulletin 118. Bureau of American Ethnology, Washington, D.C.
1952 The Jonathan Creek Village: Site 4, Marshall County, Kentucky. University of Kentucky Reports in Anthropology, Vol. 8, No. 1. Lexington.

Webb, William S., and David L. DeJarnette
1942 An Archeological Survey of Pickwick Basin in the Adjacent Portions of the States of Alabama, Mississippi, and Tennessee. Bulletin No. 129. Bureau of American Ethnology, Washington, D.C.

Weigand, Phil C., and Jon Muller
1967 Preliminary Report on Investigations at the Kincaid Site. Manuscript on file, Center for Archaeological Investigations, Southern Illinois University, Carbondale.

Welch, Paul D.
1994 The Occupational History of the Bessemer Site. *Southeastern Archaeology* 13(1):1–26.
1998 Outlying Sites within the Moundville Chiefdom. In *Archaeology of the Moundville Chiefdom,* edited by V. J. Knight, Jr. and V. P. Steponaitis, pp. 133–166. Smithsonian Institution Press, Washington, D.C.
2006 Archaeology at Shiloh Indian Mounds: 1899–1999. University of Alabama Press, Tuscaloosa.

Wesler, Kit
2001 *Excavations at Wickliffe Mounds.* University of Alabama Press, Tuscaloosa.

Wilk, Richard R.
1990 The Built Environment and Consumer Decisions. In *Domestic Architecture and the Use of Space: An Interdisciplinary Cross-Cultural Study,* edited by Susan Kent, pp. 34–42. Cambridge University Press, Cambridge.

Wilk, Richard R., and William J. Rathje
1982 Household Archaeology. *American Behavioral Scientist* 25(6):617–639.

Williams, Roger
1963 [1643] A Key into the Language of America, edited by J. Hammond Trumbull. In *Complete Writings of Roger Williams,* Vol. 1, pp. 61–284. Russell and Russell, New York.

Williams, Stephen
1990 The Vacant Quarter and Other Late Events in the Lower Valley. In *Towns and Temples along the Mississippi,* edited by David H. Dye and Cheryl Anne Cox, pp. 170–180. University of Alabama Press, Tuscaloosa.

Wilson, Gregory D.

2005 Between Plaza and Palisade: Household and Community Organization at Early Moundville. Unpublished Ph.D. dissertation. Department of Anthropology, University of North Carolina, Chapel Hill.

Wissler, Clark

1938 *The American Indian: An Introduction to the Anthropology of the New World.* Oxford University Press, London.

Wobst, Martin H.

1978 The Archaeo-Ethnology of Hunter-Gatherers or the Tyranny of the Ethnographic Record in Archaeology. *American Antiquity* 43(2):303–309.

Worth, John E.

2000 The Lower Creeks. In *Indians of the Greater Southeast: Historical Archaeology and Ethnohistory,* edited by Bonnie G. McEwan, pp. 265–268. University Press of Florida, Gainesville.

Wray, Donald E.

n.d. The Shryock Site, Fulton County, Illinois. Manuscript on file at Dickson Mounds Museum, Lewiston, Illinois.

Wylie, Allison

1985 The Reaction against Analogy. *Advances in Archaeological Method and Theory* 8:63–111.

# Contributors

**Dennis B. Blanton** received his M.A. in Anthropology from Brown University in 1983 and is the Curator of Native American Archaeology at the Fernbank Museum of Natural History in Atlanta, Georgia. His duties include care of the extensive St. Catherine's Island and Edward John Noble Collection of archaeological material from coastal Georgia.

**Tamira K. Brennan** is currently in the Ph.D. program at Southern Illinois University at Carbondale, where she received her M.A. in 2005. She is currently involved in ongoing investigations at the Kincaid Mounds site in the Black Bottoms of extreme southern Illinois, both revisiting old collections and notes from the 1930s and 1940s and undertaking new excavations.

**Ramie A. Gougeon** is senior archaeologist at Panamerican Consultants, Inc., Durham, North Carolina. His dissertation research at the University of Georgia was an examination of three domestic structures from the Little Egypt site (9MU102) in northwest Georgia.

**Thomas H. Gresham** received his M.A. from the University of Georgia and is president of Southeastern Archaeological Services, Inc., a consulting firm in Athens, Georgia. He is also a long-time officer and board member of the Society for Georgia Archaeology. He has directed a range of projects in the Southeast, mostly in Georgia.

**Vernon J. Knight, Jr.** is a Professor of Anthropology at the University of Alabama. Among his research interests are indigenous late prehistoric and early historic period social structure, religion, and politics in the Southeast and Greater Antilles.

**Cameron H. Lacquement** is a Ph.D. candidate in Anthropology at the University of Alabama. His interests include Native architecture, experimental archaeology, structural and geotechnical engineering, and architectural energetics.

**Robert H. Lafferty, III** is the president of Mid-Continental Research Associates, Inc. in Springdale, Arkansas. He received his Ph.D. in Anthropology from Southern Illinois University at Carbondale in 1977. Lafferty has conducted prehistoric research in numerous places in the southeastern United States on topics including fortifications, settlement patterns, exchange systems, site preservation, and dating ancient earthquake activity.

**Mark A. McConaughy** is a regional archaeologist for the Pennsylvania Bureau for Historic Preservation. He received his Ph.D. in Anthropology in 1979 from the University of Pittsburgh. As a student at the University of Pittsburgh, he participated in the excavations of the Watson Farm site under Patrick and Cheryl Munson. He also was a Teaching Assistant at Meadowcroft Rockshelter and the Avella Mound, Pennsylvania. After graduation McConaughy directed excavations of the Rench site, Illinois; Horseshoe Rockshelter, Pennsylvania; and Graeme Park, Pennsylvania. He has also conducted research along the Paita Peninsula of Peru and at the Early Bronze Age sites of Bab edh Dhra and Numeirah, Jordan.

**Nelson A. Reed** graduated from Washington University in 1950. He has done land and underwater survey in Guatemala, research in the Yucatán, and excavated in Illinois. He was introduced to archaeology by Preston Holder; he organized and later led four seasons of excavations on Monks Mound as a research associate of Washington University. He also taught there and ran a three-month project in experimental archaeology with students living and practicing primitive technology, house building, tool making, and agriculture.

**Robert J. Scott** is an archaeologist with the Arkansas Archeological Survey and research assistant to Dr. Marvin D. Jeter at the University of Arkansas at Monticello. He obtained his B.A. in Anthropology at Southern Illinois University at Carbondale in 2000 and completed his M.A. at the University of Alabama in 2004. He is currently involved in research related to the historic

Lower Creeks and the late prehistory of the Lower Mississippi Valley and Trans Mississippi South.

**Lynne P. Sullivan** is Curator of Archaeology at the Frank H. McClung Museum and Research Associate Professor in the Department of Anthropology at the University of Tennessee. She received her Ph.D. in anthropology from the University of Wisconsin–Milwaukee and has published numerous books and articles on southeastern archaeology, the history of archaeology, and the curation of archaeological collections.

# Index